The Reality of Assisted Dying: Understanding the Issues

The Reality of Assisted Dying: Understanding the Issues

Edited by

Julian C. Hughes and Ilora G. Finlay

Open University Press

Open University Press
McGraw Hill
Unit 4
Foundation Park
Roxborough Way
Maidenhead
SL6 3UD

Email: emea_uk_ireland@mheducation.com
World wide web: www.mheducation.co.uk

Executive Editor: Sam Crowe
Associate Editor: Hannah Church
Content Product Manager: Graham Jones

British Library Cataloguing in Publication Data
A catalogue record of this book is available from the British Library

ISBN-13: 978-0-33-525317-3
ISBN-10: 0-33-525317-2
eISBN: 978-0-33-525318-0

Typeset by Transforma Pvt. Ltd., Chennai, India
Printed and bound by CPI Group (UK) Ltd, Croydon, CR0 4YY

Praise for this book

"A much needed, timely compendium covering the main issues underlying and surrounding Assisted Dying. The 'bite size' chapters constitute a cornucopia of well-distilled information and valuable insights. A must-read for healthcare professionals, but also for legislators and others wanting to go beyond the sound bites of the lobbyists and the typically shallow discussion in much of the media. As the editors say, 'The purpose of this book is to encourage us to ponder these points profoundly, thoughtfully, with care, compassion and in detail."

Robert Twycross, Emeritus Clinical Reader in Palliative Medicine, University of Oxford, UK; former Head, WHO Collaborative Centre for Palliative Care, Oxford, UK

"This powerful collection of essays brilliantly unpacks the legal, ethical and practical issues around the assisted dying debate. Opening up new lines of argument and demonstrating the real challenges with reforming the law this is a crucial contribution to the current arguments around euthanasia."

Jonathan Herring, Professor of Law, University of Oxford, UK

"This book is an essential exploration of the complexities behind the sound bites. The authors come from across all sides of the debate and recognise that even the strongest people become vulnerable when faced with unwanted news. They also acknowledge that disabled people are disproportionately disadvantaged across both acute and primary healthcare. The authors are aware that able-bodied people often express horror and fear at the thought of becoming disabled, yet when it occurs they invariably want support to live well. This book helps us all to look at the uncertainty we live with every day and the momentous decisions that politicians are facing as they seek to protect every citizen in our current ableist society. Becoming better informed about the multifaceted reality of changing the law on assisted dying will help people make better choices. As a disabled person I want those who are tasked with keeping me safe and well to fully comprehend the facts about legalising doctors or caregivers to assist someone to end their life prematurely. Our life is literally in your hands!"

Baroness Campbell of Surbiton DBE, UK

"The law in this country has always been that deliberate killing of a human being is prohibited, except in war and other special circumstances. In recent times suggestions have been made that this should be

modified to deal with certain cases of suffering. It appears likely that after the General Election there will be a debate in the Westminster Parliament and the other Parliaments. It is vitally important that these debates should be conducted with knowledge of the detail circumstances proposed for the changes. The arguments on the issues are extremely detailed and it is important that the participants in the debates have access to the detailed information supporting or opposing the proposals. There have been a number of books and other publications to which a participant can have access. I have recently understood that this volume has been published with a view to supplying this need. It is, in my view, a balanced treatment of the subject, but of course is based upon the views of the many well informed contributors, and I recommend it to a participant in the debates who seeks detailed information on the full circumstances that apply to the different detailed proposals that will probably be the subjects of these debates."

The Rt Hon. the Lord Mackay of Clashfern KT,
House of Lords, Westminster, UK

"Wherever your views lie on the very real and topical issue of assisted dying, you should read this book. If you believe that improved, more equitable, and better-funded palliative care should be provided for the dying, this well-structured, logical, yet passionate work will strengthen your resolve. On the other hand, if you begin with the conviction that assisted dying is the right solution, by the end of these two hundred pages, Baroness Ilora Finlay and Professor Julian Hughes will present you with difficult questions that demand better answers. For others, it may even lead to a complete change of mind."

Dr Matt Morgan, Honorary Visiting Professor, Cardiff University,
UK; Intensive Care Medicine Consultant, University Hospital of Wales,
Cardiff, UK; Adjunct Clinical Professor, Curtin University, AU

"The current discussions of "assisted dying" both in popular media and medical ethics are generally superficial and confused conceptually, historically, and philosophically. This fine book is clarifying and balanced. It successfully raises serious questions about the too-easy endorsement of both assisted suicide and euthanasia in recent decades, drawing significantly from some of the very best critical thinkers on both sides of the Atlantic. It provides among other things a deep dive into the experience of euthanasia and assisted suicide as the physician engages with these against the background of professional identity formation. Hopefully, readers will be asking themselves throughout what really are the goals or ends of medicine, and can assisted suicide or euthanasia be made consistent with them. The general tone of these chapters, all of them well constructed and carefully edited, is that the profession and the wider society run considerable risks if these practices are legalized. While treatment refusal and withdrawal are consistent with professional identity because the healing art by no means requires that those who are

dying be subjected to a technological assault when they could instead have a peaceful and natural death, the healing art and the act of killing are incompatible. Whether the reader believes this to be true, this book is a refreshing and altogether needed contribution in a time when too many are too easily endorsing a departure from received moral and professional wisdom without deep consideration of the implications."

Stephen G Post, PhD, Professor and Director, Center for
Medical Humanities, Compassionate Care & Bioethics,
The Renaissance School of Medicine, Stony Brook University, USA

"This book, under the careful guidance of Julian C. Hughes and Ilora Finlay, provides up to date information and candid reflection on the experiences in countries where assisted dying has become a daily reality. For every year that passes, the claim that Britain can successfully navigate the dangers and slopes of legal euthanasia becomes harder to believe. Perhaps more than the way we die, it influences the way we live: our solidarity with vulnerable people, our preparedness to invest in accessible and high-quality health care and, perhaps most importantly, our capacity to preserve hope in the face of our own frailty."

Theo Boer, Professor of Health Care Ethics, Former Member
of a Euthanasia Review Committee in the Netherlands, NL

"Few topics are more controversial, and few are more important. Whilst powerful and emotional descriptions of death and dying resonate with us all, assisted dying is not just a matter of individual rights and choices, but is a topic with profound societal impacts. This remarkable and very welcome book examines assisted dying from both perspectives and unpicks both the risks to our society if we fail to fully understand the implications and risks of assisted dying, and the benefits to us all of a greater focus on high quality palliative care."

Sir David Haslam, CBE; Past Chair, National Institute for
Health and Care Excellence (NICE), UK; Past President,
British Medical Association and Royal College of General Practitioners, UK

"All legislators in the new parliament should take the time to read this volume, before they begin to decide how they will vote on any bill to introduce what should more properly be described as state-aided suicide. Theirs is an awesome responsibility and above all, our MPs need to study carefully what has happened in other jurisdictions when such laws have been introduced: it is all set out here, dispassionately and methodically. Nor is every contribution from the same viewpoint: this is public service, not propaganda."

Dominic Lawson, Award-winning columnist for the Sunday Times and Daily
Mail, former editor of the Spectator and Sunday Telegraph, UK

"For any citizens as yet undecided about assisted dying, please read this book. It brings together those from the front line of palliative care

with other clinicians, and with leaders in the fields of law, philosophy and ethics who are not driven by politics or faith, but just by a certain knowledge gained from years of experience and thought that no legislation, however well drafted, can prevent exploitation of patients facing their last days. They make the case against assisted dying with first hand evidence gathered from around the world. Legislation is not the answer, better palliative care is."

The Lord Grade of Yarmouth CBE, House of Lords, Westminster, UK

"A remarkable resource for serious and nuanced engagement with this vital debate. The breadth of knowledge and experience represented, including crucial advocacy for improvement of - and access to - palliative care, ensures rigorous exploration of the issues, alongside deep empathy for all whose lives are affected."

The Rt Revd and Rt Hon Dame Sarah Mullally DBE, Bishop of London, UK

"This collection of essays is evidence based, reasoned and comprehensive: medical, social, legal, political and philosophical aspects of current practice and debate are clearly described and carefully assessed in their global context; the contributors' conclusions, often counter-cultural, make you think, and think again, what assisted dying really means for individuals, medicine and society."

Kenneth M Boyd, Professor Emeritus of Medical Ethics, College of Medicine and Veterinary Medicine, University of Edinburgh, UK

"With mounting calls for legalizing euthanasia and assisted suicide, it would be reckless not to seriously ponder how this may impact health care and society, and how it relates to existing end-of-life health care. With 34 chapters written by a host of eminent UK and international medical, policy, ethics, and law experts, this accessible yet comprehensive book provides a crucial reality check on what it means to give physicians such unprecedented powers in the name of patient autonomy and compassionate relief of suffering. The editors of this book, two prominent voices in this debate, brought together leading UK scholars and experts from carefully selected jurisdictions which already opted for some form of legalization. The international experts hold up a mirror for what the UK and other countries should expect if they decide to go that route. Others provide insight into how palliative care already offers support in dying, the challenge of designing proper safeguards, and the impact on specific populations, such as disabled persons, elderly, and persons with mental illness. With further chapters critically analyzing the key ethical and policy arguments invoked in this debate, and others providing diverse religious and secular humanist perspectives, it is hard to think of anything that is not addressed in this book. While the dominant tone of this book is critical of legally permitting physicians to directly support suicide or kill patients, several chapters provide other nuanced perspectives, with at least two chapters asking appropriately: even if some form of

legalization of 'assisted dying' would be desirable, should this be part of mainstream medicine? Every policy maker and citizen willing to go beyond the slogans that are all-too-easily thrown around in this debate should read this book. It should definitely strengthen the quality of the debate."

Trudo Lemmens, Professor and Scholl Chair in Health Law and Policy, University of Toronto, Ontario, Canada

"This book is essential reading for anyone concerned with serious illness and end of life care. It shines a light on a complex issue, revealing that decisions to end life are far from simple. Even the strongest have vulnerable times. It is relatively easy for those with a high profile to access good care, but many in our population are frightened of not being heard and of being discriminated against. Those in our parliaments need to read this book carefully before deciding on such legislation."

Mr Barry Sheerman, British Politician and Former Member of Parliament for Huddersfield (formerly Huddersfield East), UK

"Assisted dying (a blanket phrase for assisted suicide and euthanasia) are 'hot topics' in several countries at present. Those advocating such legal change present simple 'soundbite' messages, as if death will be the solution to the plight of those who are dying. Yet death comes to us all. Advances in palliative care, combined with meticulous attention to patients' concerns, can restore great quality to life. This book reveals the reality of assisted dying by drawing on the evidence of those countries that have legislated for assisted dying. Each chapter provides great insights, including suggestions on ways to improve safety. It is a book to be read by all involved in either side of this heated debate."

Dr C Fourcade, President of the French Association for Palliative Care, France

The book is dedicated to all those who work in the field of palliative care and give so much to ensure that death is as peaceful, pain-free and dignified as possible.

Contents

List of boxes, figures and tables

Boxes

Figures

Tables

About the editors

Julian C. Hughes is an Honorary Professor at Bristol University, UK. He was a consultant in old age psychiatry in the National Health Service (NHS) for over 20 years. He first studied Philosophy, Politics and Economics (PPE) at the University of Oxford prior to studying Medicine at Bristol. He gained his PhD from the University of Warwick. He was appointed Honorary Professor of Philosophy of Ageing at Newcastle University in 2009; and was Professor of Old Age Psychiatry at the University of Bristol from 2016 to 2019. He was elected Fellow of the Royal College of Psychiatrists and of the Royal College of Physicians of Edinburgh. He was the deputy chair of the Nuffield Council on Bioethics until March 2019. Palliative care in dementia was an area of special interest. He now concentrates on writing in the areas of ageing, dementia, ethics and philosophy. His most recent book was *Dementia and Ethics Reconsidered*, published by Open University Press in 2023.

Ilora G. Finlay, Baroness Finlay of Llandaff, is an independent Crossbench Peer in the House of Lords, where she has spearheaded a number of healthcare initiatives, including the statutory recognition that palliative care is a core NHS service and establishing the Chief Coroner post. She is actively involved in tobacco control and child protection. A consultant in palliative medicine since 1987, she has cared for thousands of dying patients and their families, developing seven-day-a-week specialist palliative care services across Wales and establishing Cardiff University's world-renowned Palliative Medicine Diploma/MSc. She holds a Distinguished Honorary Professorship in Cardiff and held Groningen's Johanna Beijtel Chair. A past president of the British Medical Association (BMA) and the Royal Society of Medicine, she previously chaired the National Mental Capacity Forum. She helped to found and remains a board member of the independent think tank 'Living and Dying Well'. Among many appointments, she is a vice president of Marie Curie and Hospice UK, she chairs the Commission on Alcohol Harm and remains president of the Chartered Society of Physiotherapy. She also chairs the Bevan Commission, which provides independent advice on health and social care to the Welsh Government.

About the contributors

Abdul-Azim Ahmed is Secretary General of the Muslim Council of Wales and Deputy Director at the Centre for the Study of Islam in the UK, Cardiff University, UK.

Nigel Biggar is Regius Professor Emeritus of Moral Theology and Senior Research Fellow at the University of Oxford, UK.

Frank Brennan is a palliative care physician based at St George and Calvary Hospitals in Sydney and a senior lecturer in the Faculty of Medicine, University of New South Wales, Australia.

Ramona Coelho is a family physician in London, Ontario, Canada.

Leopold Curfs is Professor of Intellectual Disabilities and Director of the Governor Kremers Centre, Maastricht University Medical Centre, The Netherlands.

Adrian Dabscheck is a consultant in palliative medicine at Western Health and senior lecturer in the Department of Medicine, Melbourne University, Australia.

Sinéad Donnelly is Professor and module convenor Palliative Medicine, general medicine physician, University of Otago, Wellington, Aotearoa New Zealand.

Ilora G. Finlay, The Baroness Finlay of Llandaff, is Distinguished Honorary Professor of Palliative Medicine, Cardiff University Medical School, UK; vice president of Marie Curie and Hospice UK; Crossbench Peer in the House of Lords and a board member of Living and Dying Well.

Alice Firth is a parliamentary research assistant to Baroness Sheila Hollins, House of Lords, UK and PhD student at King's College London.

Katherine Frew is a consultant in palliative medicine, Northumbria Healthcare NHS Foundation Trust, UK.

Tanni Grey-Thompson, The Baroness Grey-Thompson, is a Paralympian, Chancellor of Northumbria University, UK and a Crossbench Peer in the House of Lords, UK.

Andrew Hawkins is a barrister and CEO, Whitestone Insight and former founder and chairman, ComRes, UK.

Cees Hertogh is Professor of Medicine for Older People, Department of Medicine for Older People, Amsterdam UMC, The Netherlands.

Leonie Herx is Clinical Professor, Palliative Medicine, Cumming School of Medicine, University of Calgary, Canada.

Sheila Hollins, The Baroness Hollins, is Emeritus Professor of Psychiatry of Disability at St George's Hospital, University of London and a Crossbench Peer in the House of Lords, UK.

Julian C Hughes is a retired consultant in old age psychiatry and Honorary Professor, Bristol Medical School, University of Bristol, UK.

Richard Huxtable is Professor of Medical Ethics and Law, and Director, Centre for Ethics in Medicine, University of Bristol, UK.

David Albert Jones is Director, Anscombe Bioethics Centre, Oxford; Professor of Bioethics, St Mary's University, Twickenham and Research Fellow, Blackfriars Hall, University of Oxford, UK.

Alex Ruck Keene is a barrister and Honorary King's Counsel; Visiting Professor at King's College, London and member of 39 Essex Chambers, UK.

John Keown is the Rose F. Kennedy Professor of Christian Ethics in the Kennedy Institute of Ethics, Georgetown University, Washington, DC, USA.

Scott Y.H. Kim is a psychiatrist and Senior Investigator in the Department of Bioethics at the National Institutes of Health, Clinical Center, Bethesda, Maryland; and Adjunct Professor of Psychiatry at the University of Michigan, USA.

John Kleinsman is a researcher in bioethics and Director of the Nathaniel Centre for Bioethics, Aotearoa New Zealand.

Flora Klintworth is a parliamentary research assistant to Baroness Grey-Thompson, House of Lords, UK.

Fiona MacCormick is a consultant in palliative medicine, NHS Lothian, Scotland, UK.

John Maher is a psychiatrist in Barrie, Ontario, Canada; President of the Ontario Association for Assertive Community Treatment & Flexible Assertive Community Treatment; and editor-in-chief of the *Journal of Ethics in Mental Health*.

Alexandra Mullock is Senior Lecturer in Medical Law, University of Manchester and Co-Director of the Centre for Social and Ethical Policy.

Onora O'Neill, The Baroness O'Neill of Bengarve, is Emeritus Professor of Philosophy at the University of Cambridge; President of the Society for Applied Philosophy and a Crossbench Peer in the House of Lords, UK.

Suzanne Ost is Professor at the Law School, Lancaster University, UK.

Paul Paes is Professor of Education and Palliative Care at Newcastle University and an Honorary Consultant in Palliative Medicine at Northumbria Healthcare NHS Trust, UK.

Conall Preston is a parliamentary research assistant to Baroness Finlay, House of Lords and researcher for Living and Dying Well, UK.

Nancy Preston is Professor of Supportive and Palliative Care in the International Observatory on End of Life Care, Faculty of Health and Medicine, Lancaster University, UK.

Robert Preston was Clerk to the Mackay Committee (2004–5) and Director of Living and Dying Well (2010–21).

Claud Regnard is a retired palliative care medicine consultant.

Katherine Sleeman holds the Laing Galazka Chair in Palliative Care, Cicely Saunders Institute, King's College London, UK; and is an Honorary Consultant in Palliative Medicine at King's College Hospital NHS Trust.

Daniel Sulmasy is the André Hellegers Professor of Biomedical Ethics and Director of the Kennedy Institute of Ethics, Georgetown University, Washington, DC, USA.

Peter Thirkell is an Emeritus Professor of Marketing in the School of Marketing and International Business, Victoria University of Wellington, New Zealand.

H Lucy Thomas is a specialty doctor in palliative medicine and a consultant in public health in the UK.

Irene Tuffrey-Wijne is Professor of Intellectual Disability and Palliative Care, Kingston University, London, UK.

Wendi Wicks is a co-founder and leader of Not Dead Yet Aotearoa (a member of Care Alliance-Te Manaaki Haumi), and a lifetime member of Disabled Persons Assembly NZ.

Leeroy William is Adjunct Clinical Professor, Eastern Health Clinical School, Monash University and Adjunct Associate Professor, Public Health Palliative Care Unit, La Trobe University, Australia.

Lesley E. Williamson is a research associate at the Cicely Saunders Institute of Palliative Care, Policy & Rehabilitation and at the NIHR Health & Social Care Workforce Research Unit, King's College London, UK.

Alexandra Wright is the senior Rabbi of the Liberal Jewish Synagogue, St John's Wood, London and President of Liberal Judaism, UK.

John Wyatt is Emeritus Professor of Neonatal Paediatrics, Ethics & Perinatology at University College London, UK.

Kevin Yuill is Emeritus Professor of History at the University of Sunderland, UK and CEO of Humanists Against Assisted Suicide and Euthanasia (HAASE).

Foreword

Currently, in the United Kingdom, discussion around the law on assisted suicide is in flux. Campaigners claim it is what progressive countries are doing and it is what people want. Yet writing a law is not easy – those of us involved in legislation and in legal oversight know that attention to detail is essential and all evidence must be scrutinized. And nowhere is this more important than in matters of life and death. Language must be clear and accurate; safeguards must work and oversight must be effective.

This book provides a fresh perspective on the many relevant issues. There is clarity in the critique of the central issue of autonomy; similarly with the notions of dignity and quality of life. The principle that there should be a prohibition of intentional killing – a principle that is of such great consequence in law and for our social and moral order – is revisited.

Words have meaning. To understand the reality of assisted dying, we need to know what it involves. The term, as the editors and others point out, is a euphemism that fudges the reality of such practices. Recently, the Federal Court of Australia concluded that the term 'suicide' does apply to their Voluntary Assisted Dying legislation.

If we are to cross the Rubicon and allow assisted suicide or euthanasia, we must do so with our eyes open, not with tinted glasses or tunnel vision. Hence the question, 'How safe are the safeguards?'.

This book contains (in Chapter 4) a memorable quote from Professor Etienne Montero giving evidence to the Supreme Court of Canada in 2015, when he said: 'paper safeguards are only as strong as the human hands that carry them'. It is not, however, simply human weakness that leads to safeguards slipping. As authors in this book point out, there are logical reasons why the eligibility criteria tend to expand. Words like 'suffering', or even 'terminal', do not have clear boundaries, and they cannot be assessed with the certainty required.

Concerns about safeguards reflect the reality of discrimination already experienced by those with disability. Many point to undetected abuse, covert coercion, and the risks to those who become vulnerable through illness or circumstance, whether young or old, and those whose despair originates from loneliness, depression or suicidal inclinations.

Without adequate palliative care or social support, true choice is an illusion. The importance of good quality palliative care is evident, as the House of Commons Health and Social Care Select Committee recognized in their 2024 report. It should be available to all, based on best research and kindness, to reduce the complexities of pain and suffering. The Danish Ethical Council concluded that euthanasia is 'in conflict with palliative care' and recommended against legal change as 'it is to a large extent possible to create a decent framework for a dignified death for seriously ill people simply by having sufficient focus on palliative care'. Hence, Denmark – renowned for its progressive attitudes across society – has set its face against a change in the law.

And, as this book shows, the problems emerging in countries that have legalized the taking of – or assistance in the taking of – people's lives by their doctors are significant and serious. Strikingly, too, it turns out that, although of course people wish to have peaceful deaths, many do not see legalizing doctor-assisted suicide or euthanasia as providing the best options.

What is most striking and original in the book, however, is the view of reality which we glean from the perspectives of those who have lived with legislative change in their own countries. Here we can read, sometimes between the lines as well as in the printed word, how the expansion of eligibility criteria is a reality, and also of the pressure – from individuals and from institutions – to conform to a new reality in which the prohibition of intentional killing no longer exists for medical people. Despite clauses to honour conscientious objection, many doctors do not want to be involved. They describe feeling forced into situations which cause them moral discomfort and injury. The experience of the Liverpool Care Pathway in the UK shows how a well-intentioned initiative to improve dying led to some coarsening of attitudes towards life and death.

The present proposals in the UK are limited to the last few months of life. It is, however, clear that once in place, the opportunity to end life would be extended as it has been in other countries.

The book contains a unique response to some of these concerns, and one which has (perhaps strangely) been taken up neither by those who actively advocate for change, nor by other bodies that have looked at the issues. This response is that medical professionals should, by and large, be kept out of any system of assisted suicide or euthanasia. Such socio-legal, or civic, models strive to keep the aims of medical practice separate from the aims of 'assisted dying', save doctors from making decisions for which they are ill-equipped by training or temperament, and prevent a misperception – or it might be a delusion – that intentional killing sanctioned by the state can be regarded as anything other than an extreme event which requires careful judicial (or at least quasi-judicial) review and oversight. This would avoid 'assisted dying' becoming normalized in routine clinical care as a therapy.

In any event, this book should help us to think again. Its premise, that we need to look more closely at the reality of assisted suicide and euthanasia, cannot be denied. The perspectives presented here are revealing. We must ponder the issues with great care. We must not wander into a world in which intentional killing, especially by the medical profession, is applauded without tremendous solicitude for all those who might be vulnerable. These pages encourage us to open our eyes and see with clarity the moral, legal and social world towards which we walk. There is nothing inevitable about which path to take.

This is a book which anyone who is concerned about or interested in end of life and assisted dying must read.

Elizabeth Butler-Sloss
The Baroness Butler-Sloss GBE
House of Lords

Acknowledgements

We should like to thank the following:

Baroness Butler-Sloss for generously giving up her time to write the Foreword, which has so deftly helped to identify critical aspects of this book; and for allowing us to quote from her interview with *The Telegraph* in 2013, recorded in Chapter 11.

Cambridge University Press for permission to use quotation from *The Theory and Practice of Autonomy* by Gerald Dworkin in Chapter 27, reproduced with permission of the Licensor through PLSclear (PLSclear Ref. No. 92877).

The Danish Nationalt Center for Etik, and Dr Frank Beck Lassen in particular, for permission to use quotations from their 2023 report, *The Ethical Council's Opinion on Euthanasia* in Chapter 4.

Ipsos UK for permission to use material from their surveys as referenced in Chapter 2.

Dr Pravin Thevathasan, Editor of the *Catholic Medical Quarterly*, for permission to use a quotation from 2013 from Alison Davis in Chapter 29.

The United Nations for permission to use quotations from the *General Comment No. 1* to the *Convention on the Rights of Persons with Disabilities* in Chapter 13.

Professor Linda Woodhead, now at King's College London, for her advice about permission to use the 2013 YouGov and University of Lancaster Survey referred to in Chapter 2, which she designed while at Lancaster University, and which was administered by YouGov and funded by the AHRC and ESRC 'Religion and Society Programme' which Professor Woodhead also directed.

We are grateful to Professor, the Baroness O'Neill of Bengarve for permission to publish an amended text from her address of 30 June 2010 at the Royal Society of Medicine in London (Chapter 27).

We must record a debt of thanks to Conall Preston for his hard work in supporting the writing of this book. In addition, we must thank Anne Hughes and Andrew Finlay for general support and proof-reading. We should also like to thank Luke Hughes, who first had the idea and encouraged us to write the book. We shall remain very grateful to Hannah Church and Sam Crowe from Open University Press for their persisting encouragement, unswerving patience and considerable support during the development of the book; and to Graham Jones for his invaluable help during its production.

We are extremely grateful to all of our authors. They have written speedily, with very tight deadlines. Their contributions have been vital, highly informative and crucial to the debate about the important contested issues around assisted suicide and euthanasia.

PART 1

Context

1 Introduction

Ilora G. Finlay and Julian C. Hughes

Many have sat by the bedside of a person they love, watching them die and wishing it was over faster. Some have experienced failings in care, others have been grateful for the kindness of modern medicine. Both advocates for a change in the law and those opposing such change are motivated by compassion. But the complexities of the issues involved are inadequately covered in the headlines or soundbites of modern media. These complexities and the unintended consequences of a change in the law are of critical concern to those responsible for designing legislation and implementing change.

The movement in favour of a change in the law to allow forms of assisted suicide or euthanasia seeks to engage the public's natural compassion and fears, suggesting that at issue is their liberty to make choices about their lives and deaths, and their right to demand assistance. According to this way of thinking, the law must be changed to allow and sanction a right to die according to our inclinations.

Against this almost daily insistence that a change in the law is required as a logical step by a liberal and compassionate democracy interested in autonomy, the opposition are often left looking like reactionary, out-of-step characters; albeit many of those opposed to change spend their lives working to improve the quality and standards of care for some of the most vulnerable in our society.

In the United Kingdom (UK) and the British Crown Dependencies (Jersey, Guernsey, the Isle of Man), the heat of the debate has been rising, as it has in other countries. Meanwhile, worrying stories emerge from the countries that have legalized 'assisted dying' in one form or another. Detailed and thoughtful consideration of the real problems that could beset a change in the law on intentional killing are relatively seldom seen except in specialized journals. At a critical moment in the UK debate, therefore, this book provides up-to-date reflections from a broad variety of international experts – some of whom support legislative change in the UK and some of whom have experience of 'assisted dying' in other countries.

Our hope is that we can inform you, the reader, about the key issues to be considered, which must be addressed, to avoid unsafe law. There are hard facts to be established and faced so we can think about matters clearly. Our aim in putting together this collection has been to clarify the debate and focus on reality.

Terminology

We have allowed authors to use their own preferred terminology without imposing uniformity. We are confident the way terms are used within the chapters is clear. We shall, nonetheless, make some brief comments here about terminology to highlight words that cause controversy or confusion.

'Assisted dying' is the term commonly used to name the debate. These words are used to refer *both* to assisted suicide *and* to euthanasia. 'Assisted dying' is, nevertheless, a euphemism. 'Assisted dying' seems better to some than talk of suicide and killing. But the term can be offensive to some who work in palliative care, or many other branches of health care, who would say that they are providing assistance in dying every day; it is just they do not aid suicide and do not kill their patients. Our own practice will be to use quotation marks whenever we talk of 'assisted dying' in order to emphasize that we see it as a euphemism.

'Medical Assistance in Dying' (MAiD) is terminology used in Canada in connection with their legislation. It has the euphemistic qualities of 'assisted dying'. The word 'medical' implies a cloak of benevolence, as if this is simply another form of medical treatment, and thus not a cause for moral concern. Some question why 'assisted dying' should require medical input at all (Twycross 2024; and see Chapters 19 and 20).

'Assisted suicide' is a straightforward term: someone (in 'physician-assisted suicide' it is a doctor) provides lethal drugs for the person to take orally or administer to themselves. Some proponents of legalization feel that 'suicide' carries the outdated stigma of pre-1961 days. It is problematic – it creates a real tension – because in mental health a lot of effort is put into suicide prevention, whereas those who promote 'assisted dying' are, in effect, engaging in suicide promotion.

'Euthanasia' is usually used to portray when the doctor (or other professional) administers the lethal drugs by intravenous injection, or rarely as a gas, intentionally to bring about the person's death. But the term is more complicated. Etymologically it means a good death and many in healthcare work to provide morally unproblematic euthanasia. Deliberately bringing about a premature death, which is how 'euthanasia' is generally used, must not be confused with the cessation of futile treatment or a patient's competent treatment refusal. Euthanasia can be voluntary, where the person asks to die; or non-voluntary, where the person is unable to say what they wish, as in the case of newborn babies or people with advanced dementia. The term 'involuntary euthanasia' is usually considered to be murder or manslaughter as the death runs counter to the person's competently expressed wishes. By 'euthanasia' we shall mean voluntary active euthanasia, when a person engages someone else to act to end his or her life.

The term 'slippery slope' is one we have tried to avoid. Enforceable boundaries and limits to the practice of one person being involved in taking the life of another are essential when considering legal safeguards. There is an empirical argument, that in practice, so-called safeguards designed to limit 'assisted dying' are mere qualifying criteria, open to wide interpretation, which cannot be objectively verified, and which result in ever-increasing types of conditions being deemed appropriate for premature death, with a resulting escalation of numbers of 'assisted' deaths in those societies (see Chapter 30). Trying to restrict the qualifying criteria can be seen as discriminatory.

There is a logical point too: if the issue is suffering, why should it only be from terminal illness and why not from longer term disability? If 'assisted dying' is available to those who are competent, why not to those who become incompetent? If it is limited to physical suffering, why not to mental or existential suffering? As we see incremental expansion of the criteria, attitudinal changes across much of society may well alter.[1] Writing in *The Irish Times*, Breda O'Brien (2024) stated: 'Once assisted dying becomes one of a menu of options, some people will opt to die rather than live believing that they are burdensome to someone else.'

The concerns for legislators and the public

So, what are the concerns and arguments that need to be considered carefully? Our intention here is not to provide a detailed summary of the chapters that follow. Instead, we wish to highlight the scale and depth of the issues that arise.

Table 1.1: Issues to be considered by legislators and the public

Concerns and issues	Chapters in the book where these are discussed
Polls suggest people want 'assisted dying', but when asked, many confuse it with normal clinical practice. When people understand the complexities, the proportion in favour of change declines.	Chapters 2 and 3
People must think carefully about the problems they are trying to solve and about the consequences that might follow from a change in the law, which must apply to everyone.	Chapters 10, 12 and 14
Subjective terminology ('unbearable suffering') opens the gate to incremental expansion away from initial safeguards.	Chapters 3, 5, 6 and 30
Current laws walk a tightrope, balancing between compassionate assistance in suicide (militating against prosecution) and the need to protect the vulnerable from mal-intent.	Chapters 3, 10, 12 and 14
Do safeguards really work for the people for whom they are intended and are they fair and equitable?	Chapters 4, 7, 11, 22, 23, 24 and 30
The assessment of capacity can be very difficult and, in some circumstances, almost impossible.	Chapters 11, 13 and 25
None of us are fully autonomous, as we discovered during the Covid-19 pandemic. Individual autonomy cannot be the primary and sure basis for legal change.	Chapters 3, 14 and 27; and see discussion here in Chapter 1

(continued)

Table 1.1: Issues to be considered by legislators and the public (*continued*)

Concerns and issues	Chapters in the book where these are discussed
Dignity, defined by Cicely Saunders as 'having a sense of personal worth', can be enhanced or undermined.	Chapter 28
Medical assistance with suicide (or agreeing to administer euthanasia) cuts across suicide prevention strategies and the rates of unassisted suicide rise.	Chapters 3, 8, 15 and 29
Diagnosis and prognosis are far from exact sciences. Do errors result in wrongful decisions and avoidable premature death?	Chapters 11 and 16
What is the role of palliative care in enabling true choice?	Chapters 3, 4, 17 and 18
Should 'assisted dying' be delivered by a socio-legal model, separate from health care, and prove easier and safer to administer and monitor than existing proposals? No medical skills are required in prescribing or administering a fixed dose of lethal drugs and doctors are poor at detecting coercion or abuse.	Chapters 19 and 20
What are the potential psychological, emotional and moral impacts on all those who witness 'assisted dying'?	Chapters 5 and 15
The lethal drugs are not licensed for use in euthanasia or in assisted suicide; their use is not regulated; there are failure rates and complications.	Chapters 14 and 21
Those with disabilities, including intellectual disabilities, feel particularly vulnerable. They already feel stigmatized in society by ableist policies and attitudes.	Chapters 3, 6, 8, 22, 23 and 24
Elder abuse and coercive threats are sadly rife, but mostly undetected by professionals.	Chapters 11, 25 and 26
In the face of poor care, choice is an illusion – where realistic choices do not exist, coercion can masquerade as choice.	Chapters 5, 9, 25 and 26
Once legalized, 'assisted dying' quickly becomes normalized and can be seen as a solution to social and economic problems.	Chapters 4, 7, 9 and 15
A tolerant society must be open to rational arguments and to examining evidence carefully.	Chapters 3, 31, 32, 33 and 34

Legislators and the public must think hard and carefully about the implications of changing the law. All in all, it is hard to see how steps can be taken in the direction of legalizing 'assisted dying' without considerable caution and much deeper debate than we usually see in the media.

Discussion: the pillars of the debate

In the remainder of this Introduction, we shall hang our thoughts on the main pillars of the arguments in favour of and against 'assisted dying'. [These arguments can be found in many publications, including Dworkin et al. (1998), Finlay and Preston (2020), Graham and Hughes (2014), Keown (1995) and the other books listed in our bibliography.] Our intention is simply to highlight facts and ramifications that are important but are easily overlooked.

We have identified four pillars in the arguments that surround 'assisted dying': (1) autonomy and choice; (2) intentional killing and personal safety; (3) safeguards and incremental extension to expand eligibility; and (4) palliative care.

Autonomy and choice

Both in theory and in practice, autonomy is frequently highlighted as the main reason for 'assisted dying'. The concept originally arose in medical practice to protect patients from interventions they did not want and to which they had not consented. However, the philosopher, John Harris, pointed to a broader understanding:

> Respect for persons, something we all wish to show, requires us to acknowledge the dignity and value of others and to treat them as ends in themselves, not merely instrumentally. This means respecting their autonomy. Autonomy is the ability to choose and the freedom to choose between competing conceptions of how to live. ... When we are denied control at the end of our lives, we are denied autonomy. (House of Lords 2004–5)

Not only is autonomy important in theory, it is also seen as important by those facing death. In Oregon, losing autonomy was the main concern for those availing themselves of 'assisted dying': 90.8 per cent of people gave it as a concern between 1998 and 2001; the figure in 2023 was 91.6 per cent (Oregon Health Authority 2024). Hence, both theoretically and in reality, autonomy is a crucial plank in the argument for a change in the law.

Some of the conceptual problems surrounding autonomy are clearly set out in Chapter 27 (see also Chapters 3 and 14). No one person is an island – we are interdependent in almost everything we do, as our decisions and actions have implications for others. Hence we should really think in terms of 'relational autonomy'. My deciding that I must die now, even if through non-assisted suicide, still impinges on others.

A change in the law, therefore, has consequences for other people, not just for those who can make their views known. Legal change, as reported in Part 2, increases the sense of vulnerability, particularly in some patient and ethnic groups, as well as impacting on those expected to assist in 'assisted dying'. This is one of the reasons why socio-legal models (Chapters 19 and 20) have their appeal. Many doctors and other healthcare professionals feel uneasy about assessing patients' eligibility for and participating in 'assisted dying' and want no involvement.

Relational autonomy recognizes how our choices are influenced and how they impinge on others. Individualistic autonomy can be characterized as being derived from colonialist attitudes rather than societal respect for each and every citizen, providing an unstable foundation for something as significant as a change in the law to allow 'assisted dying'. Take, for instance, the deep issues around 'suicide' and 'rational suicide', considered in Chapters 15 and 29. It has been asserted that the difficulties with rational suicide stem from 'a profound fear of ageing and dying rooted in seeing ourselves as individual selves, separate from the collective' (Pope 2017: 72). As David Brooks (2023) wrote in *The Atlantic*: 'Autonomy-based liberalism leaves people alone. Its emphasis on individual sovereignty inevitably erodes the bonds between people.'

Yet the impetus to have control over our lives, including choices about how we die, is strong, suggesting that we should have *a right* to die. However, rulings in the case of Diane Pretty (in the Law Lords in 2001 and the European Court of Human Rights in 2002) roundly rebutted this: it was not possible to derive a right to die from the right to life.

It is usual when thinking of rights to think of duties and obligations. When legislation is passed there is evidence that a conscience clause becomes eroded as it is increasingly challenged by those who claim a right to die at a time and place of their choosing. This raises issues around conscientious objection, as described in the Netherlands (Chapter 5), Canada (Chapter 7), New Zealand (Chapter 8) and Australia (Chapter 9). It sounds simple enough to say that professionals would have the right to follow their consciences, but if 'assisted dying' starts to be seen as part of normal health care – and in Canada normalization of MAiD within health care has been rapid – then it is a small step for unwillingness to participate (on the part of individuals or institutions) to be framed as a breach of contract (Chapters 7 and 9).

Intentional killing and personal safety

If autonomy is the philosophical foundation for calls for 'assisted dying', the prohibition of intentional killing is the cornerstone to its opposition. Even among those who are against 'assisted dying', the debate too readily turns to consider safeguards and palliative care. But the prohibition of intentional killing is fundamental.

The clearest statement was made by Lord Walton in the House of Lords in 1994. He acknowledged the moving plight and painful experiences of many facing death, as well as the salience of autonomy in connection with death and dying. Then he stated:

> Ultimately, however, we concluded that such arguments are not sufficient reason to weaken *society's prohibition of intentional killing which is the cornerstone of law and of social relationships*. Individual cases cannot reasonably establish the foundation of a policy which would have such serious and widespread repercussions. The issue of euthanasia is one in which the interests of the individual cannot be separated from those of society as a whole. (House of Lords 1994; added emphasis)

We all generally accept the rule that we should not intentionally kill each other – a rule that allows us to live our lives safely and peacefully. Moreover, the prohibition of intentional killing is deeply rooted in our society: morally, legally, socially, historically, culturally, and so on.

The prohibition of intentional killing explains 'the stern face' of the assisted suicide policy issued by the Crown Prosecution Service in England and Wales

(Chapter 12). Yet those compelled out of compassion to act should be approached with 'a kind heart'. Although the policy sees hardly any prosecutions, its deterrence role can be regarded as an inevitable feature of a policy that must seek out actual cases of homicide (see also Chapter 10).

Our prohibition of intentional killing explains why there are concerns about missing data in the reports about 'assisted dying' from various countries. In the Netherlands, Groenewoud et al. (2021) raised the possibility of 'misuse' of euthanasia. In Belgium, 'Independent research shows that only around 50 per cent of cases of euthanasia are reported, and the unreported cases are those that are more ethically and legally problematic' (Jones et al. 2017: 278). In Flanders, Chambaere et al. found that 'the rate of hastening death without an explicit request from the patient remained stable at 1.7 per cent in 2013' (2015: 1179). But this small percentage represents over 1,000 deaths annually. Moreover, we must remember that the reporting of 'assisted dying' relies on the professionals involved to report the details of the case and *only after the event*. It is no surprise that there have been virtually no prosecutions in any country that has legalized 'assisted dying'.

The use of the word 'intentional' brings to mind the confusion that sometimes exists about the doctrine, or principle, of 'double effect'. Double effect suggests it is morally licit to do something *foreseeing* a bad outcome as long as it was not *intended*. It is almost axiomatic in medicine. When we give chemotherapy, the intention is to treat a specific cancer, even if a foreseeable consequence might be neutropenia and sepsis. We do not intend fatal organ failure. Yet double effect is still criticized by some who think it mere semantics to talk of a difference between foreseeing and intending.

We do not need to delve deeper into the principle of double effect (see Gillon 1986: 133–39). Except, for years, people have continued to think: (a) that the use of morphine for people in pain kills them; and, therefore, (b) the principle of double effect is required to justify doctors killing their patients with morphine. But the appropriate and judicious use of morphine does not kill people, so the double effect argument in this context is pointless.

Our intentions are embedded in our actions. The aim in both assisted suicide and euthanasia is to bring about the person's death as rapidly as possible. Hence 'assisted dying' breaks the prohibition of intentional killing. But through the proper use of analgesics, or sedatives, or antidepressants, or anticonvulsants, or surgery – these things do not *aim at the death* of patients. Some people argue that 'assisted dying' can be thought of as a part of palliative care, and this is the reality in some jurisdictions (Chapters 7 and 9). But the two things are radically different. The intentional nature of one set of activities is to reduce suffering and distress; the intentional nature of the other is to end the person's life.

The same considerations are at play when we think of withholding or withdrawing treatment, including cardiopulmonary resuscitation. The aim is not to kill the patient, but to lessen the burden of futile treatments. Nevertheless, it is easy for an over-acceptance of death to emerge, as was seen during Covid-19 when the use of 'Do Not Attempt Cardio-Pulmonary Resuscitation' (DNACPR) orders was too often taken to mean 'do not resuscitate at all' – and mistrust of clinicians developed in some care homes and pressurized clinical services.

Some years ago in the UK, there was great public and media consternation about the use of the Liverpool Care Pathway (LCP). The LCP was a well-intentioned compassionate initiative to take the best aspects of hospice care at the end of life and roll them out across the wider National Health Service (NHS). A financial incentive was given to NHS Trusts to speed up the LCP adoption, but this encouraged the impression in some that the LCP was covertly intended to bring about death rather than being a response to recognizing imminent death (within hours). Accusations of wrongful deaths arose, which led to Baroness Neuberger being asked to undertake an in-depth inquiry (Neuberger et al. 2013).

For those contemplating legislative change towards assisted suicide and euthanasia, the lesson is clear: a well-intentioned carefully thought-out approach failed when rolled out across the NHS and this was compounded by a perception of incentives to 'put patients on the pathway'. The ease with which some staff failed to question the way their own services were implementing the LCP revealed a susceptibility to devaluing life and seeing death as a solution to workplace pressures.

Many healthcare professionals wish to have nothing to do with 'assisted dying'. For others, socio-legal models (Chapters 19 and 20) would be a compromise because at least they would not involve a contradiction of purpose. The naturally felt prohibition of intentional killing also explains the emotional upset that doctors who take part in euthanasia can feel, especially when their participation seems forced (Chapters 5 and 15). The pressure to participate becomes more intense when people claim they have a *right* to 'assisted dying' as seen in Canada (Lemmens 2023). The further step is that regulators start to see it as their job to encourage MAiD, increasing the pressure on individuals and institutions, such as hospices, to participate (Lemmens 2023). Similar developments have been seen in other countries, such as Belgium, where euthanasia has moved from being 'an exceptional act, a last resort for extreme cases' to being a normal part of end-of-life care, where 'patients apparently believe they have a right to euthanasia' (Montero 2017: 37).

Of course, not all doctors object to 'assisted dying'. In every country where it is legal, there is always a cadre of doctors and other health professionals who are more involved in assisted suicide and euthanasia than most. No doubt many of these professionals act out of a sense of compassion. But one charge against 'assisted dying' is that it leads to a coarsening of society.

Lyon (2024) records some of the expressions used by 'some prolific public-facing MAID providers in Canada and other countries'. Euthanasia leaves them 'hyped up on adrenaline' and feeling 'very good'. It is 'heartwarming', 'liberating' or like taking part in a 'crusade'; it even causes an 'urgent and pressing need for sex'. This last is a frank and somewhat shocking admission on the part of Philip Nitschke, a leading advocate of 'assisted dying' in Australia (Simons 2013). Lyon (2024) also describes laughter being provoked 'in providers discussing how to force provision on resisting patients or upset families'. He goes on to say, 'The providers experiencing these emotions are among those with the highest known provision rates (hundreds of deaths each) and vocal advocates for MAiD' (Lyon 2024).

The shocking thing about these revelations is that they originate from people involved in ending the lives of others. The prohibition of intentional killing is deeply ingrained in our DNA, so we find it profoundly disquieting. Or at least we should do, unless our sensibilities have indeed been coarsened. Matthew Parris (2024), writing in *The Times*, said this: 'As … the practice spreads, social and cultural pressure will grow on the terminally ill to hasten their own deaths so as "not to be a burden" on others or themselves. I believe this will indeed come to pass. And I would welcome it.' But what we thereby welcome (if we do) is exactly a weakening of '*society's prohibition of intentional killing … which is the cornerstone of law and of social relationships*' (House of Lords 2004–5). Reflecting on 14 years of euthanasia in Belgium, Benoit Beuselinck, an oncologist, said: 'An important value of our society, the unconditional respect of human life, has been overruled' (2017: 113).

Safeguards and incremental extension to expand eligibility

Parris (2024) accepts the idea that initial safeguards will eventually be replaced by broader criteria allowing more people to access 'assisted dying'. We should, to be more exact, talk about expanding the eligibility criteria – already a reality in many countries and proposed in others (Chapters 3, 4, 6, 7, 8, 9 and 15; and see Montero 2017). We can explain this in terms of what O'Neill (in Chapter 27) refers to as 'mere sheer choice', where a simple form of autonomy rules, so that if someone chooses something they should get it. Or we can explain it in terms of what Kim (in Chapter 30) describes as 'a desire for equality'; so, if the eligibility criteria allows you to have 'assisted dying' for terminal cancer, on the grounds of equality – given that I also suffer – I should be allowed access to 'assisted dying' for my chronic (non-terminal) condition. Or we can explain it in terms of rights, as we have seen in the Netherlands (Chapter 6), Canada (Chapter 7) and Belgium (Montero 2017), where talk about 'assisted dying' as a right has gradually pushed to expand the eligibility criteria by incremental extension. Hence, in various countries the criteria include, or there is pressure to include, mental health conditions, children, people living with dementia, people who have not made a request to die, older people who are simply tired of life, and so on.

Before MAiD was passed in Canada, in response to the worry that the law would endanger 'people who were depressed, stressed, or just poor and overwhelmed … Citing studies from jurisdictions elsewhere … Prime Minister Justin Trudeau declared that this "simply isn't something that ends up happening"' (Brooks 2023). Yet in 2024, Canada is being called 'the world capital of assisted dying' (*The Times* 2024), a view supported by several chapters in this book (e.g. Chapters 7, 15 and 26), which reflects the view that safeguards have all but disappeared. Seemingly in response to the widespread concerns, the Canadian government has paused the expansion of the eligibility criteria to include people suffering purely from mental health conditions.

Powerful pressure groups advocate for ever wider changes in the law as a political issue. But, as we have suggested, that pressure needs to be tempered by reality. Els Borst was the health minister in the Netherlands from 1994 until 2002, so oversaw the passing into law of their euthanasia bill. Later, it is reported, she decided that the government acted 'far too early'. In an interview, she said she thought the government did not pay attention to the need for palliative care and support for people who were dying. She said: 'In the Netherlands, we first listened to the political and societal demand in favour of euthanasia. ... Obviously, this was not in the proper order' (Liaugminas 2009).

One way in which the eligibility criteria for 'assisted dying' can be expanded is to allow or include organ donation. Organ donation after euthanasia is practised in both the Netherlands and Belgium. In a controversial paper, Wilkinson and Savulescu suggested that 'although most arguments for euthanasia are distinguished from questions of organ donation, it may be that the benefits of donation, for the individual and for others, provide the *strongest case* for euthanasia' (2012: 41). We cannot discuss this further in sufficient detail, but simply note the possibility that organ donation might be a motivation for 'assisted dying', which raises a host of ethical, legal, social and medical questions. Organ donation and euthanasia is a real issue in the transplant literature (van Dijk et al. 2023). There are now discussions of organ donation by anaesthetized patients: 'organ donation euthanasia'. This is where 'The patient does not die as a result from the administered euthanasia drugs, but receives anesthesia before the organs, including the heart, are taken out, which then causes death' (Bollen et al. 2020: S298). For a fuller discussion, see Stammers, who concluded: 'There appears to be a very thin line between a "last act of grace" and a final act of desecration' (2017: 130).

Palliative care

The House of Commons Health and Social Care Committee's report, Assisted Dying/Assisted Suicide (2024), highlighted the general importance of 'a good death'. Most of its recommendations were about palliative care: there should be universal coverage, with an increase in funding to hospices, and better mental health support to those who are terminally ill, with improved health literacy and support for those facing a terminal illness.

This resonates with those who call for improved palliative care for all those who fear pain and suffering, particularly when they are near death (Chapters 3, 4, 8, 10, 17, 25, 26 and 28). Not only does this require that palliative care is available to all, which it is not (Chapter 17), it also requires ongoing funding of high-quality research, looking at end-of-life care in all settings. Research funding for palliative care has long been a low priority (Higginson 2016). But it is important, partly because a common response to those who think it is better to pursue good quality palliative care than 'assisted dying' is that palliative care does not 'work' for everyone.

It is true that some people receiving palliative care die in pain, with estimates based on relatives' reports ranging between 1.4 per cent and 12 per cent (Zamora et al. 2019: 11). However, this depends on where they receive palliative care and from whom. Palliative care, however, is complex. In microbiology, we know that certain bacteria will be killed by certain antibiotics. It is not the same with pain. As Cicely Saunders emphasized, pain is a result of physical, psychological, social and spiritual components occurring in a unique individual. So palliative care needs time and expertise. Too often patients only meet a palliative care professional when they are very close to death. Hence the need for both more research in symptom control and medications (Chapter 18) and better use of resources (Chapter 17).

Finally, we must face what people actually fear. There are certain conditions which people dread and feel that death would be preferable to enduring the suffering associated with them. What should our response be to people living with these conditions who feel they simply cannot cope? Genuine compassion is essential; and every form of clinical, practical and emotional support to the people themselves and to their families and friends. To make this support realistically useful will, again, require resources as well as research. But what if despite all this the person says he or she cannot continue? Might not 'assisted dying' then be the answer?

Your response to that question will depend on your response to the information, opinions and arguments set out in this book. For this very particular group – those for whom literally nothing else will do – will it be possible to pass a law that allows them to access 'assisted dying' without any risks to others, to those vulnerable groups identified in these pages? Are we willing to take the risk that we shall seem like Prime Minister Trudeau denying that bad things happen? Is it worth passing a law that might lead to a profound change in the values of society? Once normalized, will we start to feel that certain people or groups of people would be better off dead; moreover, that they should seek 'assisted dying' for the sake of their friends, family and society as a whole? Should we lift the prohibition of intentional killing that has been the cornerstone of our law, our relationships and our social and civil lives? The purpose of this book is to encourage us to ponder these points profoundly, thoughtfully, with care, compassion and in detail.

Note

1. For fuller discussion of many of these terms, see Keown (2018).

References

Beuselinck, B. (2017) 2002–2016: fourteen years of euthanasia in Belgium, in D.A. Jones, C. Gastmans and C. MacKellar (eds) *Euthanasia and Assisted Suicide: Lessons from Belgium.* Cambridge: Cambridge University Press.

Bollen, J., Shaw, D., de Wert, G. et al. (2020) Organ donation euthanasia (ODE): performing euthanasia through living organ donation, *Transplantation*, 104 (S3): S298. Available at: https://doi.org/10.1097/01.tp.0000700004.43157.0a (accessed 10 April 2024).

Brooks, D. (2023) The outer limits of liberalism, *The Atlantic*, 4 May. Available at: https://www.theatlantic.com/magazine/archive/2023/06/canada-legalized-medical-assisted-suicide-euthanasia-death-maid/673790/ (accessed 25 February 2024).

Chambaere, K., Stichele, Mortier, F. et al. (2015) Recent trends in euthanasia and other end-of-life practices in Belgium, *New England Journal of Medicine*, 372 (12): 1179–81. Available at: https://doi.org/10.1056/NEJMc1414527.

Dworkin, G., Frey, R.G. and Bok, S. (1998) *Euthanasia and Physician-Assisted Suicide: For and Against.* Cambridge: Cambridge University Press.

Finlay, I. and Preston, R. (2020) *Death by Appointment: A Rational Guide to the Assisted Dying Debate.* Newcastle upon Tyne: Cambridge Scholars.

Gillon, R. (1986) *Philosophical Medical Ethics.* Chichester: Wiley.

Graham, P. and Hughes, J.C. (2014) Assisted dying – the debate: *videtur … sed contra*, *Advances in Psychiatric Treatment*, 20 (4): 250–57. Available at: https://doi.org/10.1192/apt.bp.112.010744.

12   The Reality of Assisted Dying

Groenewoud, A.S., Atsma, F., Arvin, M. et al. (2021) Euthanasia in the Netherlands: a claims data cross-sectional study of geographical variation, *BMJ Supportive & Palliative Care*, 4: e867–77 (updated 2024). Available at: https://doi.org/10.1136/bmjspcare-2020-002573 (accessed 8 April 2024).

Higginson, I.J. (2016) Research challenges in palliative and end of life care, *BMJ Supportive & Palliative Care*, 6: 2–4. Available at: https://doi.org/10.1136/bmjspcare-2015-001091.

House of Commons (2024) *Assisted Dying/Assisted Suicide*, Health and Social Care Committee: Second Report of Session 2023–24, 20 February. Available at: https://publications.parliament.uk/pa/cm5804/cmselect/cmhealth/321/report.html (accessed 27 March 2024).

House of Lords (1994) *Medical Ethics: Select Committee Report*, Hansard, vol. 554, Col. 1346, debated 9 May. Available at: https://hansard.parliament.uk/lords/1994-05-09/debates/40522656-8041-4d6f-a2a0-d7f9a9cbc3db/MedicalEthicsSelectCommitteeReport (accessed 8 April 2024).

House of Lords (2004–5) *Assisted Dying for the Terminally Ill Bill – Minutes of Evidence*, Question 1. Available at: https://publications.parliament.uk/pa/ld200405/ldselect/ldasdy/86/4090903.htm (accessed 6 April 2024).

Jones, D.A., Gastmans, C. and MacKellar, C. (2017) Final conclusions on final solutions, in D.A. Jones, C. Gastmans and C. MacKellar (eds) *Euthanasia and Assisted Suicide: Lessons from Belgium*. Cambridge: Cambridge University Press.

Keown, J. (ed.) (1995) *Euthanasia Examined: Ethical, Clinical and Legal Perspectives*. Cambridge: Cambridge University Press.

Keown, J. (2018) *Euthanasia, Ethics and Public Policy: An Argument Against Legalisation*, 2nd edn. Cambridge: Cambridge University Press.

Lemmens, T. (2023) When death becomes therapy: Canada's troubling normalization of health care provider ending of life, *American Journal of Bioethics*, 23: 79–84. Available at: https://doi.org/10.1080/15265161.2023.2265265.

Liaugminas, S. (2009) Euthanasia pioneer now admits it's wrong, *Mercator*, 4 December. Available at: https://www.mercatornet.com/euthanasia_pioneer_now_admits_its_wrong (accessed 29 March 2024).

Lyon, C. (2024) Words matter: 'enduring intolerable suffering' and the provider-side peril of medical assistance in dying in Canada, *Journal of Medical Ethics*. Available at: https://doi.org/10.1136/jme-2023-109555 (accessed 27 March 2024).

Montero, E. (2017) The Belgian experience of euthanasia since its legal implementation in 2002, in D.A. Jones, C. Gastmans and C. MacKellar (eds) *Euthanasia and Assisted Suicide: Lessons from Belgium*. Cambridge: Cambridge University Press.

Neuberger, J., Aaronovitch, D., Bonser, T. et al. (2013) *More Care, Less Pathway: A Review of the Liverpool Care Pathway*, Independent Review of the Liverpool Care Pathway. Available at: https://www.gov.uk/government/publications/review-of-liverpool-care-pathway-for-dying-patients (accessed on 8 April 2024).

O'Brien, B. (2024) Only Irish exceptionalism can explain the rush to legislate for assisted dying, *The Irish Times*, 24 March. Available at: https://www.irishtimes.com/opinion/2024/03/24/breda-obrien-only-irish-exceptionalism-can-explain-the-rush-to-legislate-for-assisted-dying/ (accessed 25 March 2024).

Oregon Health Authority (2024) *Oregon Death with Dignity Act: 2023 Data Summary*, Oregon Health Authority, Public Health Division, Center for Health Statistics, 20 March. Available at: https://www.oregon.gov/OHA/PH/ProviderPartnerResources/EvaluationResearch/DeathwithDignityAct/Pages/index.aspx (accessed 6 April 2024).

Parris, M. (2024) We can't afford a taboo on assisted dying, *The Times*, 29 March. Available at: https://www.thetimes.co.uk/article/we-cant-afford-a-taboo-on-assisted-dying-n6p8bfg9k (accessed 9 April 2024).

Pope, A. (2017) A psychological history of ageism and its implications for elder suicide, in R.E. McCue and M. Balasubramaniam (eds) *Rational Suicide in the Elderly: Clinical, Ethical, and Sociocultural Aspects*. Cham: Springer.

Simons, M. (2013) Between life and death, *The Sydney Morning Herald*, 31 August. Available at: https://www.smh.com.au/lifestyle/between-life-and-death-20130826-2skl0.html (accessed 9 April 2024).

Stammers, T. (2017) 'A last act of grace?': Organ donation and euthanasia in Belgium, in D.A. Jones, C. Gastmans and C. MacKellar (eds) *Euthanasia and Assisted Suicide: Lessons from Belgium*. Cambridge: Cambridge University Press.

The Times (2024) Lessons from the world's assisted dying capital, Sarah Baxter speaking on *The Story*. Podcast available at: https://www.thetimes.co.uk/podcasts/the-story (accessed 10 April 2024).

Twycross, R. (2024) Assisted dying: principles, possibilities, and practicalities. An English physician's perspective, *BMC Palliative Care*, 23: 99. Available at: https://doi.org/10.1186/s12904-024-01422-6 (accessed 20 April 2024).

van Dijk, N., Stärcke, P., de Jongh, W. et al. (2023) Organ donation after euthanasia in patients suffering from psychiatric disorders: 10-years of preliminary experiences in the Netherlands, *Transplant International*, 36: 10934. Available at: https://doi.org/10.3389/ti.2023.10934 (accessed 10 April 2024).

Wilkinson, D. and Savulescu, J. (2012) Should we allow organ donation euthanasia? Alternatives for maximising the number and quality of organs for transplantation, *Bioethics*, 26: 32–48. Available at: https://doi.org/10.1111/j.1467-8519.2010.01811.x.

Zamora, B., Cookson, G. and Garau, M. (2019) *Unrelieved Pain in Palliative Care in England*, OHE Consulting Report, London: Office of Health Economics. Available at: https://www.ohe.org/publications/unrelieved-pain-palliative-care-england (accessed 10 April 2024).

2 Polling on assisted suicide: the misuse of public opinion

Andrew Hawkins[1]

Introduction

Most public opinion polls, with one or two notable exceptions, have shown consistent and generally extensive public support for assisted suicide. For the past 5 years, YouGov has tracked two questions bimonthly. The first asks whether people 'think the law should or should not be changed to allow someone to assist in the suicide of someone suffering from a terminal illness'. Since 2019 support has varied between 64 per cent and 71 per cent (YouGov 2024). A second regular question seeks views on whether the law 'should be changed to allow someone to assist in the suicide of someone suffering from a painful, incurable but NOT terminal illness?'. Support for that over the same period has been markedly lower, varying between 41 per cent and 47 per cent (YouGov and University of Lancaster 2013).

Taking much of the published polling on assisted suicide at face value, we might mistakenly believe that much of the British public have taken to heart the kind of large-scale extermination described in P.D. James's 1992 dystopian novel *The Children of Men*, where on reaching 60, those no longer useful to society are forced to take part in the *Quietus*, a council-sanctioned mass drowning.

Misleading the public

But the picture is not as simple as many proponents of assisted suicide would like. Notwithstanding that the issue of assisted suicide is *literally* one of life and death, as with any complex issue spanning legal, socio-economic and medical issues, the public can be easily misled.

If hard cases make bad law, they also make for sensationalist media stories that can tug on heartstrings but do not always reflect the reality of the science or the human stories behind each tragic article. As with polling on the death penalty, to produce a poll showing public 'support' is easy, but to design and conduct a poll which takes account of the many complex arguments and facets that its reintroduction would involve is far harder.

Let us now address the problems with the recent history of polling on assisted suicide, the first of which is poor questioning and imperfect information. Pollsters have for years posed questions that contain within them dangerous assumptions. These assumptions are often easily debunked, and the premises of the questions flawed. Added to this is the problem of imperfect information, which can help explain why public opinion diverges so dramatically from that of, say, Members of Parliament or doctors. Both of these problems combine to create a heavily misguided debate and therefore the need for a renewed focus, on both sides, towards reasoned and rational arguments.

The reluctance of Parliament to legislate to permit assisted suicide reflects the fact that, despite many attempts to change the law, members of each House have had the chance to hear arguments for and against, in objective terms. Those arguments cannot be communicated simply or easily in a public poll.

Some believe it is too late for a debate on this topic – the argument is over. In a 2013 poll of 4,437 adults, YouGov found that 70 per cent supported a change in the law to allow assisted suicide (YouGov and University of Lancaster 2013). Ten years later, YouGov carried out another survey, this time for Dignity in Dying, which claimed an increase in support to 74 per cent (YouGov and Dignity in Dying 2023). Other surveys have shown similar results. For example, a 2009 poll by Ipsos MORI found that 76 per cent thought someone should not be prosecuted for helping a family member commit suicide (Ipsos and Dignity in Dying 2009). Apparent support for euthanasia is hard to deny, and indeed any criticism of the polling, of the sort here, ought to bear this in mind. That said, when reviewing afresh the polling for this chapter, several repeated and problematic semantic terms are evident.

Semantic issues

The first issue is reference to assisted suicide being for those who have an 'incurable illness', '6 months to live' or are experiencing 'unbearable pain'. Doctors themselves assert that such guarantees are often wildly inaccurate (see Chapter 16). Patients often do not die within the forecast timeline. And what does 'unbearable' pain mean in the modern era of effective palliative care?

This is all the more resonant as many survival rates rapidly improve. In the UK over the last 50 years, the cancer survival rate has doubled and improves with each new development. Moreover, pain should never be 'unbearable' given modern palliative care practices.

The second type of problematic phrasing is reference to 'family members' or 'relatives'. Hypothetical emotive scenarios elicit a highly emotive response in what should otherwise be a rational and objective moral debate. Pollsters have a description for such questions and it is not a polite one: they are called 'heartless bastard' questions because respondents answer in the way intended by the client or risk being regarded as cold-hearted. 'Do you want your nearest and dearest to be in unnecessary agony?' No, I thought not.

The third problem is the guarantee that patients who receive assistance to commit suicide always express a 'clear indication of a willingness to die'. As with the (wrong) assumption that no miscarriage of justice can ever occur in the debate around capital punishment, the reality for assisted suicide is that informed, unpressured consent can virtually never be guaranteed.

Indeed, in a 2005 poll (YouGov and Daily Telegraph 2005), respondents were told: 'Some people say that allowing euthanasia would have one or more undesirable consequences.' They were then asked: 'Which, if any, of the following undesirable consequences do you think it would have?' More than half

(51 per cent), including those who had supported euthanasia previously, agreed that 'old people might feel under pressure to seek euthanasia'. Almost the same proportion, 47 per cent, said that an undesirable consequence would be that 'it would lead to the commission of a significant number of murders disguised as mercy killings'. If even people who support assisted suicide concede that some vulnerable older people could be manipulated into it, then it is clearly misleading for questions to imply that the decision to choose assisted suicide would never be influenced by external pressure. That is all the more salient as memories of Dr Harold Shipman recede.

A further problem is that assisted suicide is often presented as a pain-free, immediate and peaceful option. Evidence suggests this simply is not the case (see Chapter 21). Deaths can take hours and, in some horrific cases, patients can regain consciousness and die days later. Others will write about those cases in more detail (see Chapter 4) but the point here is that polls conducted to advance the policy end-point almost never address such (false) assumptions.

It is concerning that these words and phrases appear repeatedly in questions asked by pollsters on behalf of pressure groups. For example, the 2013 YouGov survey referred to above reads as follows:

> Euthanasia is the termination of a person's life, in order to end suffering. Do you think British law should be kept as it is, or should it be changed so that people with incurable diseases have the right to ask close friends or relatives to help them commit suicide, without those friends or relatives risking prosecution? (YouGov and University of Lancaster 2013)

This combines many of the problems identified above, including as a final flourish a hypothetical familial context.

The 2009 Ipsos MORI poll again cites family involvement:

> Think of a situation where a terminally ill but mentally competent adult travels abroad to have an assisted suicide in a country where this is legal. This adult asks a family member or friend to enable or assist them to travel abroad to die. In your opinion, do you think this family member or friend should or should not be prosecuted if they enable or assist that adult to travel abroad and die? (Ipsos and Dignity in Dying 2009)

Frame your question

One of the more egregious examples of framing a question to achieve a specific answer was in a Populus poll for Dignity in Dying (2015). The poll question contained a mind-numbing 139-word introduction setting out the safeguards under which assisted suicide would be conducted, without balancing with any of the downsides. The poll, which found 82 per cent in support of assisted suicide, was hailed as 'the largest ever' on the subject, as if the sample size of 5,000 would magically compensate for its flawed wording.

Worse still, Dignity in Dying hailed the claim that 80 per cent of 'Christians' supported it too, by using a frankly lazy filter question akin to the one used when someone is admitted to hospital and ticks 'CofE' on the form, namely: 'to which of the following religious groups do you consider yourself to be a member of?'. That approach has been widely criticized elsewhere, but it is a poor habit that tends to be used to show that a proposed policy or law change is so reasonable that *even* 'Christians' support it.

At ComRes, the polling company I founded and chaired for over 20 years, we ran many polls on this issue, one of which it is helpful to highlight in demonstrating the power of question wording and how alternative scenarios and better information can measure public opinion more accurately.

Most striking of these surveys was a deliberative poll for Christian Action Research and Education (CARE) in 2014, which showed that opinions on assisted suicide change when the information in the context to the question is improved (ComRes and CARE 2014). In essence, the more people know about what assisted suicide entails, the more squeamish they feel about it.

We first asked if respondents agreed or disagreed with a Bill then going through the House of Lords to legalize assisted suicide in certain circumstances: 73 per cent agreed while 12 per cent disagreed. Of those who agreed, we asked a series of follow-up questions providing additional information. We then asked whether they still supported assisted suicide or if the new information had changed their mind.

This careful approach involved, for example, telling respondents that the country's major disability rights advocacy groups such as SCOPE, Disability Rights UK and Not Dead Yet UK all opposed a change to the law. As a result, more than one in ten (12 per cent) previous supporters of assisted suicide changed their minds and a further quarter said they did not know. We then offered respondents the claim that some vulnerable people might access assisted suicide so as not to be a burden on family (in line with a report covering 2016 which found almost 50 per cent of patients in Oregon whose lives were ended under the Oregon Death with Dignity Act cited 'being a burden' as one of their concerns (Oregon Health Authority 2017)). This led to a further decrease in support to 47 per cent among a hitherto 100 per cent supportive cohort. In other words, with just modest additional information reflecting actual experience in jurisdictions where assisted suicide is already legal, hypothetical supporters reconsidered their position very dramatically indeed.

Public opinion

More thoughtfully designed polls consistently show two important realities about public opinion. First, the public are highly susceptible to excessively emotive language. Second, the more people are made aware of some of the unintended consequences of assisted suicide, support for it decreases. This shows just how important information is to the debate: too many polls have replaced fact (both moral and, less controversially, scientific) with emotion, and their results often reflect this.

Even if we were to dismiss all of the above criticisms, there is one further factor seldom considered but which can be fatal to over-simplistic polling. It is that the public are indeed compassionate, but that compassion appears often wrongly directed at support for what is defined as assisted suicide by lobby groups but in reality is something altogether different.

The most recent evidence for this claim was a Survation poll of 1,032 British adults in July 2021 asking what people understood by the term 'assisted dying' (Survation 2021). Just over four in ten (43 per cent) correctly thought it meant 'providing people who have less than six months to live with lethal drugs to end their life'. Importantly, though, more than half of the sample – 52 per cent – thought that the term either meant 'providing hospice-type care to people who are dying' (10 per cent) or 'giving people who are dying the right to stop life-prolonging treatment' (42 per cent). Importantly for the public debate, this suggests that more than half of the people answering polls about assisted suicide or 'assisted dying' are mistaken about the very thing they are being asked about.

If half the public conflate assisted suicide with palliative care, the poll suggests we should treat all simple one-question polling on the issue with scepticism, unless terms are defined much more carefully than is often the case.

The power of debate on the issue is underlined by comparisons between polling of MPs and real (free) votes. MPs, who have had numerous opportunities to debate this issue, have consistently opposed legalizing assisted suicide. In 2004, ComRes polled MPs with a very simple question: 'In principle, would you support or oppose a Bill to legalize voluntary euthanasia?'. Seventy-nine per cent of MPs opposed and 21 per cent supported.

In 2015, when Rob Marris MP brought his Private Member's Bill to the House of Commons, MPs voted by 330 to 118 against legalizing assisted suicide. One MP anonymously reported, going into that debate intending to vote one way but, having listened to the arguments on both sides, ended up changing their mind and voting against the Bill. That, after all, is the job of a 'parliament'. Parliamentary debate shows the power that reasoned argument has to change minds and reminds of the power of persuasion in politics.

Conclusion

Pro-euthanasia groups have been highly effective at positioning emotive and relatable stories in the media. To an extent, it is right to envelop this debate about life and death in human terms. But we must continue making the case by disseminating facts, because once rational arguments are made, and when the public consider the consequences of legalizing assisted suicide from an informed perspective, they are far less willing to support it.

This has been the key difference between the debate that has taken place in Parliament and that in more public spaces, on social media, broadcast networks and in newspapers. In Parliament, the debate has centred around argument; in the media, it has focused on personalities and emotions.

Some will claim that it is disrespectful to argue that the public lacks the information to have an informed view about the merits or otherwise of assisted suicide. We do not agree. Rather, we believe it is both disrespectful and dangerous to abuse people's innate sense of compassion by over-simplifying this complex issue and framing questions to elicit a particular response.

Polls which meet the standard necessary to inform policy-makers of the public mood must take full account of the limits of public understanding of the terminology and implications of what they are being asked to offer a view on. Those implications should include the experiences of the few jurisdictions that have already legalized assisted suicide, in order that any polling on the issue in the UK can look at the final end-point of progressive liberalization. To make the case about public opinion on anything less than this is tantamount to deception.

Note

1. Andrew Hawkins would like to acknowledge the contribution of Lachlan Rurlander to this chapter.

References

ComRes and CARE (2014) *CARE – Assisted Suicide Poll*, 11–13 July 2014. Available at: https://savanta.com/wp-content/themes/savanta/poll/Care_Assisted_Suicide_Poll_July_2014_(with_summary_table).pdf (accessed 19 February 2024).

Ipsos and Dignity in Dying (2009) *Public Opinions on Assisted Dying*, 16 December 2009. Available at: https://www.ipsos.com/en-uk/public-opinions-assisted-suicide (accessed 19 February 2024).

Oregon Health Authority (2017) *Oregon Death with Dignity Act, Data Summary 2016*, 10 February. Available at: http://www.oregon.gov/oha/PH/PROVIDERPARTNERRESOURCES/EVALUATIONRESEARCH/DEATHWITHDIGNITYACT/Documents/year19.pdf (accessed 19 February 2024).

Populus (now Yonder) and Dignity in Dying (2015) *Dignity in Dying Poll*, 11–19 March 2015. Available at: https://yonderconsulting.com/poll-archive/dignity-in-dying.pdf (accessed 19 February 2024).

Survation (2021) *Survation APPG for Dying Well Survey July 2021*, 8 September 2021. Available at: https://www.survation.com/archive/2021-2/ (accessed 19 February 2024).

YouGov (2024) *Should the law be changed to allow someone to assist in the suicide of someone suffering from a terminal illness?* YouGov UK. Available at: https://yougov.co.uk/topics/politics/trackers/should-the-law-be-changed-to-allow-someone-to-assist-in-the-suicide-of-someone-suffering-from-a-terminal-illness (accessed 19 February 2024).

YouGov and Daily Telegraph (2005) *YouGov/Daily Telegraph Survey Results*, 19–24 August 2005. Available at: https://d3nkl3psvxxpe9.cloudfront.net/documents/YG-Archives-lif-dTel-AborEuthCloning-050830.pdf (accessed 19 February 2024).

YouGov and Dignity in Dying (2023) *YouGov/Dignity in Dying Survey Results*, 13–14 January 2023. Available at: https://docs.cdn.yougov.com/sdx2ypu7cf/DiD_Inquiry_230114.pdf (accessed 19 February 2024).

YouGov and University of Lancaster (2013) *YouGov/University of Lancaster Survey Results*, 25–30 January 2013. Available at: https://d3nkl3psvxxpe9.cloudfront.net/documents/YG-Archive-University-of-Lancaster-300113-faith-matters-euthanasia.pdf (accessed 19 February 2024).

3 Voluntary euthanasia and physician-assisted suicide: seven prominent but weak arguments for legalization[1]

John Keown

Introduction

This chapter outlines seven prominent arguments in favour of legalizing voluntary euthanasia and/or physician-assisted suicide and explains why they fail.

First, however, some definitions. 'Physician-assisted suicide' involves a doctor intentionally helping a patient to suicide, typically by prescribing lethal drugs. 'Euthanasia' involves a doctor intentionally killing a patient, typically by administering a lethal injection. (It is 'voluntary' euthanasia if the patient consents; 'non-voluntary' if the patient is incapable of consenting.)

The debate is *not*, then, about withholding or withdrawing treatment because it is futile, too burdensome or refused by the patient. Nor is it about administering palliative medication with intent to ease serious pain and suffering, even if the doctor foresees that the patient's life may or even will end sooner. Those practices have always been legal and accepted as ethical. To help keep this crucial moral and legal distinction clear, we will avoid the vague and misleading phrase 'assisted dying'.

Now to the seven arguments, the most prominent of which are the first two: respect for autonomy, compassion, legal hypocrisy, a right to suicide, public opinion polls, legal failure, and religion.

Respect for autonomy

The law should respect a patient's right to decide the time and manner of their death, at least if they are 'terminally ill' and/or experiencing 'unbearable suffering'.

Limits to respect for autonomy

There simply is no 'right to decide the time and manner of one's death'. While autonomy is an important human capacity, respect for autonomy has its limits (see also Chapter 27). The law places, and sound ethics justifies, various reasonable restrictions on one's choices. This is particularly true when one's choices would require the involvement of other people, such as doctors, and would have adverse effects on other people, whether on relatives or on society in general.

Endorsing the choice to be medically killed would have profound effects on the medical profession and on society's view of the value of human life. It is, then, a profoundly public – rather than 'private' – matter.

Patients no more have the right to a lethal injection from their physician than to the amputation of a healthy limb, and no more the right to a prescription for lethal drugs than to a prescription for antibiotics. Patients *do* have a right to refuse treatment, but that is a negative right, not a positive right; a shield, not a sword.

One key limit on respect for autonomy is set by the foundational principle of the inviolability (or 'sanctity') of life, the historic legal principle that prohibits the intentional killing of the innocent. That prohibition is grounded in a recognition of our fundamental equality-in-dignity, however sick or disabled or marginalized we may be. As the preamble to the UN Declaration of Human Rights (1948) puts it: 'recognition of the inherent dignity and of the equal and inalienable rights of all members of the human family is the foundation of freedom, justice and peace in the world'.

We *all*, then, equally enjoy the 'right to life', the inalienable right not to be intentionally killed. We also enjoy a right to be protected from suicide. Suicide prevention is an important aspect of social policy and we need to do much more to improve it (Chapter 29). Significantly, there is evidence that, far from reducing the rate of unassisted suicide, the legalization of physician-assisted suicide leads to an increase in both assisted and unassisted suicide (Boer 2017; Girma and Paton 2022).

In its 1994 report unanimously rejecting the case for voluntary euthanasia and physician-assisted suicide, the House of Lords Select Committee on Medical Ethics defended the prohibition on intentional killing. It declared: 'That prohibition is the cornerstone of law and of social relationships. It protects each one of us impartially, embodying the belief that all are equal' (House of Lords 1993–94: para. 237). Moreover, how many requests for voluntary euthanasia/physician-assisted suicide would be *truly* autonomous, especially when suicidal ideation is often associated with mental illness? The Select Committee concluded: '[W]e do not think it possible to set secure limits on voluntary euthanasia … It would be next to impossible to ensure that all acts of euthanasia were truly voluntary, and that any liberalization of the law was not abused' (House of Lords 1993–94: para. 238).

Protecting the vulnerable

Concern for the vulnerable is another powerful reason for limiting individual autonomy. The Select Committee stated: 'We are also concerned that vulnerable people – the elderly, lonely, sick or distressed – would feel pressure, whether real or imagined, to request early death … [T]he message which society sends to vulnerable and disadvantaged people should not, however obliquely, encourage them to seek death, but should assure them of our care and support in life' (House of Lords 1993–94: para. 239).

Similarly, the eminent philosopher Onora O'Neill has observed: 'Legalising "assisted dying" amounts to adopting a principle of indifference towards a special and acute form of vulnerability: in order to allow a few independent folk to get others to kill them on demand, we are to be indifferent to the fact that many less independent people would come under pressure to request the same' (O'Neill 2006; see also Chapter 27 in this volume).

Judging patients 'better off dead'

Even campaigners, for all their trumpeting of autonomy, would limit choice to only *some* patients. Typical proposals for legalization require patients to satisfy some additional criterion, such as 'terminal illness' or 'unbearable suffering'. In other words, doctors would have to judge *which* autonomous requests to grant. And how would the doctor decide, other than on the basis of a judgement that death would benefit the patient; that the patient would be 'better off dead'? The patient proposes but the doctor disposes.

It is no surprise, then, that disability groups (like 'Not Dead Yet') are at the forefront of opposition to decriminalization. They appreciate that legalization is not fundamentally about individual choice but reflects a social judgement that *some* patients' choices should be granted because *their* lives are not 'worth living'.

Compassion

Physicians have a duty of compassion, a duty to relieve their patients' suffering, even if that means administering a lethal injection or writing a prescription for lethal drugs.

Limits to compassion

The doctor's duty of beneficence includes a duty to relieve suffering but, just like the duty to respect autonomy, it is not unlimited. It is trumped by the duty not intentionally to kill, or help kill, his or her patient. This duty not to kill has formed the bedrock of professional medical ethics since the Hippocratic Oath. The core vocation of the physician is to try to heal or to make whole, not to make dead.

This vocation includes a duty to alleviate suffering even if, as an unintended side-effect, life is shortened. But it rules out intentional killing. Traditional professional ethics, then, walks hand in hand with the long-standing criminal prohibition on voluntary euthanasia and physician-assisted suicide. If physicians were to embrace killing as a 'therapeutic' intervention, this would endanger the trust that patients now have that their physician will never abandon them by judging them 'better off dead'. As a leading US health lawyer once starkly put it, he never wanted to have to wonder whether the physician entering his room was wearing the white coat of the healer or the black hood of the executioner.

Palliative care

Not only is killing unethical; it is unnecessary. The enormous progress that has been made in palliative care, not least since the establishment of the hospice movement over 50 years ago, means that no patient need suffer unbearably. Even in rare cases of refractory pain, there is the option of palliative sedation. In 2014, a poll of the Royal College of Physicians showed that over 60 per cent of its members agreed that patients could die with dignity under the existing law, and that relaxation of the law was not needed.

'Unbearable suffering'?

Although euthanasia advocates typically use emotionally charged cases of dying patients with painful symptoms to front their campaign, the reality is that, after legalization, voluntary euthanasia and physician-assisted suicide come to be condoned in a *much* wider, and expanding, range of cases.

Take, for example, the Netherlands, the country with by far the longest experience of legalized voluntary euthanasia and physician-assisted suicide. In 1984, the Dutch Supreme Court declared them lawful for patients with 'unbearable suffering', the focus being on the dying. In 1994, the same court held that a somatic illness was not necessary and that even patients whose suffering arose solely from a mental illness were eligible. And in 2016, the Dutch government proposed to extend the law to allow elderly people with a 'completed life' access to suicide pills. The slipperiness of the slope could scarcely be more apparent.

Moreover, the main reasons people tend to give for accessing voluntary euthanasia and physician-assisted suicide are not agonizing, unrelieved pain and suffering. The official reports from the US State of Oregon, where physician-assisted suicide has been practised since 1997, have consistently shown that by far the two main reasons for requesting such assisted suicide have been 'losing autonomy' and being 'less able to participate in activities making life enjoyable'. And around half of patients have cited being a burden on family, friends and caregivers.

Compassion, autonomy and the logical slippery slope

Campaigners in the UK model their proposals for legalization on the law in Oregon, which allows only physician-assisted suicide, not voluntary euthanasia, and only for the 'terminally ill' (a vague concept). But these proposals would prove but a foot in the door. For, if the relief of suffering and respect for autonomy justify physician-assisted suicide, then:

- they also justify voluntary euthanasia (especially for those unable to kill themselves even with assistance, such as the totally paralysed); and
- they equally justify physician-assisted suicide and voluntary euthanasia for those suffering from a chronic illness, such as arthritis, who may have much longer to suffer than the 'terminally ill'; and
- compassion would justify non-voluntary euthanasia, as in the case of suffering infants or people with advanced dementia. Although they lack autonomy, the absence of patient autonomy does not cancel the doctor's duty to relieve suffering. Why should compassion be confined to the competent? (Keown 2022). Following this logic, the Dutch courts, 12 years after ruling voluntary euthanasia lawful, declared non-voluntary euthanasia lawful, in the case of disabled infants. In short, *anyone who supports voluntary euthanasia is committed in principle to supporting non-voluntary euthanasia.*

Legal hypocrisy

The law allows doctors to end lives by withholding/withdrawing life-prolonging treatment or by administering drugs which, as a side-effect, shorten life, so it is hypocritical of the law to prohibit them from performing voluntary euthanasia/physician-assisted suicide.

Leaving aside the fact that, properly titrated, palliative drugs do not hasten death, the short answer to this argument is that, even if they did, there is a cardinal ethical and legal distinction between *intending* and merely *foreseeing* the shortening of life.

In 1997, in its landmark ruling rejecting a constitutional right to physician-assisted suicide, the US Supreme Court dismissed the argument that respecting a patient's refusal of life-prolonging treatment is the same as physician-assisted suicide. It observed that in physician-assisted suicide, the physician *intends* to assist the patient's death but that this need not be the case with respecting a refusal of treatment. The Chief Justice noted that the fact that General Eisenhower foresaw on D-Day that he was sending many American soldiers to certain death did not mean he intended their death: his purpose was to liberate Europe from the Nazis. Even Dutch law accepts that euthanasia involves intentional, not merely foreseen, life-shortening. This distinction drawn by English law and by professional medical ethics is not, then, hypocritical: it is Hippocratic.

It is also argued that the law unfairly discriminates against the rich, who can afford to fly to Switzerland to obtain physician-assisted suicide at *Dignitas*. This argument proves too little and too much. Too little because the mere fact that some people can afford to circumvent the law is no argument against the law. The rich can, for example, fly abroad to access a ready supply of recreational drugs or to engage in underage sex. Too much because by no means all of those who travel to Dignitas are 'terminally ill'. For example, one young man had been paralysed from the chest down in a rugby accident and did not want to lead 'a second-class existence' (Booth 2008); and one elderly woman with arthritis was still active and simply wished to avoid 'prolonged dwindling' (Savill 2011).

A right to suicide

> In many countries, suicide has been decriminalized. The law now recognizes, therefore, a right to suicide. If there is a right to suicide, it should be legal to assist someone to exercise that right.

The argument is misconceived. It does not follow that decriminalization represents a condonation of suicide, let alone recognition of a 'right' to suicide. In the UK, for example, legislators enacting the Suicide Act 1961 made it crystal clear that decriminalization did not imply condonation. Decriminalization was the result of other factors, including an appreciation that the social problem of suicide, to which people were often driven by mental health problems, was better addressed by the healthcare system than the criminal justice system. Moreover, assisting or encouraging suicide remained a serious crime, confirming that suicide remained contrary to public policy.

Public opinion polls

> Opinion polls show that a clear majority of the public supports legalization. The law should reflect the will of the people.

Polls do tend to show a clear majority in favour of legalization. However, polls can be misleading: much can turn on the phrasing of questions and on the amount of background information, if any, given to those polled (see Chapter 2). A House of Lords Select Committee commissioned research which concluded that the polls tended to reflect 'kneejerk' reactions to simple options rather than informed opinion (House of Lords 2004–5: para. 232). Indeed, the polls may largely reflect the influence of the mass media and 'celebrities'. In any event, as history amply demonstrates, majority opinion is no guarantee of sound ethics or social policy.

Legal failure

The law is ineffective. Voluntary euthanasia and physician-assisted suicide are practised illegally. Decriminalization would bring them out into the open and subject them to effective legal control.

All criminal laws are broken to some extent, sometimes (like the law against exceeding the speed limit) to a considerable extent, but that is hardly by itself a reason to repeal them. And there is little evidence that laws against voluntary euthanasia/physician-assisted suicide are any less effective than many other criminal laws. For example, research by medical sociologist Professor Clive Seale (2006) found that the incidence of voluntary euthanasia/physician-assisted suicide in the UK was 'extremely low' (and significantly lower than in the Netherlands, which permits them).

There will be breaches of the law, to a greater or lesser extent, in different jurisdictions, depending on a range of cultural factors. This is not by itself an argument for repeal, especially when repeal is very likely to provoke significant increases in voluntary euthanasia/physician-assisted suicide, as we have seen in countries like the Netherlands and, more recently, Canada, which legalized voluntary euthanasia/physician-assisted suicide in 2016. In both countries, around one in 20 deaths is now by voluntary euthanasia or physician-assisted suicide.

Moreover, the claim that legalization subjects voluntary euthanasia/physician-assisted suicide to effective legal control is inconsistent with the evidence. The Dutch have carried out repeated surveys into end-of-life decision-making, surveys that have shown that since legalization, doctors have failed to report thousands of cases to the Dutch euthanasia review committees, and that thousands of patients have been euthanized without request, both practices in clear breach of the law.

It is not surprising that the Dutch law has been criticized, twice, by the UN Human Rights Committee. In 2001, the Committee expressed concern not only about the adequacy of the regulatory system but about the extension of the law to minors, and the practice of infanticide. In 2009, it remained concerned about the extent of voluntary euthanasia/physician-assisted suicide and the fact that a physician could terminate a patient's life without any independent review by a judge to guarantee that the decision was not the subject of undue influence or misapprehension.

What of Canada, which like the Netherlands permits both voluntary euthanasia and physician-assisted suicide? It is skiing down the slippery slope even faster than the Dutch have. Since legalization in 2016, it has already ditched the legal requirement that the patient's death be 'reasonably foreseeable' and has legislated to make the mentally ill eligible at a future date. In 2019, the UN Special Rapporteur on the rights of people with disabilities expressed her extreme concern at the operation of the Canadian law (United Nations 2019; see also Lemmens 2023).

As for Oregon and the US states that have followed its model, there have been no comprehensive surveys, so any claims that its law is ensuring effective control simply lack substantiation. Absence of evidence of abuse is not evidence of absence of abuse, and the Oregon model is not even designed to detect abuse. Its so-called 'safeguards', which are even laxer than those in the Netherlands, have been aptly described by a leading US health law expert as 'largely illusory' (Capron 1996). And, if a critical mass of US states follows Oregon (significantly, only a fifth have so far done so), the obviously arbitrary limitations to physician-assisted suicide and to the 'terminally ill' will be increasingly criticized as 'barriers to access', will buckle under the force of the logic of legalization, and those states will join the Netherlands and Canada hurtling down the slope.

The regulatory mechanism in all three jurisdictions, we should add, depends very largely on self-reporting by the physicians involved, after the event. It is, therefore, intrinsically ineffective. How many physicians are going to volunteer that they have broken the law?

Religion

Opposition to decriminalization is essentially religious, and religious views should not be imposed in secular societies.

This argument is as feeble as it is frequent (see also Chapter 31). Three key arguments against legalization – that it would undermine 'the cornerstone of law and of social relationships' that protects us all equally; that it would threaten vulnerable patients; and that it would resist effective legal control – are all philosophical, not theological. Moreover, many secular bodies, from the UK Parliament to the American Medical Association, have long rejected legalization (and see Chapter 34).

Conclusion

Campaigners for voluntary euthanasia/physician-assisted suicide, abetted by their many allies in the mass media, persistently press the above arguments on legislators, the professions and the public. As we have seen, however, those arguments, either separately or in combination, are weak and they gain no force through repetition. By contrast, both in principle, and because of the inevitable and dangerous consequences of legalization, the case for maintaining the legal bright-line prohibition on intentional killing or assisting suicide remains strong.

Note

1. This chapter is based on Keown (2016), which contains further relevant citations. See also Keown (2018).

References

Boer, T. (2017) Does euthanasia have a dampening effect on suicide rates? Recent experiences from the Netherlands, *Journal of Ethics in Mental Health*, 10: 1–9. Available at: https://jemh.ca/issues/v9/documents/JEMH%20article%20Boer%20final%20proof.pdf (accessed 21 March 2024).

Booth, R. (2008) 'He wasn't prepared for a second-class life': why injured rugby star went to Switzerland to die, *The Guardian*, 18 October. Available at: https://www.theguardian.com/uk/2008/oct/18/11 (accessed 21 March 2024).

Capron, A.M. (1996) Legalizing physician-aided death, *Cambridge Quarterly of Healthcare Ethics*, 5 (1): 10–23.

Girma, S. and Paton, D. (2022) Is assisted suicide a substitute for unassisted suicide?, *European Economic Review*, 145: 104113. Available at: https://www.sciencedirect.com/science/article/pii/S0014292122000551 (accessed 21 March 2024).

House of Lords (1993–94) *Report of the Select Committee on Medical Ethics*, HL Paper 21. London: HMSO. Available at: https://api.parliament.uk/historic-hansard/lords/1994/may/09/medical-ethics-select-committee-report (accessed 28 February 2024).

House of Lords (2004–5) *Report of the Select Committee on the Assisted Dying for the Terminally Ill Bill*, HL Paper 86-I. Available at: https://publications.parliament.uk/pa/ld200405/ldselect/ldasdy/86/8602.htm (accessed 21 March 2024).

Keown, J. (2016) Voluntary euthanasia and physician-assisted suicide: should the WMA drop its opposition?, *World Medical Journal*, 62 (3): 103–7.

Keown, J. (2018) *Euthanasia, Ethics and Public Policy: An Argument Against Legalisation*, 2nd edn. Cambridge: Cambridge University Press.

Keown, J. (2022) The logical link between voluntary and non-voluntary euthanasia, *Cambridge Law Journal*, 81 (1): 84–108.

Lemmens, T. (2023) When death becomes therapy: Canada's troubling normalization of health care provider ending of life, *American Journal of Bioethics*, 23 (11): 79–84.

O'Neill, O. (2006) *A Note On Autonomy And Assisted Dying*. An unpublished memorandum circulated to members of the House of Lords during their consideration of Lord Joffe's *Assisted Dying for the Terminally Ill Bill*.

Savill, R. (2011) British woman takes own life at Dignitas because she did not want to die of old age, *The Daily Telegraph*, 3 April. Available at: https://www.telegraph.co.uk/news/uknews/8424665/British-woman-takes-own-life-at-Dignitas-because-she-did-not-want-to-die-of-old-age.html (accessed 22 March 2024).

Seale, C. (2006) National survey of end-of-life decisions made by UK medical practitioners, *Palliative Medicine*, 20 (1): 3–10.

United Nations (1948) *Universal Declaration of Human Rights*. Available at: https://www.un.org/en/about-us/universal-declaration-of-human-rights.

United Nations (2019) *Visit to Canada: Report of the Special Rapporteur on the Rights of Persons With Disabilities*, A/HRC/43/41/Add.2, 19 December 2019. Available at: https://www.ohchr.org/en/documents/country-reports/ahrc4341add2-visit-canada-report-special-rapporteur-rights-persons (accessed 11 July 2024).

4 | Assisted dying: the evidence from abroad

Conall Preston

Introduction

When deciding whether or not to pursue a policy, it is prudent to examine the results from those who have already tried it. In this chapter, I examine the assisted dying experience abroad. Assisted dying covers both assisted suicide and euthanasia.

The first jurisdiction to implement assisted dying was the US state of Oregon in 1998. In 2002, Belgium and the Netherlands followed suit. Since then, several other jurisdictions have done so. However, relatively few publish comprehensive data reports. I therefore focus on the following eight jurisdictions: Oregon (USA), Washington State (USA), California (USA), Canada, Belgium, the Netherlands, Victoria (Australia) and New Zealand. They provide good quality data on an annual basis and they offer a range of different models of assisted dying.

In October 2023, the Danish Council of Ethics published a report on assisted dying (commissioned by the Danish Parliament's Health Committee), noting that, 'you cannot answer what the consequences of legalising euthanasia will be without specifying which model you are talking about' (Nationalt Center For Etik 2023). The report, to which I shall return, substantiates the importance of this statement.

To start, we need to establish three definitions:

Assisted suicide: where lethal drugs are self-administered by the patient, e.g. the patient swallows a cocktail of drugs.

Euthanasia: where lethal drugs are administered to the patient by a third party, e.g. a doctor injects a patient with lethal drugs.

Assisted dying: an umbrella term referring to both assisted suicide and euthanasia. But assisted dying – as a term – is problematic because, while used as a euphemism, it can also be correctly applied to good quality palliative care. Meanwhile, in Canada the term 'medical assistance in dying' (MAiD) is also used, which in 99 per cent of cases means euthanasia.

Individuals, not just statistics

Before exploring available data which can seem to reduce people to statistics (as so often happens), here are some real-world examples of unintended consequences from assisted dying legislation:

- Tine Nys was a 38-year-old woman euthanized in 2010 in Belgium. Her sisters subsequently challenged the decision because they did not feel she was incurably ill. She had a recent diagnosis of autism, but no treatment, and had applied for euthanasia shortly after a relationship failed. In 2020, the three doctors involved were acquitted of unlawfully poisoning her (BBC 2020).
- In 2013, a Belgian transgender man (assigned female at birth) named Nathan Verhelst was euthanized after undergoing a series of failed gender-reassignment surgeries. The newspaper *Het Laatste Nieuws*, which interviewed him on the eve of his death, reported that he had been rejected by his parents who had wanted another son. Nathan was not at risk of death by natural causes. He needed support and help from those around him, not a lethal injection (BBC 2013).
- In 2018, Roger Foley took legal action against his local hospital, other health agencies, and both the state and federal governments on the grounds that he was not provided with the assisted home care support he wished for, but was instead offered MAiD. His lawyer, Ken Berger, commented: 'Here he is, needing society's help and care and we turn our back on him and we're in essence … asking him if he is interested in assisted dying rather than working with him to provide the services he needs' (CTV News 2018).
- In 2019, a 74-year-old patient with dementia in the Netherlands was euthanized after being covertly sedated and restrained by her relatives (this is the 'coffee euthanasia' referred to in Chapter 5; see also Chapter 25; Miller et al. 2019; Rankin 2019).
- In 2022, Canadian Paralympian and armed forces veteran, Christine Gauthier, requested a new wheelchair ramp to her house. She was instead asked if she had ever considered MAiD. Other veterans seeking support for post-traumatic stress disorder (PTSD) have also been offered MAiD unprompted (Edington 2023).
- In 2022, two individuals diagnosed with multiple chemical sensitivities (MCS) applied for MAiD. Both blamed their decision not on their illness, but on a lack of support to access affordable housing compatible with MCS. One wrote: 'I've applied for MAiD essentially because of abject poverty' (Wiebe and Mullin 2023).
- In a further case from Canada, a 71-year-old man was told he was terminally ill with end-stage chronic obstructive pulmonary disease (COPD) and offered MAiD. He was euthanized within 48 hours of his first assessment, but autopsy revealed he did not have COPD (Coelho 2022).
- In Belgium in 2022, Shanti De Corte, a survivor of the 2016 Brussels airport terrorist bombing, opted for euthanasia after years battling PTSD. She was 23 years old. In Belgium, euthanasia is legal for mental illness if every treatment has been exhausted. However, in psychiatry it is 'difficult, if not impossible' to

know that someone will never recover from their condition (Canadian Parliament 2024). While we can be in no doubt of the scale of Shanti's suffering, it is impossible definitively to say she would not have recovered with continued treatment (Soumois 2022).

- Donna Duncan, a 61-year-old woman who suffered a severe concussion after a car crash, could not get treatment over the course of many months at the local clinic for complex chronic diseases. She was, however, able to receive MAiD within a few days in 2022. But her daughter has maintained that she did not have the requisite capacity to decide to have MAiD (Smith 2024).
- In March 2022, Alexina Wattiez, a 36-year-old Belgian woman with cancer was to be euthanized by lethal injection. Her partner and daughter, outside the room, heard screaming. She was dead when they entered the room, but there were reported to be signs of suffocation and it is alleged that the two nurses involved smothered her with a pillow when the lethal injection failed to work (Cook 2023).
- A 27-year-old woman with autism from Alberta in Canada (known as MV) applied for and was granted MAiD, having previously been refused on two occasions. Her father has sought an injunction on the grounds that she has an undiagnosed mental illness (Cecco 2024).

These are several examples from many, but they suggest assisted dying has become a stop-gap measure effectively to 'deal' with socio-economic issues, as well as being used as a replacement for underfunded mental health and end-of-life care services. The data from our eight jurisdictions support this conclusion.

Why do people seek assisted dying?

The US states of Oregon and Washington offer only assisted suicide and have the most complete datasets. Their models are almost identical, and pro-assisted dying campaigners in the UK often point to Oregon as the example to follow.

When society normalizes assisting suicide or euthanasia in clinical settings, a covert pressure seems to develop for those who are ill or vulnerable to consider ending their lives.

Washington State reports show that, from 5 March (when the law came into force) to 31 December 2009, in the 44 people (36 of whom had ingested lethal drugs, the others had been prescribed the drugs but not taken them) for whom there was an After Death Reporting Form, 23 per cent reported feeling a burden on their family, friends or caregivers, while 2 per cent had concerns over the financial implications of treatment (Washington State Department of Health 2010). Fast-forward 13 years, and there is a shift in the reasons people sought death. In 2022, 446 people were known to have died (363 had died after ingesting lethal drugs) and there were After Death Reporting Forms on 433 people. Of these 433, a majority (59 per cent) cited concern with being a burden on family, friends or caregivers; and 10 per cent cited financial implications of treatment as a concern (Washington State Department of Health 2023). Hence, in the context of increasing numbers of people seeking assisted suicide in Washington State, there was a shift in the end-of-life concerns among those who had died, with proportionally more citing both financial concerns and worries about being burdensome. Both of these show how coercion, perhaps covert and unconscious (see Chapters 25 and 26), might operate; and both are concerns which might be ameliorated by psychosocial interventions.

Oregon's data show a similar trend.[1] In 1998, the first year of implementation, 13 per cent of those dying from prescribed lethal drugs reportedly had applied because they felt a burden to their families or carers (Oregon Health Authority 1999). In 2023, this had risen to 43.3 per cent. Over the whole period from 1998 to 2021, the figure was 48.3 per cent. Similarly, between 1998 and 2021, the proportion of people expressing a concern about the financial implications of treatment had also climbed to 5 per cent, while in 2023 it was 8.2 per cent (Oregon Health Authority 2024).

Canada differs in that it offers both assisted suicide and euthanasia, whereas Oregon and Washington only offer the former. In Canada in 2022, 35.3 per cent of those who died from MAiD said they felt a burden on family, friends or caregivers (Health Canada 2023). While this is proportionally lower than Oregon and Washington, Canada's raw numbers are significantly higher. There were 13,102 cases of MAiD where reports had been received by the end of January 2023, out of a total of 13,241 MAiD 'provisions' (i.e. deaths) in 2022. This suggests that 4,625 people described the nature of their suffering as feeling burdensome. In the same year, 17.1 per cent (or about 2,240 people) gave 'loneliness or isolation' as the nature of their suffering (Health Canada 2023).

While not everyone who applies for assisted suicide does so out of loneliness, or because they feel a burden, or for financial reasons, it is clear a considerable proportion do. The proportion has increased, suggesting that socio-economic factors, which could be alleviated in other ways, have a real impact on an applicant's decision-making.

Concerns: safeguards, impact and consequences

Safeguards

The erosion of safeguards and widening interpretation of the law is something many pro-assisted dying campaigners dismiss. When confronted with the evidence seen in Canada, Belgium and the Netherlands, they instead point to Oregon, Australia or New Zealand, claiming these jurisdictions have not expanded their legislation. However, New Zealand only implemented assisted dying in November 2021, which is too recent to allow time for much expansion or for analysis of data trends to be considered (NZ Ministry of Health 2023). In the Australian Capital Territory, there is currently a bill aiming to legalize assisted dying modelled on laws passed in other Australian states. However, the human rights commissioner, the children's rights commissioner and the disabilities commissioner conducted an inquiry that recommended expansion to allow access to children and those with dementia (Select Committee on Voluntary Assisted Dying Bill 2023). In Oregon, from March 2022, you no longer need to be a resident to apply for assisted suicide.[2] They have also waived the 15-day 'cooling-off' period between a patient's (first) oral request to a physician and their next (written) request for those who are expected to die within the 15-day period. While Oregon's expansions are relatively small and even understandable, it would be disingenuous to suggest it has not expanded at all (Zimmerman 2024).

Further afield, the Netherlands, Belgium and Canada have expanded their laws much more significantly. In 2002, the Netherlands and Belgium restricted assisted dying for adults with terminal and incurable physical illnesses. As of 2024, both countries allow access solely on mental health grounds (once every treatment has been exhausted) and for children (van Veen et al. 2022; Reuters 2023). In 2015, when Canada's Supreme Court debated assisted dying, warnings about the expansion seen in Belgium were dismissed: 'the permissive regime in Belgium is the product of a very different medico-legal culture'. As Professor Etienne Montero said while giving evidence to the Court, 'paper safeguards are only as strong as the human hands that carry them' (Supreme Court of Canada 2015). Just as in Belgium, assisted dying has expanded in Canada. In 2024, Canada temporarily postponed their implementation of assisted dying for the mentally ill (Kim and Yousif 2024). However, Canada remains on course to have the world's most permissive system of assisted dying.

Impact

Over time, jurisdictions which legalized assisted dying have seen significant increases in the number of such deaths. Jurisdictions which permit euthanasia document far greater numbers than those with only assisted suicide. For example, in 2016 both Canada and California passed assisted dying laws. Both are progressive jurisdictions with roughly 39 million inhabitants. California allows only assisted suicide, whereas Canada allows both assisted suicide and euthanasia. In 2017, a year after implementation, California recorded 407 assisted suicides to Canada's 2,838 assisted deaths (California Department of Public Health 2018; Health Canada 2023). In 2022, California recorded 853 deaths as a result of ingesting 'aid-in-dying' drugs to Canada's 13,241 (California Department of Public Health 2023; Health Canada 2023). Fewer than seven of Canada's 13,241 assisted deaths in 2022 were assisted suicides – the remainder were all euthanasia. However, in a recent development, California, which originally only legalized assisted dying for terminally ill individuals, has tabled a bill to expand their law. It proposes scrapping the terminal illness criteria and replacing it with 'a grievous and irremediable medical condition', meaning any incurable physical condition would be permitted. Additionally, those with early-to-mid-stage dementia will become eligible, while administration of lethal drugs via intravenous injection will be permitted too (Blakespear 2024).

Figure 4.1 compares the raw numbers of Canada, Belgium, the Netherlands and Oregon. Of the four, only Oregon restricts their laws to assisted suicide. When patients can choose between assisted suicide or euthanasia, not only do the vast majority choose euthanasia, but far more opt for an assisted death.

Although assisted dying is frequently portrayed as an option for only the most extreme cases, in 2022, 4.1 per cent of all Canadian deaths were euthanized (Health Canada 2023). Similarly, during 2023 it was responsible for 5.4 per cent of all deaths in the Netherlands (Regional Euthanasia Review Committees 2024).

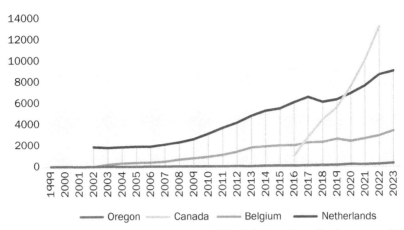

Figure 4.1 Numbers of assisted deaths, 1999–2023: Belgium, Canada, Oregon and the Netherlands.

Note: Figures for Canada for 2023 were not available at the time of going to print.

Another worrying trend seen in the Netherlands has been the significant increase in people receiving an assisted death because of psychological suffering. In 2023, 138 people were euthanized for this reason – more than double the same figure in 2019 (Waterfield 2024).

Unintended consequences

People worry about the unintended consequences of assisted dying. This chapter started with examples of people who represent some of those consequences. But the data also suggest that there are systemic consequences, including both a rise in 'unassisted' suicides and the variable quality of palliative care.

Victoria, Australia, implemented assisted dying in 2019. Campaigners in Victoria argued strongly that, if it were legalized, the 'unassisted' suicide rate would decrease. However, figures from the Coroners Court of Victoria (2024) show such suicides increased from 697 in 2019 to 801 in 2023. A detailed analysis of the figures for Victoria, looking in particular at suicides among those who were 65 or over, led to the conclusion 'that rates of unassisted suicide among people 65 and over have increased, not only in absolute terms but also relative to the older population and have increased more than unassisted suicides in the younger population … these results do not show any evidence of a beneficial effect due to [voluntary assisted dying]' (Jones 2023: 12). This suggests the possibility that once a society facilitates suicide in certain circumstances, suicidal thinking as a whole might become normalized.

Campaigners for assisted dying often claim that greater availability and quality of palliative care go hand-in-hand with assisted dying. However, between 2015 and 2022, the palliative care rankings of countries with assisted dying laws decreased (see Table 4.1) – Belgium fell 21 places. In all these jurisdictions, assisted dying has been medicalized and become a treatment option. All except

Table 4.1: Comparison of national rankings for palliative care and assisted dying legislation

Nation	2015 ranking (The Economist Intelligence Unit 2015)	2021 ranking (Finkelstein et al. 2022)	Comment
UK	*1st*	*1st*	*No assisted dying legislation*
Ireland	*4th*	*2nd*	*No assisted dying legislation*
Australia	2nd	4th	Declined
Netherlands	8th	No data	Declined
New Zealand	3rd	12th	Declined
Switzerland	15th	13th	Improved
Canada	11th	22nd	Declined
Belgium	5th	26th	Declined

Switzerland, where assisted dying is not part of mainstream health care and its palliative care ranking increased.

Financial incentives

There is a financial incentive for governments to pursue assisted dying. In 2020, the Canadian Parliament Budget Office predicted that its 2016 assisted dying law (Bill C-14) was producing a net reduction in healthcare costs of C$86.9 million annually. Their 2021 expansion of the law, to people whose death was not expected in the relatively near future (Bill C-7), was being predicted to save C$149 million (Office of the Parliamentary Budget Officer 2020). Since then, the number of assisted deaths has only increased, thereby increasing savings.

Conclusion: the example of Denmark

Finally, the Danish report. In 2023, the Danish Parliament commissioned the Danish Council of Ethics to investigate 'assisted dying'. They chose two models to analyse: the permissive Dutch model, and the more restrictive Oregon model. After an in-depth investigation, they not only recommended that Denmark adopt neither of these systems but that it shouldn't legalize assisted dying at all. They said, 'On the present basis, there are no members of the Ethics Council who find the Oregon model or the Dutch model sufficiently clear in their delineations, fair in their justifications for access, or sound in terms of control mechanisms' (Nationalt Center for Etik 2023: 7). The Council considered, 'euthanasia to be in conflict with palliative care and are therefore against the legalization of euthanasia as long as we as a society have not exhausted the possibilities for relief' (2023: 8). Furthermore, 'The very existence of an offer of euthanasia will decisively change our ideas about old age, the coming of death, quality of life and what it means to take others into account. If euthanasia becomes an option, there is too great a risk that it will become an expectation aimed at special groups in society' (2023: 7). Denmark, a modern and progressive country, looked at the evidence and did not like what it saw. We must do the same.

Notes

1. For access to all the Annual Reports, go to Oregon Health Authority, *Death with Dignity Act Annual Reports.* Available at: https://www.oregon.gov/oha/ph/providerpartnerresources/evaluationresearch/deathwithdignityact/pages/ar-index.aspx (accessed 11 March 2024).
2. For further details, see Oregon Health Authority, *Frequently Asked Questions: Oregon's Death With Dignity Act (DWDA).* Available at: https://www.oregon.gov/oha/ph/providerpartnerresources/evaluationresearch/deathwithdignityact/pages/faqs.aspx (accessed 11 March 2024).

References

Blakespear, C. (2024) *SB 1196: End of Life Option Act*, Office of Senator Catherine Blakespear, SB 1196 Factsheet, updated 3 April. Available at: https://img1.wsimg.com/blobby/go/cd607dce-3325-492b-b030-b0a22331af65/downloads/SB%201196%20(Blakespear)%20Factsheet.pdf?ver=1709839292696 (accessed 11 April 2024).

British Broadcasting Corporation (BBC) (2013) Belgian helped to die after three sex change operations, *BBC News*, 2 October. Available at: https://www.bbc.co.uk/news/world-europe-24373107 (accessed 11 March 2024).

British Broadcasting Corporation (BBC) (2020) Belgium euthanasia: three doctors cleared in landmark trial, *BBC News*, 31 January. Available at: https://www.bbc.co.uk/news/world-europe-51322781 (accessed 2 April 2024).

California Department of Public Health (2018) *California End of Life Option Act 2017 Data Report.* Available at: https://www.cdph.ca.gov/Programs/CHSI/CDPH%20Document%20Library/2017EOLADataReport.pdf (accessed 11 March 2024).

California Department of Public Health (2023) *California End of Life Option Act 2022 Data Report.* Available at: https://www.cdph.ca.gov/Programs/CHSI/CDPH%20Document%20Library/CDPH_End_of_Life%20_Option_Act_Report_2022_FINAL.pdf (accessed 11 March 2024).

Canadian Parliament (2024) *MAiD and Mental Disorders: The Road Ahead*, Report of the Special Joint Committee on Medical Assistance in Dying. Available at: https://www.parl.ca/Content/Committee/441/AMAD/Reports/RP12815505/amadrp03/amadrp03-e.pdf (accessed 11 March 2024).

Cecco, L. (2024) Canadian man says daughter, 27, lacks ability to fully consent to assisted death, *The Guardian*, 13 March. Available at: https://www.theguardian.com/world/2024/mar/13/canada-medical-assisted-death (accessed 2 April 2024).

Coelho, R. (2022) Medical assistance in dying overused in Canada even before expansion, *The London Free Press*, 11 July. Available at: https://lfpress.com/opinion/columnists/coelho-medical-assistance-in-dying-overused-in-canada-even-before-expansion (accessed 11 March 2024).

Cook, M. (2023) Euthanasia nurses in Belgium smother patient when lethal drugs fail to work, *Bioedge*, 14 September. Available at: https://bioedge.org/end-of-life-issues/euthanasia/euthanasia-nurses-in-belgium-smother-patient-when-lethal-drugs-fail-to-work/ (accessed 2 April 2024).

Coroners Court of Victoria (2024) *Coroners Court 2023 Annual Suicide Data Report*, 16 February. Available at: https://www.coronerscourt.vic.gov.au/sites/default/files/2024-02/Coroners

%20Court%202023%20Annual%20Suicide%20Data%20Report%20-%20December%202023.pdf (accessed 3 April 2024).

CTV News (2018) Chronically ill man releases audio of hospital staff offering assisted death, *CTV News*, 2 August. Available at: https://www.ctvnews.ca/health/chronically-ill-man-releases-audio-of-hospital-staff-offering-assisted-death-1.4038841#:~:text=An%20Ontario%20man%20suffering%20from,requests%20to%20live%20at%20home (accessed 2 April 2024).

Edington, S. (2023) Canadian Paralympian: I asked for a disability ramp – and was offered euthanasia, *The Telegraph*, 2 September 2023. Available at: https://www.telegraph.co.uk/world-news/2023/09/02/canada-paralympian-christine-gauthier-stairlift-euthanasia/ (accessed 11 March 2024).

Finkelstein, E.A., Bhadelia, A., Goh, C. et al. (2022) Cross country comparison of expert assessments of the quality of death and dying 2021, *Journal of Pain and Symptom Management*, 63 (4): e419–29.

Health Canada (2023) *Fourth Annual Report on Medical Assistance in Dying in Canada 2022*. Available at: https://www.canada.ca/content/dam/hc-sc/documents/services/medical-assistance-dying/annual-report-2022/annual-report-2022.pdf (accessed 3 April 2024).

Jones, D.A. (2023) Did the Voluntary Assisted Dying Act 2017 prevent 'at least one suicide every week'?, *Journal of Ethics in Mental Health*, 11: 1–20. Available at: https://jemh.ca/issues/open/documents/Did%20the%20Voluntary%20Assisted%20Dying%20Act%202017.pdf (accessed 12 March 2024).

Kim, C. and Yousif, N. (2024) Canada again delays assisted dying for the mentally ill, *BBC News*, 1 February. Available at: https://www.bbc.co.uk/news/world-us-canada-68120380 (accessed 11 March 2024).

Miller, D.G., Dresser, R. and Kim, S.Y.H. (2019) Advance euthanasia directives: a controversial case and its ethical implications, *Journal of Medical Ethics*, 45 (2): 84–89.

Nationalt Center for Etik (2023) *The Ethical Council's Opinion on Euthanasia*. Available at: https://livinganddyingwell.org.uk/wp-content/uploads/2023/11/Denmarks-Ethics-Council-Report-on-Euthanasia-October-2023-2.pdf (accessed 11 March 2024).

NZ Ministry of Health (2023) *Assisted Dying Service Reporting*. Available at: https://www.health.govt.nz/our-work/regulation-health-and-disability-system/assisted-dying-service/assisted-dying-service-reporting (accessed 12 March 2024).

Office of the Parliamentary Budget Officer (2020) *Cost Estimate for Bill C-7 'Medical Assistance in Dying'*, 20 October. Available at: https://distribution-a617274656661637473.pbo-dpb.ca/241708b353e7782a9e5e713c2e281fc5ed932d3d07e9f5dd212e73604762bbc5 (accessed 12 March 2024).

Oregon Health Authority (1999) *Oregon's Death with Dignity Act: The First Year's Experience*. Available at: https://www.oregon.gov/oha/PH/PROVIDERPARTNERRESOURCES/EVALUATIONRESEARCH/DEATHWITHDIGNITYACT/Documents/year1.pdf (accessed 11 March 2024).

Oregon Health Authority (2024) *Oregon Death with Dignity Act: 2023 Data Summary*. Available at: https://www.oregon.gov/oha/PH/PROVIDERPARTNERRESOURCES/EVALUATIONRESEARCH/DEATHWITHDIGNITYACT/Documents/year26.pdf (accessed 2 April 2024).

Rankin, J. (2019) Netherlands euthanasia case: doctor 'acted with best intentions', *The Guardian*, 26 August. Available at: https://www.theguardian.com/world/2019/aug/26/doctor-on-trial-landmark-euthanasia-case-netherlands-dementia (accessed 11 March 2024).

Regional Euthanasia Review Committees (2024) *Annual Report 2023*, Regional Euthanasia Review Committees. Available at: https://www.euthanasiecommissie.nl/de-toetsingscommissies/uitspraken/jaarverslagen/2023/april/4/index (accessed 18 April 2024).

Reuters (2023) Dutch to widen 'right-to-die' to include terminally ill children, *Reuters*, 14 April, 2023. Available at: https://www.reuters.com/world/europe/dutch-widen-right-to-die-include-terminally-ill-children-2023-04-14/ (accessed 11 March 2024).

Select Committee on Voluntary Assisted Dying Bill (2023) *Inquiry into the Voluntary Assisted Dying Bill 2023*, Legislative Assembly for the Australian Capital Territory. Available at:

https://www.parliament.act.gov.au/__data/assets/pdf_file/0008/2358116/VAD-Submission-073-ACT-Human-Rights-Commission.pdf (accessed on 11 March 2024).

Smith, L. (2024) Canada has revealed the horror of assisted dying, *Spiked*, 15 January. Available at: https://www.spiked-online.com/2024/01/15/canada-has-revealed-the-horror-of-assisted-dying/ (accessed 2 April 2024).

Soumois, F. (2022) Brussels terror attack victim euthanised at age 23, *Medscape*, 25 October. Available at: https://www.medscape.com/viewarticle/982984?form=fpf (accessed 11 March 2024).

Supreme Court of Canada (2015) *Carter v. Canada (Attorney General)*, 6 February. Available at: https://scc-csc.lexum.com/scc-csc/scc-csc/en/item/14637/index.do (accessed 11 March 2024).

The Economist Intelligence Unit (2015) The 2015 Quality of Death Index: ranking palliative care across the world, *The Economist*. Available at: https://impact.economist.com/perspectives/sites/default/files/2015%20EIU%20Quality%20of%20Death%20Index%20Oct%2029%20FINAL.pdf (accessed 12 March 2024).

van Veen, S.M.P., Widdershoven, G.A.M., Beekman, A.T.F. and Evans, N. (2022) Physician assisted death for psychiatric suffering: experiences in the Netherlands, *Frontiers in Psychiatry*, 13: 895387. Available at: https://www.ncbi.nlm.nih.gov/pmc/articles/PMC9251055/pdf/fpsyt-13-895387.pdf (accessed 11 March 2024).

Washington State Department of Health (2010) *Washington State Department of Health 2009 Death With Dignity Act Report*. Available at: https://doh.wa.gov/sites/default/files/legacy/Documents/Pubs/422-109-DeathWithDignityAct2009.pdf (accessed 12 March 2024).

Washington State Department of Health (2023) *2022 Death With Dignity Act Report*, Chapter 70.245 RCW. Available at: https://doh.wa.gov/sites/default/files/2023-10/422-109-DeathWithDignityAct2022.pdf (accessed 12 March 2024).

Waterfield, B. (2024) Number of Dutch people euthanised due to mental illness up 20%, *The Times*, 5 April. Available at: https://www.thetimes.co.uk/article/number-of-dutch-people-euthanised-due-to-mental-illness-up-20-percent-w0xmfz3s2 (accessed 18 April 2024).

Wiebe, K. and Mullin, A. (2023) Choosing death in unjust conditions: hope, autonomy and harm reduction, *Journal of Medical Ethics*, 50:407–412. Available at: https://doi.org/10.1136/jme-2022-108871 (accessed 11 March 2024).

Zimmerman, S. (2024) Oregon removes assisted suicide wait for certain patients, *CTV News*, 24 July. Available at: https://www.ctvnews.ca/world/oregon-removes-assisted-suicide-wait-for-certain-patients-1.4522686 (accessed 11 March 2024).

5 Making euthanasia legal in the Netherlands: implications for the doctor–patient relationship

Cees Hertogh

Introduction: a long road ...[1]

In 1973, the first case of active termination of life by a physician (Dr Postma) in the Netherlands was brought to court. As described in Chapter 6, the court sympathized with arguments about Dr Postma alleviating suffering, but concluded that it was not reasonable to use a lethal injection to achieve this goal; hence his provisional prison sentence.

Intensive discussions and court cases followed, making euthanasia a Dutch societal and political issue. In 1984, the executive board of the Royal Dutch Medical Association (KNMG) issued a position statement emphasizing that the question of euthanasia should be dealt with exclusively within the context of the doctor–patient relationship, and not be about whether or not euthanasia was permissible; rather, the question was under what conditions medical assistance in dying (euthanasia and assisted suicide) could be acceptable. Accordingly, due care criteria were proposed. A State Commission report in 1985 clarified that euthanasia is restricted to 'intentionally terminating another person's life at the person's request', formulated due care criteria and urged the government to enact legislation on medical ending of life quickly.

The societal debate shifted away from a focus on the competent patient with serious and unacceptable suffering from physical disease, towards discussion of life termination in incompetent patients. It was not until 1998 that the left-wing liberal party D'66 introduced a Bill that became the Termination of Life on Request and Assisted Suicide Act of 2002. A crucial element for D'66, which had long been lobbied for by the Dutch Right to Die Society (NVVE), was Article 2.2 of the law, which made active life termination of patients who lack decisional capacity on the basis of an advance euthanasia directive (AED) legal. This law therefore offered more options for active termination of life than medical ethics and also went further than the existing medical expertise regarding end-of-life practice: doctors had never been willing to execute an AED of an incompetent patient.

Several experts on this subject, including myself, have repeatedly pointed out that Article 2.2 is actually a flaw in the law because it is at odds with the due care criteria (van Delden 2004, Hertogh 2009). Also – with hindsight – the inclusion of the advance directive in the law was a first step towards a change in euthanasia practice and its moral foundation, resulting in increased pressure on doctors to perform euthanasia.

Core of the law and its moral foundation

The law on euthanasia and assisted suicide does not legalize these acts, but codifies an exception to the penal code. Euthanasia and assisting suicide remain criminal offences, except when performed by a physician who follows the rules of due care and reports the case to the statutory review committee. Key to this legal solution is a 'conflict of duties' between the duty to relieve suffering and the moral prohibition of killing. Thus, although a patient's request is crucial to the concept of euthanasia, the law does not create a right to a self-chosen death. Strictly speaking, the law is not about patient rights, but about the actions of doctors and their accountability. This is reflected in the formulation of the due care criteria (see Box 5.1).

Box 5.1: Statutory due care criteria – The Netherlands

In order to remain unpunished, the doctor who performs euthanasia or assists in suicide must:

1. be satisfied that the patient's request is voluntary and well considered;
2. be equally satisfied that the patient's suffering is 'hopeless' and 'unbearable';
3. have informed the patient about their situation and prospects;
4. have arrived at the conclusion, together with the patient, that there is no reasonable alternative to relieve the suffering;
5. have consulted at least one other independent physician who has seen the patient and has given a written assessment of the previous requirements;
6. have performed the life termination in a professional and careful way.

These six criteria distinguish between the more procedural and technical ones (criteria 5 and 6) and the substantive rules that refer to the decision-making process (criteria 1–4). Thus, the first rule requires that the patient is *fully informed* of his or her condition and prognosis (the third criterion), while the subjective criterion of hopeless and unbearable suffering (the second criterion) requires doctor and patient to engage in a *dialogue* in which alternatives to alleviate the situation are discussed and weighed. Only after arriving at the *joint conviction*, that for this specific patient no alternative solutions are feasible or acceptable (the fourth criterion), can the conclusion be drawn that the second due care criterion has been met.[2]

The advance directive in the law

However, Article 2.2 stipulates that in the event of incapacity, an AED can replace the oral request as an alternative to comply with the first due care criterion. How, then, can doctors meet the other (substantive) due care criteria, given that these criteria are essentially based on shared decision-making and dialogue? This was one of the most debated themes during the parliamentary discussions of the Bill, particularly with reference to patients with advanced dementia. The legislator 'solved' this problem, by adding to Article 2.2 that, in the case of euthanasia based on an AED, the due care criteria were to be applied '*mutatis mutandis*',[3] a cryptic formula that has become a source of ambiguity and discussion since 2002.

Research among nursing home physicians showed that, for a doctor to be able to comply with an AED of a patient with dementia, 'meaningful communication' with and at least a confirmation by the patient of his or her advance directive remained essential (de Boer et al. 2011). The KNMG, referring to this research, took this position but the Review Committees criticized the KNMG for being too restrictive in practice. The NVVE made similar accusations against doctors and the media regularly drew attention to distressing cases of patients whose AED was ignored by doctors. This medical reluctance was poorly understood by the public. After all, it was argued, legally, doctors no longer had anything to fear, so why not just execute the AED?

The moral burden on doctors

Missing from this debate was a thorough understanding of the burden that euthanasia places on doctors. They are not just instruments to administer death on request, they are moral agents with their own emotions and conscience. Hence the emphasis in the substantive due care criteria on *joint* decision-making as a practical and moral precondition for a physician to be able to kill another person to relieve suffering – a precondition that, according to many doctors, cannot be met when meaningful communication is no longer possible and the patient's voice is only expressed through the AED.

Routinization of physician-assisted death

Reluctance of doctors to perform euthanasia led to the NVVE opening the so-called 'End of Life Clinic' in 2012, with affiliated doctors who have a special affinity with euthanasia. The objectives of this initiative are twofold. First, to support patients whose request for termination of life have been refused by their own doctor, either by entering into a conversation with their unwilling doctor to persuade him or her to provide the desired assistance, or by having the euthanasia performed by a doctor of the End of Life Clinic – provided that the due care criteria can be met. And secondly, to carry out 'difficult' requests for life termination from which other doctors shy away and thus to use the options offered by the law more broadly.

This 'clinic' – in 2018 renamed the 'Euthanasia Expertise Centre' – articulates a significant change in euthanasia practice. Originally rooted in a reciprocal (and often longstanding) relation of trust between a patient and his or her attending physician (most frequently a general practitioner), the performance of euthanasia can increasingly be delegated to 'specialized' physicians. For doctors hesitant to grant a request, or who feel overburdened by increasing numbers of requests, the Euthanasia Expertise Centre offers an alternative to which they can refer patients. Conversely, pressure on doctors to comply with requests from their own patients also increases, because the Euthanasia Expertise Centre frames many of these requests as 'uncomplicated' and calls upon doctors to deal with these 'simple' and 'normal' requests themselves in order not to overburden the Centre. This framing, together with a tendency to remove euthanasia from the relationship of trust between doctor and patient and an ongoing societal debate on euthanasia as a patient right, results in the routinization of euthanasia as a normal medical procedure, without acknowledging what this ultimate form of end-of-life care means in terms of emotional burden and moral distress for doctors.

Pressure on doctors: research findings

Euthanasia significantly interferes with daily medical practice and consultations with other patients – after all, it requires a lot of preparation and co-ordination and one is not actually capable of undertaking 'normal' consultations immediately after a euthanasia. Also, medical assistance in dying always interferes with the private lives of doctors: it is something you never get used to and that you always take home with you (de Boer et al. 2019). A conscientious physician who has just performed euthanasia always hopes that – at least for the time being – he or she will be spared another request. A new request relatively close to a recently granted euthanasia or assisted suicide therefore creates a feeling of pressure. And this feeling is fuelled by doubt as to whether you can be free to say 'no'. Although formally a physician is never obliged to perform euthanasia/assisted suicide, even when all criteria are met, the policy position of the KNMG and – especially – the legalization of medical assistance in dying, have made it more difficult to reject a request or transfer it to another doctor.

Over the years, physicians have gradually experienced increasing pressure to grant requests for euthanasia. This is an under-exposed effect of the legislation that has received little attention in scientific research. Our qualitative studies, however, reveal several forms and sources of pressure (de Boer et al. 2019; Coers et al. 2023). In addition to the ones just mentioned, this research shows that a misbalance in valued aspects of the doctor–patient relationship, such as trust, reciprocity and mutual understanding, constitutes a major source of pressure. This pressure can take the form of emotional blackmail, such as when patients threaten to commit suicide if their euthanasia request is not granted. Pressure is also felt when control is taken over by the patient or others and the doctor experiences him- or herself more as an instrument to ensure the autonomy of the patient. As an example, a physician sketched how he was overwhelmed by the scene he found when arriving at the patient's house: a living room full of people with a glass of wine in their hand to toast with the patient on the upcoming euthanasia. Also relatives, although they formally do not play a role in a highly personal issue such as euthanasia/assisted suicide, can put pressure on the doctor, either to grant a request or to reject it. The potentially most extreme form of imbalance with regard to the values underpinning a good practice of medical assistance in dying occurs in relation to termination of life on the basis of a written advance directive in a patient with advanced dementia. Our recent research shows that, compared with our earlier findings (de Boer et al. 2011), many doctors still hold that without meaningful communication the due care criteria in these situations cannot be met. However, they also feel growing pressure to provide euthanasia based on an AED, especially following the developments described below, and fear that they will be forced to cross their personal moral boundaries (Coers et al. 2023).

'Sneaky' euthanasia

The most recent development – which had been expected since 2002 – occurred in 2016, when a doctor performed euthanasia on a nursing home resident with advanced dementia based on an AED. In this 'coffee euthanasia', the patient was sedated prior to ending her life using a strong sedative covertly in her coffee. She was unaware of the impending euthanasia. She was told that after coffee with her family, she would go shopping with them. The physician who ended her life later stated that communication about euthanasia and an attempt to verify her AED would have been pointless, because the person concerned was completely incapacitated owing to dementia. When, despite the sedation, she seemed to resist the administration of the lethal injection, the doctor continued to end her life while the patient was restrained by her family.

Public debate, and fierce opposition from physicians, resulted in full-page national newspaper advertisements and a website petition supported by over 450 physicians, stating their strong disapproval of this 'sneaky euthanasia'. The review committee concluded that the due care criteria were not met and the case was referred to the public prosecutor. Consequently, for the first time since the enactment of the euthanasia law, a doctor stood trial for possible unlawful euthanasia. Following a district court ruling, the case went to the Supreme Court to elicit its verdict on the '*mutatis mutandis*' application of the due care criteria.[4]

The Supreme Court ruling came as a shock to many. Although criticized for lacking a human rights perspective, this new legal reality was immediately adopted by the regional review committees in their so-called 'code of practice' through the following adjustments:

- If a patient is incapacitated due to dementia, the physician does not need to inquire about that patient's current wish, nor is it necessary to discuss the moment and manner in which euthanasia will be carried out, because a patient in that situation will no longer understand such a conversation and may only become upset or agitated by it.
- Determining whether such a patient is suffering from hopeless and unbearable suffering involves a medical professional judgement that is reserved to the doctor.
- If there are indications that the performance of euthanasia may be accompanied by restlessness, agitation or aggression, administration of sedative premedication is permitted.

The Supreme Court ruling places the doctor in a lonely position and leaves the determination of hopeless and unbearable suffering entirely up to him or her.

This development[5] has moved euthanasia practice far from its origins in trust between doctor and patient and its moral foundation in dialogue and joint decision-making.

Conclusion

The legalization of medical euthanasia in the Netherlands has changed the role of the doctor, because legislation went further than medical ethics. Because the legislation wanted, unwisely in my view, to regulate life-ending actions by doctors in both competent and incapacitated patients in one law, a distorted construct has emerged that puts increasing pressure on doctors and potentially undermines the embedding of euthanasia in a reciprocal relationship of trust between doctor and patient. This potential effect is further reinforced by the fact that the evolution of practice and societal debate have placed more emphasis on patient autonomy and self-determination at the end of life.

Notes

1. A full and nuanced account of the history of euthanasia in the Netherlands can be found in Youngner and Kimsma (2012). See also Chapter 6 in this volume.
2. The relevance of the fourth due care criterion and its relation to the second was also underscored by the ministers of health and justice in the preamble to the Bill, where it is stated that careful life termination is only possible if *the physician together with the patient* have come to the conclusion that the only way left to alleviate the patient's suffering is active medical assistance in dying.
3. *Mutatis mutandis* suggests that necessary changes are to be made depending on the situation; it literally means 'things being changed that have to be changed' (*Shorter Oxford English Dictionary*).
4. For a detailed description of the case and a critical discussion of the Supreme Court ruling, see Buijsen (2022). For an analysis of the motives for physicians to support the 'no sneaky euthanasia' petition, see Coers et al. (2023).
5. For example, based on the High Court's ruling, the KNMG has formulated a new euthanasia position, which strongly emphasizes the importance of communication about the performance of euthanasia, also in cases of patients with decision-making disability. In addition, a new professional guideline on decision-making capacity was recently published under my chairmanship, which underscores the relevance of human rights protection of people with decision-making disabilities and promotes a paradigm shift from substitute decision-making on the basis of an advance directive towards supported decision-making.

References

Buijsen, M. (2022) *Mutatis mutandis* … On euthanasia and advanced dementia in the Netherlands, *Cambridge Quarterly of Healthcare Ethics*, 31 (1): 40–53.
Coers, D.O., de Boer, M.E., Sizoo, E.M. et al. (2023) Dealing with requests for euthanasia in incompetent patients with dementia: qualitative research revealing underexposed aspects of the societal debate, *Age and Ageing*, 52 (1): afac310. Available at: https://doi.org/10.1093/ageing/afac310.

de Boer, M.E., Depla, M.F.I.A., den Breejen, M. et al. (2019) Pressure in dealing with requests for euthanasia or assisted suicide: experiences of general practitioners, *Journal of Medical Ethics*, 45 (7): 425–29.

de Boer, M.E., Dröes, R., Jonker, C. et al. (2011) Advance directives for euthanasia in dementia: how do they affect resident care in Dutch nursing homes? Experiences of physicians and relatives, *Journal of the American Geriatrics Society*, 59 (6): 989–96.

Hertogh, C.M.P.M. (2009) The role of advance directives as an aid to communication and shared-decision making in dementia, *Journal of Medical Ethics*, 35 (2): 100–3.

KNMG (1984) Standpunt inzake euthanasie [Position on euthanasia], *Medisch Contact*, 31: 990–97.

State Commission on Euthanasia (1985) *Rapport van de Staatscammissie Euthanasic* [Report of the State Commission on Euthanasia]. The Hague: Staatsuitgeverij.

van Delden, J.J. (2004) The unfeasibility of requests for euthanasia in advanced directives, *Journal of Medical Ethics*, 30 (5): 447–51.

Youngner, S.J. and Kimsma, G.K. (eds) (2012) *Physician-Assisted Death in Perspective: Assessing the Dutch Experience*. New York: Cambridge University Press.

6 The Dutch experience: from the perspective of lifelong disability

Irene Tuffrey-Wijne and Leopold Curfs

Introduction

The Netherlands was the first country in the world to introduce assisted dying legislation. This covers 'termination of life on request' (where a physician administers a fatal dose of a drug at the person's express request) and 'assisted suicide' (where the physician supplies the drug, but the person administers it); the term 'euthanasia' is used in the Netherlands to refer to both forms of assisted dying. In this chapter, we summarize Dutch euthanasia law, practice and societal debates within a historical context (further details can be found in Chapter 5). The possibility of euthanasia is not limited to patients with an incurable illness acquired in later life who wish to avoid suffering associated with the terminal phase. We examine the ethical dilemmas and potential unintended consequences of current Dutch law and practice in relation to adults with lifelong impairments or disabilities. Our focus is on people with an intellectual disability, autism or both (see also Chapter 23). The issues with regards to newborns with serious and multiple disabilities are outside our scope (but see Chapter 24); there are separate medical protocols for this.

The Dutch law on assisted dying

The issues around assisted dying have been fiercely and openly debated within Dutch society for many decades, which is reflected within changing laws. Several milestone court cases preceded the 2002 euthanasia legislation. In 1973, a doctor who had carried out euthanasia (Dr Postma) was found guilty of breaking the law, but given a short suspended sentence in recognition of the fact that he had prevented serious and inescapable suffering. In 1984, the Supreme Court ruled that doctors would not be penalized if they acted out of 'necessity', where the medical professional agrees that a patient's request to die is the only way available to end unbearable and hopeless suffering. Ten years later, in a 1994 court case, the Supreme Court ruled that both physical and mental suffering could justify euthanasia. These developments were accompanied by a growing recognition of a gap between the law and the practice of doctors performing euthanasia under certain circumstances. The Termination of Life on Request and Assisted Suicide Act ('the Act') was passed in 2002. Ending another person's life or assisting a suicide was, and remains today, a criminal offence, but the Act provides that the Criminal Code would not apply if the six 'due care' criteria (set out in Chapter 5) have been observed. These include the criterion that the patient's suffering is 'unbearable and hopeless'.

In the same year, the Supreme Court ruled that unbearable suffering should stem from a medical condition, either physical or psychiatric. This was in response to a case of a general practitioner assisting the suicide of an 86-year-old man who had no serious mental or physical illness, but suffered from physical decline and was 'tired of life'.

It is important to note that a life-limiting condition is not a prerequisite for granting a euthanasia request. Dutch law also permits euthanasia for unbearable suffering caused by psychiatric conditions, dementia, multiple geriatric syndromes, chronic pain syndromes or genetic conditions.

Euthanasia Review Committees, reports and Code of Practice

Doctors must report all cases of euthanasia to a euthanasia review committee (Regionale Toetsingscommissie Euthanasie, RTE), explaining how they have observed each of the six due care criteria. For example, in connection with the unbearable and hopeless suffering criterion, doctors must describe what the person's suffering consisted of, why they were convinced it was unbearable, and how they could reasonably have come to the conclusion that there was no prospect of improvement. The RTE is tasked with adjudicating whether the requirements of 'due care' have been met; if they decide that the criteria were not met, the case is referred to the public prosecutor for further investigation.

The RTE produces an annual report, available on their website (including English, French and German translations from 2010), along with further selected case summaries (in Dutch only) (https://www.euthanasiecommissie.nl/). The case summaries and annual reports are written in lay language. They are explicitly meant to give an impression of how the committees apply and interpret the due care criteria for euthanasia and doctor-assisted suicide as set out in the Act.

The RTE publishes a Code of Practice, which provides guidance to doctors on how to interpret the statutory due care criteria. The Code of Practice is not set in stone, but is updated – most recently in 2022 (Regional Euthanasia Review Committees 2022) – to reflect case law and RTE review findings of euthanasia notifications over the years, which in turn are affected by shifting societal opinion.

Incidence of euthanasia

The RTE has reported a year-on-year increase in euthanasia cases, from 1,815 in 2003 to 4,829 in 2013 and 8,720 in 2022 (5.1 per cent of all deaths in the Netherlands, a rise from 4.6 per cent in 2021). It can be said, therefore, that euthanasia is no longer exceptional in the Netherlands. It is very rare for the RTE to find that the due care criteria had not been met (0.15 per cent of cases in 2022).

Ethical dilemmas and shifting societal opinion

The move towards euthanasia legislation in the 1970s, 1980s and 1990s was accompanied by changing attitudes towards conflicting principles of medical ethics: respect for patient autonomy and self-determination (a 'right to die'); and a doctor's duty to protect human life and do no harm (a 'duty of compassion'). The 2002 Act was based on a recognition that assisting someone to die could be justified as an act of compassion, as it relieved unbearable and hopeless suffering.

Since then, there has been intense interest in cases where the boundaries of what is acceptable and permissible within the Act were not totally clear-cut. Those with a terminal illness have always made up the majority of people receiving euthanasia, but this is shifting. In 2013, 84 per cent of euthanasia cases were people with incurable cancer; in 2022, the figure was 58 per cent. Over the years, growing numbers of people requested and received euthanasia for chronic (rather than terminal) illness, mental health conditions, dementia, an accumulation of age-related conditions or lifelong disability.

The current societal debate around the 'right to die' shows a shift in attitude towards giving more weight to the ethical principle of autonomy and self-determination, placing an increasingly heavy emphasis on the first of the six due care criteria ('voluntary and well-considered request') and the patient's own assessment of their suffering being unbearable and without hope. There are proposals, both within advocacy groups and within political parties, to extend the right to an assisted death to generally healthy older people who feel that they have lived long enough and no longer experience or envisage any quality of life. Proposals to change the law to allow this have been rejected by Parliament so far, but the debate continues.

What constitutes 'unbearable and hopeless suffering'?

The Euthanasia Code of Practice acknowledges that 'unbearable suffering' is a subjective notion: what is bearable for one patient may be unbearable for another, depending on the patient's medical history, life history, personality, values and stamina. The Code stipulates that while the suffering must have a medical dimension, it can result from an accumulation of mental and physical factors, or a combination of factors, including a fear of future suffering. Suffering can stem not only from physical symptoms, but also from growing dependence, feelings of humiliation or loss of dignity. The Code's guidance to doctors is that the patient's own perception that the situation is hopeless is part of what makes their suffering unbearable. However, doctors must be able to empathize with the patient and find the suffering 'palpable' – in other words, they must be able to put themselves in the patient's shoes.

Euthanasia for people with lifelong disabilities

An examination of euthanasia cases involving people with non-terminal conditions highlights the complexities and difficulties in assessing whether the due care criteria are met, and whether euthanasia is the right (which implies, the only acceptable) response. We studied 39 case reports published on the RTE website where euthanasia was given to people who had intellectual disabilities, autism or both (Tuffrey-Wijne et al. 2018, 2023). For the majority of these people, the suffering that led to their euthanasia request was associated mostly (and in some cases solely) with their feelings of loneliness, social isolation, dependence, and difficulties in coping with the world, coping with life or coping with changes in circumstances. The case reports highlighted a lack of flexibility and resilience. Some doctors were explicit in saying that the situation met the criteria for being hopeless, because the suffering was closely associated with the person's intellectual disability or autism, which is lifelong and cannot be treated (see Chapter 23).

In most of the cases, the reasons people wanted to die could be summarized as 'poor quality of life', closely associated with the characteristics of their disability (for discussion of 'quality of life', see Chapter 28). The debate around assisted deaths for non-medical conditions has not yet led to a change in the law to permit euthanasia solely for poor quality of life and being 'tired of life'; however, the 'poor quality of life' argument and accompanying hopelessness is more readily accepted when people have disabilities. Such suffering can be described in terms that others (including non-disabled doctors) may sympathize with, such as dependence and a perceived lack of dignity (see Chapter 28). While we do not dispute the reality of people's suffering, which was indeed clear from the case descriptions, it does raise concerns about the boundaries of euthanasia practice if this is closely associated with feeling unwanted and unable to function within society.

We know that people with disabilities experience severe inequalities in opportunities and in health and social care provision, which may well play a part in their poor quality of life and the experience of their situation being 'hopeless'. Society currently is not a level playing field, where everyone has a full range of life choices and can make autonomous choices about them. This makes it perhaps all too easy for people to be granted their wish for an assisted death as a 'way out' of painfully difficult situations and circumstances, rather than addressing underlying issues of inequality and a lack of adequate support for people with very complex needs. Indeed, in several case reports, it was clear that the specialized support systems which might enable the person to cope with life were not available.

In the Netherlands, it has become normal to ask for and receive an assisted death when you find that your suffering is hopeless. The fact that one in 20 Dutch people currently have an assisted death means that many people will have experience of euthanasia within their own social circle. Growing numbers of people will be conscious of the realistic option of receiving euthanasia for non-life-limiting conditions. It is inevitable that people with lifelong disabilities will ask for it too.

Once euthanasia for disability-related reasons is acceptable, it becomes much more likely for that option to be put on the table as a possibility, whether by the patient or (even inexplicitly) by those around them. We found several examples of rigid thinking, where people with mild intellectual disability or autism were fixated on the idea of euthanasia and unable or unwilling to consider alternatives. Doctors explained that the persistence and rigidity of their euthanasia request meant there were no viable alternatives from the perspective of the patient. However, it is not easy to establish whether a person has the mental capacity to make such a far-reaching decision, for example, because of their lack of ability to consider alternatives (see Chapter 13). Assessing this requires intimate and long-standing knowledge of the person within their social and relational environment, as well as their non-verbal communication.

These are complex situations. It will not be easy to decide whether euthanasia requests are truly voluntary and uninfluenced by external pressures. If there are precedents of euthanasia for people – including young people – who no longer feel able to live with the effects of their disability, then it will invariably be increasingly requested and subsequently granted; and invariably, societal opinion of what is acceptable will shift.

Conclusion

The requirement of formal review and public reporting within the Dutch system for assisted dying is unique in the world and deserves praise. We believe that all jurisdictions where assisted dying is legalized should adopt compulsory reporting and review of all cases. It enables close scrutiny of the way in which euthanasia is practised and the way in which it evolves, the reasoning behind euthanasia decisions, the dilemmas doctors face when confronted with complex situations, and the tensions between different ethical principles. Introducing assisted dying legislation is never the end of the debate, as laws (and how they are interpreted) change over time. It is therefore essential to have an open societal debate about these issues, without polarization or easy dismissal of minority views.

Our investigation of euthanasia for people with lifelong disabilities has raised questions around the extent to which legal criteria for euthanasia, even with careful and extensive accompanying guidance, can act as sufficient safeguards. It remains too difficult to decide conclusively and safely whether someone's suffering is unbearable and hopeless, without a viable alternative (the principle of compassion), as well as whether people are truly free from influence (the principle of autonomy). The suffering leading to some euthanasia requests could be seen to result from society's failure to accommodate and support the needs and characteristics of people with disabilities or autistic people.

Within western societies, people's perceived value and dignity, as well as their feeling of self-worth or of 'being a burden', may be affected by their measurable contribution to society. This can lead to an unconscious bias against disabled people (Chapter 22). This inevitably influences the way in which euthanasia requests are considered. It is exacerbated by the fact that they are less visible within society – many doctors in the cases we studied, for example, were unfamiliar with people with intellectual disability or autism. The very real experience of suffering described by disabled people in our studies cannot be fully understood in isolation of these facts.

We believe that it is a societal and governmental responsibility to build communities where disabled people are included, welcomed and their needs supported – and that this, rather than assisted dying for people who feel they have no place in society, should be the main focus of future debate.

References

Regional Euthanasia Review Committees (2022) *Euthanasia Code 2022: Review Procedures in Practice*. Available at: https://english.euthanasiecommissie.nl/the-committees/euthanasia-code-2022 (accessed 27 February 2024).

Tuffrey-Wijne, I., Curfs, L., Finlay, I. and Hollins, S. (2018) Euthanasia and assisted suicide for people with an intellectual disability and/or autism spectrum disorder: an examination of nine relevant euthanasia cases in the Netherlands (2012–2016), *BMC Medical Ethics*, 19: 17. Available at: https://doi.org/10.1186/s12910-018-0257-6 (accessed 5 February 2014).

Tuffrey-Wijne, I., Curfs, L., Hollins, S. and Finlay, I. (2023) Euthanasia and physician-assisted suicide in people with intellectual disabilities and/or autism spectrum disorders: investigation of 39 Dutch case reports (2012–2021), *BJPsych Open*, 9(3): e87. Available at: https://doi.org/10.1192/bjo.2023.69 (accessed 5 February 2014).

7 The rapid expansion of euthanasia and assisted suicide: the view from Canada

Ramona Coelho and Leonie Herx

Introduction

In less than 5 years Canada moved from its initial legislation, which allowed medical assistance in dying (MAiD) for those whose natural death was reasonably foreseeable (i.e. an end-of-life context), to its expansion in 2021, to allow MAiD for those with chronic illness or disability who are not dying. Although both assisted suicide and euthanasia are allowed under the MAiD legislation, almost all the cases in Canada are euthanasia. Legislation is already in place for MAiD for mental disorders as a sole underlying medical condition to become legal in the future, while parliamentary recommendations from 2023 suggest children and advance directives for euthanasia are next. There has been widespread, high-level concern that Canada's approach to euthanasia and assisted suicide puts Canadians at risk of wrongful and premature death when they would have benefitted from time, care and resources.

This chapter provides a summary of the Canadian MAiD regime, a brief outline of the landmark court challenges leading to progressive interpretations and changes to MAiD legislation, and examines how rapidly MAiD discourse and eligibility have changed in Canada over a relatively short time.

What is medical assistance in dying?

In Canadian law, MAiD is defined as a medical exemption in the Criminal Code to allow doctors and nurse practitioners to assist in the culpable homicide or suicide of a patient. MAiD in Canada includes both assisted suicide, where lethal drugs are provided by a practitioner and self-administered, and euthanasia, where lethal drugs are directly administered by the practitioner, which comprises over 99 per cent of such deaths.

The process of legalizing MAiD

The fight by proponents to legalize MAiD began as a series of legal battles, spanning decades. In 1993, Sue Rodriguez, who suffered from amyotrophic lateral sclerosis (ALS), went to court arguing that she had a right to end her life with assistance from a physician. The justices of the Court upheld the Criminal Code, stating that legalizing physician-assisted suicide would devalue life. In December 2009, the Quebec legislature mandated a Select Committee on Dying with Dignity to consult the public on the issue. Despite the majority of submissions being against legalization, the Quebec National Assembly passed a Bill in 2014 to legalize MAiD. They defined it as a form of health care to allow it to fall under provincial jurisdiction because criminal acts such as homicide and assisted suicide come under federal jurisdiction. MAiD was promoted to the public as a measure of last resort for use in exceptional circumstances with predictions that it would be little used.

Meanwhile, in the province of British Columbia, a court case made its way to the Supreme Court of Canada, which came to a unanimous decision to allow an exemption to the Criminal Code for culpable homicide and assisted suicide if done with consent of the patient and carried out by a physician for exceptional circumstances meeting specified criteria. The judges ruled that allowing physician-assisted death would prevent premature suicides of people who later would be unable to do so. They did not offer empirical evidence for this.

In June 2016, the federal government enacted Bill C-14 MAiD legislation. It attempted to balance the availability of assisted death for competent patients with a foreseeable death and intolerable suffering, while adding safeguards to try to minimize harm and prevent wrongful death. These safeguards included the requirement for death to be foreseeable, a 10-day waiting period, and a require-ment for capacity to consent at the time of request and assessment for MAiD as well as immediately prior to administration of lethal drugs.

Progressive interpretations and expansion of MAiD law

When the federal government enacted the MAiD law, no definition was provided for what is a 'reasonably foreseeable' death and this became progressively inter-preted through court challenges.

In one such court challenge, a 77-year-old patient (patient AB) with osteoar-thritis was approved to qualify for MAiD. The Superior Court Justice ruled there was no specific prognosis requirement for a 'reasonably foreseeable death' and thereby a patient's death does not have to be imminent or their condition terminal (Germano 2017). Hence, someone with a prognosis of many years of life could have their life ended through MAiD. In another case, *Lamb v Canada*, the case was adjourned in 2019 when an expert for the attorney general clarified that Julia Lamb (who lived with a degenerative neuromuscular disorder) could refuse regular treatment to make herself sick enough that her death would become rea-sonably foreseeable and thereby she would qualify for MAiD under the existing Bill C-14 regime.

At the same time, a court in Quebec ruled that the Canadian Charter of Rights and Freedoms was breached by limiting MAiD to those whose natural death is reasonably foreseeable. The federal government did not appeal this provincial lower court's decision and instead introduced Bill C-7, in 2021, allowing for death to be administered to those not dying but with chronic illness or disability, and removing a number of additional safeguards, including the 10-day waiting period and the requirement for capacity to consent at the time of lethal injection, which had come to be seen as barriers to accessing MAiD.

The Passing of Bill C-7

Bill C-7 was introduced by the Liberal government in February 2020. Support and opposition to Bill C-7 by members of Parliament tended to depend on party affiliation. The Liberals largely supported Bill C-7, arguing that suffering was being prolonged by denying MAiD immediately to Canadians.

However, all national disability advocacy and many social justice and Indigenous organizations raised concerns about a lack of resources to live, discrimination and the direct risks these inequalities pose to their communities while simultaneously being offered death as a solution for life suffering. Liberal disability inclusion minister, Carla Qualtrough, seemed to acknowledge such concerns and admitted to the Justice Committee that, 'it is easier to access MAiD than to get a wheelchair in some parts of the country' (Qualtrough 2020). She nonetheless voted in favour of Bill C-7.

Shifting perceptions and discourse surrounding MAiD

Throughout the early years of the debate, the Canadian Medical Association's Committee on Ethics was consistent in affirming its stance against euthanasia and assisted suicide. This was clearly stated in its Canadian Medical Association (CMA) policy in 2007 and upheld in 2013. However, when the CMA intervened in the Supreme Court of Canada *Carter* case, it emphasized that it would change its ethical policy based on the conclusions of the justices. The CMA therefore conceded and changed its policy to approve physician-assisted suicide and euthanasia, subject only to legal constraints.

Following enactment of the original MAiD legislation in 2016, many people initially took issue with the choice of the terms 'medical aid in dying' and 'medical assistance in dying' as being confusing to the public. Balfour Mount, founder of palliative care in Canada, stated in an interview, 'The first thing I would say is that the very name of that intervention, 'medical aid in dying', is misleading … Medical aid in dying is what I have been doing for 50 years. This bill is not talking about medical aid in dying' (Phillips 2021).

Inadequacy of reporting and oversight of MAiD

Politicians had promised Canadians that the expansion of MAiD was well considered. However, these claims are disputable. The parliamentary review the government had committed to undertake before any further expansion was never conducted prior to the enactment of Bill C-7. Moreover, the politicians who supported expansion quoted and drew most of their conclusions from a 2019 report on MAiD (Health Canada 2020). The evidence from this report was acquired from

MAiD providers self-reporting after MAiD deaths and was, therefore, unlikely to uncover abuses. For example, the report claimed that patients dying by MAiD had high rates of access to palliative care. In contrast, a study by Munro et al. (2020) demonstrated that palliative care access prior to having MAiD is much lower than was purported in the Health Canada Report on MAiD, and Munro's study was in a location with better access to palliative care than most places in Canada.

Also, Canadian evidence up to 2019 offered no insights into what would happen when MAiD was offered outside of the reasonably foreseeable death context and could offer no reassurance regarding what would happen when Bill C-7 allowed access for those with chronic illness and disability.

An independent review article concluded that oversight of MAiD has been grossly inadequate (Kotalik 2020). Furthermore, abuses of MAiD legislation have been documented in law and policy by different oversight bodies.[1]

In August 2023, the Commission on End-of-Life Care in Quebec issued a memo warning MAiD assessors to follow the law. Their head, Dr Michel Bureau, said in an interview, 'We're now no longer dealing with an exceptional treatment, but a treatment that is very frequent.' Bureau also said he had witnessed a slight increase in the number of cases that violate legislation (Serebrin 2023). And shortly thereafter, the Chief Coroner of Ontario announced that he was calling for applicants to form a Medical Assistance in Dying Death Review Committee (MDRC) in response to increasing health, social and intersectional complexities arising from current and pending legislative changes. The purpose of the MDRC will be to provide an expert review of MAiD deaths to assist in evaluating potential public safety.

Besides this, we are hearing of many fact-checked credible stories of MAiD abuses in the Canadian media that are in themselves a cause for concern (Coelho et al. 2023).

MAiD upends medicine

MAiD law in Canada does not require that interventions to address a person's intolerable suffering have been provided, or tried and failed, just that patients are 'informed' of their options. Other jurisdictions that allow MAiD outside the end-of-life context require all avenues to address suffering to have been exhausted.

In Canada, a person could have a readily treatable cause of their suffering but if MAiD is requested, a doctor is obligated to facilitate access through either providing MAiD or referring on to someone who will provide MAiD, even if reasonable options for care exist. This undermines the standard of medical care and the role of physicians in providing evidenced-based care recommendations (Lemmens et al. 2021).

Policies contributing to the rapid expansion of MAiD in Canada

In 2023, Health Canada produced a Model Practice Standard for Medical Assistance in Dying, which recommends that MAiD *should be raised in conversation with all those who might qualify* if the practitioner suspects it aligns with a patient's values and preferences (Government of Canada 2023). In contrast, other jurisdictions in the world, for instance Victoria in Australia, where MAiD practices are legalized, frown on or prohibit raising death as a treatment option for patients, fearing it may be coercive or reflective of the healthcare provider's feelings of hopelessness and therapeutic nihilism. The power imbalance between physician and patient, coupled with the patient's assumption that the provider will only suggest the best options for their health, makes the physician raising this option extremely dangerous.

The model practice standard's approach to 'conscientious objection' is equally troubling. Healthcare providers who object to providing MAiD, even in select circumstances, are considered conscientious objectors. The practice standard affirms physicians must follow the rules set by their provincial regulators, but it supports 'effective referral' of the patient. What does this mean? A physician who is concerned that MAiD is not a patient's best option is supposed to ignore their conscience or professional opinion and simply refer the patient so they can die by way of MAiD.

Clear examples of these problematic policies are seen in the video training sessions held by the Canadian Association of MAiD Assessors and Providers (CAMAP). CAMAP was given C$3.3 million by Health Canada to develop 'high quality MAiD training' for its delivery in Canada. Instructors in these CAMAP training videos acknowledge patients might be driven to MAiD by unmet psychosocial needs, and should that cause discomfort, 'you'll then have to refer the person on to somebody else, who may hopefully fulfill the request in the end' (Raikin 2022). Thus we see how referrals made against the physician's better judgement can funnel patients towards death, despite legitimate professional concerns and obligations that should have paused or stopped the process altogether.

In addition, despite two MAiD assessors being required to act as gatekeepers to sign off the criteria for MAiD being met, another CAMAP training video has an instructor explaining there is no need to stop if another practitioner thinks a patient doesn't qualify for MAiD, stating: 'You can ask as many clinicians as you want or need' (Raikin 2022). This implies that the safeguards and standards are non-existent or not enforced and that it is always possible to find someone to end your life eventually. This is shameful and antithetical to the noble practice of medicine.

The Disability Filibuster (2022), a national grassroots disability community initiative formed in opposition to Bill C-7 and the expansion of MAiD, stated in an open letter that members have raised fears about seeking health care if death could be offered to them when they are at their lowest. The disability community is not being alarmist. Healthcare providers have often rated the quality of life of those with disabilities as poor despite disabled persons rating their quality of life the same as aged-matched healthy individuals (Sohn 2021). Put differently, many physicians might consider patients with disabilities, especially from marginalized groups, as having lives that are no longer worth living, which might consciously or unconsciously lead them to suggest MAiD (see Chapter 22).

Canadian proponents of MAiD are primarily focused on making death more accessible, advocating for its availability in every hospital and hospice. They argue that within the context of a socialized healthcare system, institutions failing to offer MAiD should face defunding. Delta Hospice in the province of British Columbia lost funding and lost its privately funded building simply for abstaining from providing MAiD on-site, despite its availability nearby (Hall and Yuzda 2020).

The influential lobby group directing MAiD discourse in Canada has announced plans to pursue legal action against a faith-based hospital that refuses to offer MAiD services, despite the government's willingness to establish an easily accessible alternative facility off the hospital's premises (Payne 2024; Schreiber 2024). In 2023, the province of Quebec also passed a provincial law mandating the provision of MAiD in all hospices. This leaves many individuals within the disability community, who recognize the risks associated with MAiD to their lives and have requested MAiD-free spaces, with no options for access to health care in a forum that is acceptable to them. Recently, we have been made aware (personal communication) that some clinical contracts for physicians require them to undertake MAiD assessments as a condition of employment, removing any semblance of conscientious objection.

Where are we now with MAiD in Canada?

Early political commentary had stressed a very restricted pattern of use with projections of few MAiD completions. Currently, some places in Canada have MAiD rates that are the highest in the world. Within a few years of the introduction of MAiD, Canada has surpassed all other countries for its number of euthanasia and assisted suicide deaths reported. There are already emerging many cases of MAiD for psychosocial suffering in persons with disabilities (poverty, lack of access to care), while an increasing number of MAiD expansionists are openly arguing that MAiD driven by poverty and inequality is supporting choice and is a form of harm reduction (Schuklenk 2022; Wiebe and Mullin 2023).

Bill C-14 introduced MAiD as a medical act to cause death for those with intolerable suffering and whose death was reasonably foreseeable. Our current regime under Bill C-7 allows MAiD for intolerable suffering (psychological or physical), for those with disability and will include those with psychiatric diseases as well. The Special Joint Committee on MAiD has recommended expansion of MAiD for children deemed capable to consent ('mature minors') and advance directives for MAiD, along with other recommendations. Given the lack of medical research to validate these changes in law as safe, Canada is choosing to abandon caution and proceed hastily.

Conclusion

In Canada, a series of legal battles, shifting public discourse driven by wealthy lobbyists, together with political will on the part of the federal government has led to a rapid expansion of MAiD in Canada. MAiD, although being legislated as the responsibility of the medical community, is not established as such and does not operate on the same premises as the medical standard of care. Medicine is based on average responses and risks and harms, and best evidence gathered from research coupled with clinical expertise, not by court decisions or political will.

The federal Bill C-14 had assured Canadians that MAiD practice would offer assisted suicide and euthanasia for competent suffering patients at the end of their life, while safeguards would protect everyone else from premature and wrongful death. However, in less than 5 years we have seen this approach abandoned by the government with progressive expansions of the law and removal of safeguards. The emphasis has moved from protecting disabled Canadians from wrongful death while allowing exceptional access, to claiming it is discrimination to limit who can end their life with MAiD. The so-called autonomy of the individual is paramount (see Chapter 27) and MAiD has become the ready solution to almost any form of suffering.

Note

1. Such as the Chief Coroner of Ontario and the Commission on End-of-Life Care in Quebec, both in 2018; and the Correctional Investigator of Canada in 2019.

References

Coelho, R., Maher, J., Gaind, K.S. and Lemmens, T. (2023) The realities of medical assistance in dying, *Palliative and Supportive Care*, 21 (5): 871–78.

Disability Filibuster (2022) *To the Ontario Government and CPSO Policy Department*, 20 November. Available at: https://policyconsult.cpso.on.ca/wp-content/uploads/2022/11/POHR-MAID_Disability-Filibuster_20221128_Redacted.pdf (accessed 26 February 2024).

Germano, D. (2017) Judge rules Ontario woman meets requirements for medically assisted death, *CTV News*, 20 June. Available at: https://www.ctvnews.ca/health/judge-rules-ontario-woman-meets-requirement-for-medically-assisted-death-1.3467146 (accessed 11 July 2024).

Government of Canada (2023) *Model Practice Standard for Medical Assistance in Dying*. Available at: https://www.canada.ca/en/health-canada/services/publications/health-system-services/model-practice-standard-medical-assistance-dying.html (accessed 18 April 2024).

Hall, M. and Yuzda, L. (2020) Delta Hospice loses funding over refusal to provide MAiD, *Vancouver City News*, 25 February. Available at: https://vancouver.citynews.ca/2020/02/25/delta-hospice-loses-funding-over-refusal-to-provide-medically-assisted-dying/ (accessed 26 February 2024).

Health Canada (2020) *First Annual Report on Medical Assistance in Dying in Canada, 2019.* Available at: https://www.canada.ca/en/health-canada/services/publications/health-system-services/annual-report-medical-assistance-dying-2019.html.

Kotalik, J. (2020) Medical assistance in dying: challenges of monitoring the Canadian program, *Canadian Journal of Bioethics*, 3 (3): 202–9.

Lemmens, T., Shariff, M. and Herx, L. (2021) How Bill C-7 will sacrifice the medical profession's standard of Care, *Policy Options*, 11 February. Available at: https://policyoptions.irpp.org/magazines/february-2021/how-bill-c7-will-sacrifice-the-medical-professions-standard-of-care/ (accessed 26 February 2024).

Munro, C., Romanova, A., Webber, C. et al. (2020) Involvement of palliative care in patients requesting medical assistance in dying, *Canadian Family Physician*, 66 (11): 833–42.

Payne, D. (2024) Activists prepare to sue Canadian Catholic hospital over assisted suicide refusal, *Catholic News Agency*, 9 February. Available at: https://www.catholicnewsagency.com/news/256783/activists-prepare-to-sue-canadian-catholic-hospital-over-assisted-suicide-refusal (accessed 26 February 2024).

Phillips, D. (2021) Balfour Mount, *Palliative Care McGill*. Available at: https://www.mcgill.ca/palliativecare/portraits-0/balfour-mount (accessed 26 February 2024).

Qualtrough, C. (2020) Evidence to the Standing Committee on Justice and Human Rights, House of Commons, Tuesday 3 November 2020. Available at: https://www.ourcommons.ca/DocumentViewer/en/43-2/JUST/meeting-4/evidence#Int-10988133 (accessed 26 February 2024).

Raikin, A. (2022) No other options, *The New Atlantis*, 16 December. Available at: https://www.thenewatlantis.com/publications/no-other-options (accessed 26 February 2024).

Schreiber, M. (2024) The lobby group that owns the conversation around assisted deaths, *The Walrus*, 12 January. Available at: https://thewalrus.ca/dying-with-dignity-lobby/ (accessed 26 February 2024).

Schuklenk, U. (2022) Argumenta ad passiones: Canada debates access thresholds to MAiD, *Bioethics*, 36 (6): 611–12.

Serebrin, J. (2023) Quebecers no longer seeing doctor-assisted deaths as exceptional, says oversight body, *CTV News*, 15 August. Available at: https://montreal.ctvnews.ca/quebecers-no-longer-seeing-doctor-assisted-deaths-as-exceptional-says-oversight-body-1.6519503 (accessed 26 February 2024).

Sohn, R. (2021) Large majority of doctors hold misconceptions about people with disabilities, survey finds, *Stat*, 1 February. Available at: https://www.statnews.com/2021/02/01/large-majority-of-doctors-hold-misconceptions-about-people-with-disabilities-survey-finds/ (accessed 26 February 2024).

Wiebe, K. and Mullin, A. (2023) Choosing death in unjust conditions: hope, autonomy and harm reduction, *Journal of Medical Ethics*, 50:407–412. Available at: https://doi.org/10.1136/jme-2022-108871 (accessed 26 February 2024).

8 Assisted dying in Aotearoa New Zealand: a victory of politics over informed debate?

Sinead Donnelly, Peter Thirkell,
John Kleinsman and Wendi Wicks[1]

Introduction

Assisted dying came into effect in Aotearoa New Zealand on 7 November 2021, 12 months after the Act was approved by public referendum and almost 2 years after its final parliamentary vote. There had been two previous attempts to introduce similar legislation in 1995 and 2003.

In this chapter, we discuss various aspects relating to the passage of assisted dying legislation through the New Zealand Parliament as well as offering some early and brief observations regarding its impact on palliative care.

'Mind the gap': the disconnection between rhetoric and law

Throughout the 5-year parliamentary process leading to the implementation of the End of Life Choice Act 2019,[2] proponents of assisted dying continually promoted stories of bad (painful) deaths, the point being that palliative care could not alleviate the worst suffering. These stories were hard to challenge in the public forum without the challengers appearing to be lacking in compassion.

Opponents were largely limited to highlighting big-picture issues related to legalizing assisted dying, using philosophical and ethical arguments that lacked the emotional (and media) appeal of the hard cases. As Margaret Somerville has often noted: it is easy to place a suffering person in a wheelchair and our hearts rightly go out to them, but those who oppose euthanasia cannot place in a wheelchair the seriously damaged society which results (Somerville 2021).

The simplistic, emotional strategy ultimately prevailed. The deeper and more sophisticated arguments against assisted dying never gained traction, neutralized by the simple but effective appeal to people's heartstrings. While opponents worked hard to demonstrate that the scope and impact of the proposed legislation would go well beyond the so-called 'hard cases', this fact was largely lost on the wider public and many members of Parliament.

The current New Zealand law has no requirement for people to first access palliative care and is not designed as an act of last resort. The significant gap between the rhetoric of the hard cases and the much more permissive law as passed reflects a serious lack of integrity in both the public debate and the parliamentary process.

'It's what the people want!'

Members of Parliament were acutely aware of the divisive nature of assisted dying. Proponents therefore encouraged MPs to adopt the stance of 'I'm not necessarily convinced but I will support the Bill through its first reading so that the arguments can be fully considered by a Select Committee.' This gave the Bill early momentum without requiring a firm commitment from MPs.

The name, 'End of Life Choice Bill', misleadingly implied that people lacked real choice and made opponents appear to be against choice. Once the Bill passed to the Select Committee, opponents actively encouraged public submissions, resulting in a record 39,000 individual submissions (with over 90 per cent opposed). This proved to be a two-edged sword, however, making it hard to summarize the key conclusions from over 50,000 pages of complex evidence. It also allowed proponents to claim a rigorous process, while selectively highlighting carefully chosen submissions playing to their central themes of compassion, autonomy and choice.

Perhaps the most effective move by proponents was making the proposed law subject to a binding public referendum. This came about because of the New Zealand First Party's policy of requiring a referendum on any law leading to major social change, and it secured their eight votes for the second and third readings. At the same time, the referendum provision gave 'political cover' to MPs harbouring reservations by allowing them to claim that the question would be decided finally 'by the people'.

Lack of substantive engagement with the evidence

There was a noticeable lack of substantive engagement by MPs with expert witness testimony during the Select Committee stages. Hospice New Zealand (representing all 35 hospices) and the NZ Medical Association, along with 20 other organizations from the medical, aged care and palliative care sectors, all made submissions which, without exception, were opposed to the Bill. Yet the Committee's final report to Parliament on the proposed Bill stated simply that, 'Health professionals held a wide range of views on the bill'.

Similarly, their report essentially ignored that more than 93 per cent of almost 2,000 doctors, nurses and other health professionals who made individual submissions opposed to the Bill, concluding again that 'the medical community has a range of opinions on the bill'.

While it was recorded that 90 per cent of all 36,700 written submissions opposed the Bill, the report made little attempt to nuance a range of concerns or to 'weigh the evidence' based on the professional expertise, experience, insights and quality of arguments made by key professional groups, including many lawyers. It became apparent that personal anecdotes and 'hard stories' emphasizing autonomy and choice were often given equal if not greater weighting than the views of health professionals working in end-of-life care.

'Nothing about us without us': the disabled voice disabled

The presence of disabled voices in the assisted dying debate matters since every request is ultimately related to the inexorable progression of a disease and its associated disabilities. Two critical questions arise: 'Who frames what is said about disability?' and 'Who gets heard?' (see also Chapter 22).

The New Zealand experience is that it was the non-disabled who mostly defined disabled people's interests, including medical professionals, academics, disability workers, families, bureaucrats and lawyers. This happened repeatedly – non-disabled people favoured as the authoritative voice on disability. The collective stories told and repeated in the media were harmful to disabled people and highly resistant to change, tapping into entrenched ableism.

In a 2015 High Court affidavit, the plaintiff, Lecretia Seales (seeking clarification as to whether her doctor could legally assist her to end her life), specifically related her 'dignity of life' to the qualities of being independent and active, as well as continent and able to feed and wash herself, stating: 'I fear being totally immobilised and losing control of my bodily functions. I cannot bear the thought of being fully incontinent and being unable to clean myself.'[3] Meanwhile, her lawyer argued that a need for physical assistance was sufficient reason to allow assisted dying. Not Dead Yet Aotearoa, a well-established voice of disabled people on assisted dying, attempted to address the prevalence of ableist thinking in the arguments used by proponents of assisted dying while articulating the dangers of legalization for disabled persons.

During Select Committee hearings, disabled submitters were vigorously attacked by politicians, including some who were sons or fathers of disabled people, who also thought they knew better regarding disabled interests. Disability activists in Aotearoa New Zealand also found themselves the target of comments on social media, which stated that disabled persons opposing assisted dying would be better off dead.

Throughout the campaign, an authentic disabled voice was largely and persistently side-lined. Occasionally, useful segments were fitted into the existing rhetoric. But disabled peoples' concerns in large part remained, and still remain, unaddressed. The risk for disabled people under this law remains high and will only increase if efforts for a more permissive regime are successful.

An unresolved question: the relationship between assisted dying and non-assisted suicide

During the debate on assisted dying, a contentious question arose concerning the potential impact of such a law on 'non-assisted' suicide rates. The matter was a sensitive one given New Zealand's very high rates of suicide among youth, especially Māori youth, compared to other countries.

The MP sponsoring the Bill claimed that legalization would lead to a *reduction* in non-assisted suicide rates because it would give people an alternative to committing violent suicides. This logic, however, considers only those people 'in scope' of a particular assisted dying regime, while ignoring any impact on those 'out of scope'. The yet-to-be answered question remains: will State authorization of premature deaths for some suffering people have a negative effect on suicide prevention by other suffering people?

A close analysis of the statistics from Belgium and the Netherlands shows that their rates of non-assisted suicide have both risen since the implementation of assisted dying, either in real terms or relative to trends in other demographically similar countries. While no definitive conclusions can be drawn without further research, the question of a direct and/or indirect causal relationship between assisted dying and non-assisted suicides cannot be ruled out (Doherty et al. 2022).

In New Zealand, a claim regarding the Crown's failure properly to consider the effect of legalizing assisted dying on Māori suicide rates has been filed with the Waitangi Tribunal[4] and awaits consideration.

Assisted dying is not part of medicine

Opponents of assisted dying ran a media campaign garnering 1,800 doctors' signatures to an open letter affirming that assisted dying was not part of medical practice, while arguing that doctors were not necessary for assisted dying to be implemented. This argument did not take hold in New Zealand, however, with politicians and the media becoming the self-appointed moral authority on this issue. In our view, the medical profession was narrowly and simplistically regarded as the necessary vehicle for facilitating people's choices: completing paperwork, prescribing, administering and certifying death.

For proponents of assisted dying, the high public regard for the medical profession was exploited to provide a cloak of medical legitimacy for the practice while lifting the primary moral burden of an assisted death off the patient. This largely explains the preferred use of sanitized euphemisms such as 'medical aid in dying' or 'death with dignity' by proponents of change.

Paradoxically, the strongest opposition to assisted dying in the medical profession came from medical specialists most likely to be caring for people who are dying – palliative medicine doctors. Rather than being given priority, their expert voices were virtually ignored.

Lack of data for effective review

During the year leading up to the implementation of assisted dying, various physicians, ethicists and academics requested that the registering authority gather data similar to what is collected in Oregon and Canada. The registrar for assisted dying and her team were provided with a list that would allow international comparisons of this new practice for New Zealand.

As of the date of writing, this request has not been actioned. Our view is that recording the reasons individuals request assisted dying would help significantly in identifying gaps in care that lead a person to claim intolerable suffering necessitating assisted dying. Given that this information has the potential to reduce 'intolerable suffering' for persons with a life-limiting illness without them choosing a premature death, we regard it as highly unethical not to gather it.

Ironically, New Zealand's Ministry of Health has an administrative team of nine staff running the fully funded assisted dying programme compared to only two staff supporting our partially funded national palliative care service.

Response to suffering

There is emerging evidence that within the first year of assisted dying legislation in New Zealand, people are choosing euthanasia because they feel a burden to their family or because they feel alone and abandoned. There is also emerging evidence from ongoing research with palliative care staff that they are being extraordinarily 'careful' not to explore the reasons for a patient's distress if they declare an interest in assisted dying. This reticence appears to be related to health professionals' fear of legal consequences, in contrast to their previous practice of careful exploration as part of good palliative care.

One of the criteria for accessing assisted dying in New Zealand is that, in the patient's view, their suffering is intolerable. Prior to the legalization of assisted dying, people suffered because of loneliness, a sense of abandonment, social isolation, despair or meaninglessness, and the answers were seen as lying in the expert care provided by wrap-around palliative care – striving continuously to attend to the holistic needs of those who suffer.

Post-legalization, people are still suffering from these same societal shortcomings. None of these underlying causes of intolerable suffering has been relieved by assisted dying. Now the answer to such suffering is provided by the doctor ending someone's life.

The vulnerabilities associated with feeling a burden, loneliness and meaninglessness cut across all classes, races, abilities, genders and ages. With assisted dying, the societal deficits in care can be wiped out by 'wiping out' the person rather than addressing the glaring gaps in care.

Conclusion

It is still too early to be able to analyse the precise impact of assisted dying on end-of-life care in Aotearoa New Zealand, although there are some concerning trends emerging. The legislation stipulates that the Ministry of Health must review the Act within 3 years of its commencement, including whether any amendments are necessary or desirable. There is significant pressure coming from some quarters to expand the parameters of eligibility to include those who are not dying but who live with long-term debilitating diseases. Given that our law was heavily based on the Canadian legislation, we predict that there will be permissive changes that mirror what has happened, and is happening, in Canada.

Notes

1. The authors were all members of the *Care Alliance*, which, in 2012, brought together 12 organizations (palliative care providers and medical, disability, social and religious groups) to improve conversations about dying, with its members sharing an understanding that a compassionate and ethical response to suffering did not include or require assisted dying.
2. Available at: https://www.legislation.govt.nz/act/public/2019/0067/latest/DLM7285905.html (accessed 13 February 2024).
3. See paragraph 43 in: https://lecretia.org/wp-content/uploads/2015/10/redacted_affidavit_of_lecretia_seales_no_1.pdf (accessed 8 March 2024).
4. The Treaty of Waitangi Act 1975 established the Waitangi Tribunal commission to investigate possible breaches by Crown actions of promises made in the Treaty of Waitangi. See https://www.waitangitribunal.govt.nz/#:~:text=Set%20up%20by%20the%20Treaty,in%20the%20Treaty%20of%20Waitangi (accessed 13 February 2024).

References

Doherty, A.M., Axe, C.J. and Jones, D.A. (2022) Investigating the relationship between euthanasia and/or assisted suicide and rates of non-assisted suicide: systematic review, *BJPsych Open*, 8: e108. Available at: https://doi.org/10.1192/bjo.2022.71 (accessed 5 March 2024).

Somerville, M. (2021) Questioning the wisdom of legalising euthanasia, *Eureka Street*, 3 June. Available at: https://www.eurekastreet.com.au/article/questioning-the-wisdom-of-legalising-euthanasia (accessed 15 February 2024).

9 The Australian perspective

Frank Brennan, Adrian Dabscheck and Leeroy William

Introduction

In the realm of health care and ethics, few topics are as emotionally charged and morally nuanced as assisted dying. Legislation in this space raises many concerns and tensions, particularly as the desired precision of the law is at odds with the uncertainty of medicine (Brennan 2019). Assisted dying therefore requires careful consideration, seeking a balance between the autonomy of individuals and the protection of us all when we are at our most vulnerable. For some, these legislative changes provide a desired control over death, but they should not negatively affect the majority of people (Twycross 2024).

Background

Australia first introduced assisted dying in the Northern Territory in 1996, only to have this legislation overturned after 9 months. Subsequently, concerns were raised regarding the assessment of depression and prognostication in the seven assisted deaths that had occurred (Kissane et al. 1998). In June 2019, the Voluntary Assisted Dying Act 2017 became operational in the state of Victoria and paved the way for similar legislative changes in the other Australian states. The two territories (Northern Territory and Australian Capital Territory) are due to follow suit, upon which voluntary assisted dying will be accessible across the whole of Australia.

The 'Australian model'

Through this state legislation, an 'Australian model' of voluntary assisted dying has emerged. Consistent features include narrow eligibility requirements, a tightly regulated request and assessment process, pre-authorization before the administration of voluntary assisted dying in four states, mandatory reporting at every stage of the process and a conscientious objection clause (Waller et al. 2023). However, Waller et al. (2023) also highlight the significant variations between the states in criteria for eligibility, in choosing practitioner administration of voluntary assisted dying, and in different provisions regulating non-participation by facilities. These variations raise questions about the consistency and effectiveness of assisted dying laws across the country. Furthermore, the implementation of the laws in each state varies according to institutional positions on assisted dying, their associated policies and procedures, and the personal views of their staff. This has led to 'ethical variability' in clinical practice and more inconsistencies to be navigated (McDougall et al. 2023; White et al. 2023a).

Equity in end-of-life care

From a clinical perspective, voluntary assisted dying has disrupted end-of-life care in many ways. First, the contentious nature of assisted dying divides opinion and fuels debate about how care should be provided. Secondly, its implementation caused concern in terms of ethical variability, practical uncertainty about how voluntary assisted dying would work, the ability of the legislation to capture the nuances of clinical practice, and the capability of organizations to build a respectful culture for assisted dying (McDougall et al. 2023). Thirdly, equitable service delivery models for all people requiring end-of-life care need to be considered urgently, irrespective of their desire for assisted dying (Twycross 2024).

In 2017, the Productivity Commission recommended improvements to end-of-life care in Australia. Four areas were targeted: increasing community-based palliative care; better equipping of residential aged care; encouraging advance care planning; and improving the stewardship of end-of-life care services to improve integration across care settings (Australian Government Productivity Commission 2018). In the wake of the implementation of voluntary assisted dying and the Covid-19 pandemic, how has the funding of these suggested palliative care improvements been affected? While various state governments have undertaken to improve funding for palliative care, great variability continues. Hudson et al. (2024) have recently exposed the lack of publicly available information related to the implementation costs of voluntary assisted dying and have compiled a useful list of potential expenditures.

Improvements in end-of-life care are further compromised by the new landscape of health care in the post-pandemic era, where financial and workforce deficits exist amidst growing demands for end-of-life care. Patient care was already disadvantaged by the workforce's lack of palliative care knowledge and skills before the pandemic. So how will compassionate care and informed choices be offered to those who feel devastated by their life-threatening diagnosis, when this is the time they are at increased risk of suicidal ideation? (Nafilyan et al. 2023).

Healthcare professionals often avoid crucial end-of-life care conversations, partly through a lack of appropriate communication skills (Jackson and Emanuel 2024) and defensive medicine practices (Ries et al. 2022), both of which may be affected by voluntary assisted dying. This hinders the appropriate clinical exploration of desire to die statements (Adams et al. 2022) and can lead to premature and inappropriate referrals for assisted dying. By contrast, despite palliative care being explicitly recognized under the human right to health (WHO 2020), there has not been the same political and legal imperative to ensure its provision to those who need it.

For the population requiring end-of-life care in Australia, the healthcare system must facilitate access to services in a timely manner, irrespective of their location, socio-economic status, cultural background, spirituality, indigenous status or sexual orientation. Assisted dying caters for a minority of people who need this end-of-life care option, but monitoring trends to determine its effect on end-of-life care overall is problematic without standardized reporting of voluntary assisted dying (Komesaroff and Philip 2023; Worthington et al. 2024).

The Palliative Care Outcomes Collaboration (PCOC) reports on the care delivered by specialist palliative care services in approximately 25 per cent of Australian deaths annually. On average, people are seen in the last 2 months of life (Daveson et al. 2023). Some hope there will be more timely palliative care referrals, given the prognostication stipulated in assisted dying legislation, which suggests surprising accuracy. However, the absence of data on the palliative care provided outside the specialist palliative care sector is more concerning. The Australian Institute of Health and Welfare (2023) states: 'there is no nationally consistent, routinely collected primary healthcare data that enables reporting on the provision of palliative care by GPs'. Furthermore, the gaps in end-of-life care for the majority of people have been recognized by Palliative Care Australia (2021) as priorities during the Covid-19 pandemic and by the Royal Commission into Aged Care Quality and Safety.

Impact on palliative care

Palliative care has tried to demarcate its boundaries in relation to voluntary assisted dying, as recommended by the Royal Australasian College of Physicians (RACP 2018). However, conflation and misperceptions about these end-of-life options continue, and the future relationship is uncertain. Reviews of voluntary assisted dying in Victoria highlight the need for more research to answer many unanswered questions, but recognize the difficulties faced over the years (McDougall et al. 2020; Komesaroff and Philip 2023; White et al. 2023b). Importantly, patients and their caregivers have also provided insights into their experiences of barriers and facilitators to voluntary assisted dying (White et al. 2023a). The South Australian Voluntary Assisted Dying Act 2021, uniquely, expressly separated assisted dying from palliative care. This settles, at least in that state, the universal debate as to whether assisted dying should form part of palliative care.

Within a year of the legislation coming into effect, there were calls for fewer safeguards to enable greater access (McDougall and Pratt 2020). One problem was the lack of doctors willing to be involved with VAD. Consistent with the international literature, medical buy-in has been limited (Rutherford et al. 2021, 2023; Sellars et al. 2021), but some states have enabled nurses to have more involvement in order to bypass this issue.

Aspects of assisted dying legislation have caused problems for palliative care services. In those states where the topic of voluntary assisted dying cannot be raised by doctors, many conversations have been affected (Ore 2024). The dilemma for clinicians is the requirement that, in line with the principles of informed consent, they should provide all treatment options available, while not coercing the person into choosing voluntary assisted dying. Anecdotally, palliative care clinicians have been accused of attempting to persuade people against voluntary assisted dying when, in fact, they were unpacking the reasons behind a desire to die statement. Conversations have also become more convoluted as both parties try and decipher if voluntary assisted dying is really being discussed. The legal implications make clinicians wary of any such end-of-life conversations, but also more cautious when they have them.

Palliative care teams have been accused of obstructing access to voluntary assisted dying during initial conversations. But this is because of a lack of distinction between how a desire to die statement is approached in palliative care versus the perception of a first request for voluntary assisted dying. The former involves an unpacking of the statement to uncover where we may be able to help the person. The latter involves a referral to the assisted dying team.

Other anecdotal forms of obstruction relate to who should perform prognostication and capacity assessments, and which assessments should be acted on. It is usual practice in palliative care to plan end-of-life care in conjunction with these assessments. However, the legal responsibility for assessing requests for voluntary assisted dying sits with the assisted dying clinicians. Assumptions that palliative care staff are obstructing access to voluntary assisted dying can lead to miscommunication, mistrust and unnecessary actions to obtain assisted dying for patients who may die naturally before the process can be completed. At times, this may be driven by the patient or family, but having the difficult conversation with a united clinical approach can avoid distress for families at a difficult time and reduce bereavement issues.

In some cases, patients have refused medication for symptom control, for fear of losing capacity and becoming ineligible for voluntary assisted dying. The palliative care team may also be asked to withhold certain medications for symptom relief before the assisted dying assessment to avoid any impediment to the process. In other cases, the focus on attaining an assisted dying death overshadows the time that family could have been supported to be with the dying person.

There has been a lack of co-ordinated communication between teams in different services and across different settings. Privacy laws, and especially the confidentiality around voluntary assisted dying, have led to teams being unaware of assisted dying being an issue for the person entering their service. The privacy extends to the variability of assisted dying being recorded on the death certificate in different states and the lack of data on the reasons people access voluntary assisted dying in Victoria.

As in Canada, but unlike in New Zealand, specialist palliative care units have not been spared from assisted dying. There have been accusations of obstructing the right of the person having voluntary assisted dying to die in the place of their choice (Davey and Lu 2023). Nothing in the legislation supports this claim, which contrasts with the routine practice of moving patients for hospital treatment or into aged care. Many patients would prefer to die in a specialist palliative care unit, but the short-stay nature of these units may mean they need to move against their wishes. Given their predicament, and the introduction of voluntary assisted dying, many of these patients have voiced a preference to pursue assisted dying rather than move into aged care.

Any separation between palliative care and voluntary assisted dying, especially in the community, is impossible in practice. Invariably, assisted dying clinicians are not providing all the care for the people requesting voluntary assisted dying and their families. For many reasons, assisted dying cases are considered too complex for some teams and are referred to specialist palliative care services, if they are not already involved. Some referrals will have greater needs than others, but specialist palliative care services have tried to see the most complex of cases in keeping with their usual referral criteria.

Contrary to the rhetoric, palliative care services have not abandoned people requesting voluntary assisted dying; however, the ethical variability in the healthcare system contributes to this perception. The New South Wales Act expressly states that the treating team, irrespective of their response to voluntary assisted dying, must continue their usual standard of care. Bereavement care is a critical example of this ongoing support, which is often provided by community palliative care services. Assisted dying deaths and their impact on carers need to be considered (Lewis et al. 2024), especially if we are to avoid the recent tragedy of a husband taking the unused substance provided to his wife for assisted dying (Siganto 2024).

Future directions

There have been amendments to the legislation in Victoria, and a review of voluntary assisted dying over the last 5 years is in progress, with similar processes likely in other states. The number of people who have utilized assisted dying services has been increasing, especially in Western Australia, and is likely to increase over time (Willmott et al. 2023). As this occurs, it will be important to avoid the ambiguity that currently exists in Victoria. Here, the legislation does not require conscientious objectors to refer people requesting voluntary assisted dying to a willing assisted dying practitioner. However, this may be considered an obstruction to the person's access to treatment (Victoria Department of Health 2022).

A further argument made in favour of widening the eligibility criteria is the suggestion that voluntary assisted dying should align with advance care planning – perhaps to make it available to people with dementia or to those who might want to donate their organs (White et al. 2024).

In Australia, because of a Commonwealth law prohibiting the encouragement of suicide via telephone or email, assisted dying discussions are not permitted via these modes of telehealth. A recent Federal Court judgment held that voluntary assisted dying fell within the definition of 'suicide'. This ruling runs counter to a widespread argument that voluntary assisted dying does not constitute suicide (Chrysanthos 2023). It provides clarity on the legal status of voluntary assisted dying, potentially influencing future legislation and medical practices related to end-of-life care. The ruling has sparked debate on autonomy, medical ethics and public perceptions of assisted dying. Its impact extends internationally, shaping discussions on the legality and classification of similar practices worldwide. Overall, the ruling has the potential to reshape how society views and addresses end-of-life decisions, with ramifications for both medical professionals and individuals seeking control over their own deaths.

The recent editorial about the Victorian experience (Komesaroff and Philip 2023) and the review of the international evidence regarding assisted dying (Worthington et al. 2024) highlight the many unanswered questions that persist. The repercussions from the changes in legislation will take many years to evaluate, while clinicians grapple with the practical logistics of delivering effective and compassionate end-of-life care.

References

Adams, V., Katz, N.T., Philip, J.A.M. and Gold, M. (2022) Desire to die statements in the era of voluntary assisted dying: an audit of patients known to a Victorian consultation-liaison palliative care service, *American Journal of Hospice and Palliative Care*, 39 (10): 1203–9.

Australian Government Productivity Commission (2018) *Introducing Competition and Informed User Choice into Human Services: Reforms to Human Services – Inquiry Report*. Available at: https://apo.org.au/node/137956 (accessed 15 April 2024).

Australian Institute of Health and Welfare (2023) *Palliative Care Services in Australia*, Australian Government, last updated 9 November. Available at: https://www.aihw.gov.au/reports/palliative-care-services/palliative-care-services-in-australia/contents/palliative-care-in-general-practice (accessed 15 April 2024).

Brennan, F. (2019) The Victorian Voluntary Assisted Dying Act comes into operation, *Internal Medicine Journal*, 49 (6): 689–93.

Chrysanthos, N. (2023) States to push for voluntary assisted dying exemption in criminal code, *The Sydney Morning Herald*, 30 November. Available at: https://www.smh.com.au/politics/federal/voluntary-assisted-dying-is-the-same-as-suicide-federal-court-20231130-p5eo0p.html (accessed 22 April 2024).

Daveson, B., Blanchard, M., Clapham, S. et al. (2023) Population-level, patient-reported outcomes: a case study regarding a public health intervention that involves patients with life-limiting illnesses, *Frontiers in Public Health*, 11: 1232881. Available at: https://www.ncbi.nlm.nih.gov/pmc/articles/PMC10449265/pdf/fpubh-11-1232881.pdf (accessed 11 July 2024).

Davey, M. and Lu, D. (2023) 'It was cruel': dying patient denied euthanasia in Catholic-run hospital, *The Guardian*, 21 September. Available at: https://www.theguardian.com/australia-news/2023/sep/22/hospital-euthanasia-catholic-victoria (accessed 15 April 2024).

Hudson, P., Marco, D., De Abreu Lourenco, R. and Philip, J. (2024) What are the cost and resource implications of voluntary assisted dying and euthanasia?, *Australian Health Review*, 6 February. Available at: https://doi.org/10.1071/AH24016 (accessed 16 April 2024).

Jackson, V.A. and Emanuel, L. (2024) Navigating and communicating about serious illness and end of life, *New England Journal of Medicine*, 390 (1): 63–69.

Kissane, D.W., Street, A. and Nitschke, P. (1998) Seven deaths in Darwin: case studies under the Rights of the Terminally Ill Act, Northern Territory, Australia, *Lancet*, 352 (9134): 1097–1102.

Komesaroff, P. and Philip, J. (2023) Voluntary assisted dying in Victoria: the report card is mixed but we now know what we have to do, *Internal Medicine Journal*, 53 (12): 2159–61.

Lewis, S., La Brooy, C., Kerridge, I. et al. (2024) Choreographing a good death: carers' experiences and practices of enacting assisted dying, *Sociology of Health and Illness*. Available at: https://onlinelibrary.wiley.com/doi/epdf/10.1111/1467-9566.13761 (accessed 16 April 2024).

McDougall, R. and Pratt, B. (2020) Too much safety? Safeguards and equal access in the context of voluntary assisted dying legislation, *BMC Medical Ethics*, 21: 38. Available at: https://doi.org/10.1186/s12910-020-00483-5 (accessed 18 April 2024).

McDougall, R., Hayes, B., Sellars, M. et al. (2020) 'This is uncharted water for all of us': challenges anticipated by hospital clinicians when voluntary assisted dying becomes legal in Victoria, *Australian Health Review*, 44 (3): 399–404.

McDougall, R., Pratt, B. and Sellars, M. (2023) Ethical diversity and practical uncertainty: a qualitative interview study of clinicians' experiences in the implementation period prior to voluntary assisted dying becoming available in their hospital in Victoria, Australia, *Journal of Bioethical Inquiry*, 20 (1): 71–88.

Nafilyan, V., Morgan, J., Mais, D. et al. (2023) Risk of suicide after diagnosis of severe physical health conditions: a retrospective cohort study of 47 million people, *The Lancet Regional Health – Europe*, 25: 100562. Available at: https://doi.org/10.1016/j.lanepe.2022.100562.

Ore, A. (2024) Ban on doctors raising voluntary assisted dying with ill patients to remain as Victoria reviews law, *The Guardian*, 4 February. Available at: https://www.theguardian.com/

australia-news/2024/feb/04/ban-on-doctors-raising-voluntary-assisted-dying-with-ill-patients-to-remain-as-victoria-reviews-law (accessed 15 April 2024).

Palliative Care Australia (2021) *Palliative Care Australia Roadmap 2022–2027*. Available at: https://palliativecare.org.au/publication/palliative-care-australia-roadmap-2022-2027/ (accessed 15 April 2024).

Ries, N.M., Johnston, B. and Jansen, J. (2022) A qualitative interview study of Australian physicians on defensive practice and low value care: 'it's easier to talk about our fear of lawyers than to talk about our fear of looking bad in front of each other', *BMC Medical Ethics*, 23: 16. Available at: https://doi.org/10.1186/s12910-022-00755-2 (accessed 22 April 2024).

Royal Australasian College of Physicians (RACP) (2018) *Statement on Voluntary Assisted Dying*, RACP, November. Available at: https://www.racp.edu.au/docs/default-source/advocacy-library/racp-voluntary-assisted-dying-statement-november-2018.pdf?sfvrsn=761d121a_4 (accessed 22 April 2024).

Rutherford, J., Willmott, L. and White, B.P. (2021) Physician attitudes to voluntary assisted dying: a scoping review, *BMJ Supportive & Palliative Care*, 11 (2): 200–8.

Rutherford, J., Willmott, L. and White, B.P. (2023) What the doctor would prescribe: physician experiences of providing voluntary assisted dying in Australia, *OMEGA: Journal of Death and Dying*, 87 (4): 1063–87.

Sellars, M., Tacey, M., McDougall, R. et al. (2021) Support for and willingness to be involved in voluntary assisted dying: a multisite, cross-sectional survey study of clinicians in Victoria, Australia, *Internal Medicine Journal*, 51 (10): 1619–28.

Siganto, T. (2024) Inquest into voluntary assisted dying begins in Queensland after man took his wife's end-of-life medication, *ABC News*, 20 February. Available at: https://www.abc.net.au/news/2024-02-20/voluntary-assisted-dying-coronial-inquest-vad-elderly-death/103490234 (accessed 15 April 2024).

Twycross, R. (2024) Assisted dying: principles, possibilities, and practicalities. An English physician's perspective, *BMC Palliative Care*, 23: 99. Available at: https://doi.org/10.1186/s12904-024-01422-6 (accessed 22 April 2024).

Victoria Department of Health (2022) *Health Practitioner Information and Best Practice Guidance on Voluntary Assisted Dying*, 17 June. Available at: https://www.health.vic.gov.au/voluntary-assisted-dying/health-practitioner-information (accessed 22 April 2024).

Waller, K., Del Villar, K., Willmott, L. and White, B.P. (2023) Voluntary assisted dying in Australia: a comparative and critical analysis of state laws, *University of New South Wales Law Journal*, 46: 1421. Available at: https://www.unswlawjournal.unsw.edu.au/wp-content/uploads/2023/12/Issue-464-10-Waller-et-al.pdf.

White, B.P., Jeanneret, R., Close, E. and Willmott, L. (2023a) Access to voluntary assisted dying in Victoria: a qualitative study of family caregivers' perceptions of barriers and facilitators, *Medical Journal of Australia*, 219 (5): 211–17.

White, B.P., Jeanneret, R. and Willmott, L. (2023b) Barriers to connecting with the voluntary assisted dying system in Victoria, Australia: a qualitative mixed method study, *Health Expectations*, 26 (6): 2695–2708.

White, B.P., Archer, M., Haining, C.M. and Willmott, L. (2024) Implications of voluntary assisted dying for advance care planning, *Medical Journal of Australia*, 220 (3): 129–33.

Willmott, L., White, B. and Villar, K.D. (2023) Voluntary assisted dying will be available to more Australians this year. Here's what to expect in 2023, *The Conversation*, 26 January. Available at: https://theconversation.com/voluntary-assisted-dying-will-be-available-to-more-australians-this-year-heres-what-to-expect-in-2023-196209 (accessed 22 April 2024).

World Health Organization (WHO) (2020) *Palliative Care*, 5 August. Available at: https://www.who.int/news-room/fact-sheets/detail/palliative-care (accessed 15 April 2024).

Worthington, A., Regnard, C., Sleeman, K.E. and Finlay, I. (2024) Comparison of official reporting on assisted suicide and euthanasia across jurisdictions, *BMJ Supportive & Palliative Care*, 14: e1302–8. Available at: https://doi.org/10.1136/spcare-2022-003944 (accessed 16 April 2014).

PART 3

Law

10 Read the question!

Robert Preston

Introduction

When I was at school, before answering an exam question, I was always told to make sure I understood it. It's advice we would do well to heed when we think about what's being called 'assisted dying'.

The public debate is too often framed in terms of compassion or autonomy or morality. But the real question is actually about something else. It's about whether 'assisted dying' should be legalized – or, to be precise, whether doctors should be licensed by law to supply or administer lethal drugs to people who ask for them and appear to meet certain conditions.

It's a question that is often skated over by both supporters and opponents of legal change. Yet there is widespread ignorance of just what the existing law is. There-fore, in this chapter I explain what the existing law says, why it says it, and how it's applied. Only if this question of *whether* the law should change is answered in the affirmative can we move to the secondary question of *how* it might be changed.

What the law says

There are actually two laws in England and Wales that are relevant to 'assisted dying' – the 1961 Suicide Act and the 1957 Homicide Act. Under the 1961 Act, it is a criminal offence to encourage or assist another person to take his or her own life: this is the law that is engaged under one definition of 'assisted dying' – that is, supplying lethal drugs for self-administration. The 1957 law would be engaged if lethal drugs were directly administered to someone in order to bring about his or her death. Scottish law is slightly different but its overall effect is similar – knowingly supplying or administering lethal drugs is unlawful.[1]

In the interests of brevity, I will focus on the model which campaigners for 'assisted dying' most recently proposed in England and Wales, which entails the supply of lethal drugs for self-administration.

The 1961 Suicide Act decriminalized suicide, meaning that criminal charges would no longer be brought against people who attempted to take their own lives. Decriminalization is not, however, the same as legalization. Legalization implies acceptance of an act, whereas it was made clear in the parliamentary debate on the 1961 Act that that was not the case. In the words of the responsible minister at the time, 'we wish to give no encouragement whatever to suicide' (House of Commons 1961).

Decriminalization of suicide was therefore accompanied in the 1961 Act by a provision (Section 2) under which it was a criminal offence to 'aid, abet, counsel or procure' the suicide or attempted suicide of another person. This prohibition was widened in the Coroners and Justice Act 2009 (Clause 59) to one of 'encouraging or assisting' suicide in order to try and counter undesirable activity by internet websites.

Conviction by a court under Section 2 of the 1961 Act carries a penalty of up to 14 years' imprisonment. However, a court is not obliged to impose any custodial sentence, nor is the Crown Prosecution Service (CPS) obliged to undertake a prosecution (see Chapter 12). Indeed, Section 4 of the Act specifically requires that no prosecution may be undertaken without the consent of the Director of Public Prosecutions (DPP). Prosecutions are rare.

So, what's going on here? Is it, as advocates of legal change tell us, that the law is not working and that the CPS does not have the stomach to prosecute? In fact, the law is working as it should. An act may be illegal (i.e. a breach of the law) but whether it results in a prosecution depends on whether, and if so to what extent, there has been criminality (i.e. behaviour deserving of prosecution and punishment).

The discretion given to the DPP by Clause 4 of the 1961 Act recognizes that acts of assisting suicide could cover a wide range of criminality. At one end of the spectrum, the act may have involved malicious or manipulative pressure on, say, an elderly relative in order to hasten his or her death for personal gain. That is the kind of behaviour that might lead to a prosecution. At the other end of the spectrum, the act may have derived from genuine compassion, after much soul-searching and with great reluctance following earnest pleading by the person concerned. The degree of criminality attaching to such situations would be likely to be very low and not to merit prosecution. Hence the law requires the DPP to examine the facts and circumstances of any suspected act of assisting suicide and to decide whether, *in that specific instance*, a prosecution is appropriate.

Yet this is not how it is presented to the public by advocates of 'assisted dying'. They tell us that the very low prosecution rate is a sign that the law is not working. Lord Falconer, for example, told the House of Lords in 2014 that the prosecuting authorities 'have tried to steer a course between Section 2 of the Suicide Act and the desire not to enforce it' (House of Lords 2014). This is nonsense. As Sir Keir Starmer put it in 2010 when he was DPP: 'There is a residual discretion for all offences whether to prosecute or not. This is a particular version of it. But it's not unique by any stretch of the imagination; it's the way our law works' (Commission on Assisted Dying 2011: 50).

Does it work?

On average, fewer than 20 cases of assisted suicide throughout the whole of England and Wales cross the desk of the DPP annually. By any standard, that is a very low level of law-breaking. Hardly any of them are prosecuted (see Chapter 12). This is not because prosecutors are trying to avoid enforcing the law; it's because the penalties that the existing law holds in reserve are sufficient to make anyone minded to assist a suicide think very carefully indeed before proceeding. As a result, breaches of the law are rare and usually relate to situations where there has been much reluctance and soul-searching on the part of the assister and genuinely compassionate motivation. Such cases do not call for prosecution, and they are not prosecuted.

But change the law and you change the dynamic. Criminal laws are more than just regulations. They also send social messages. An 'assisted dying' law sends the subliminal message, however unintended, that if we are terminally ill, taking our own lives is an option which we should contemplate and which society accepts as reasonable. This subtle change in social messaging may not affect a minority of resolute and no-nonsense individuals – the people whose stories tend to make the headlines. But most terminally ill people are not like that. They are often struggling to come to terms with their mortality, veering between hope and despair, and worried about the care or the financial burden they are imposing on others. And, though most relatives – such as those who appear in media stories about 'assisted dying' – are loving and caring, the sad fact is that some are not. We have criminal laws, not because most of us behave decently, but because some of us don't.

Legalization changes the dynamic in another way. With the law that we have now, if a malicious or manipulative person were to consider pressuring, say, an elderly relative into suicide, he or she would have to reckon with a subsequent police investigation of all the facts and with any criminal behaviour coming to light as a result. Under an 'assisted dying' law, on the other hand, the only risk being run by a malicious or manipulative relative would be that the request for lethal drugs might be refused.

And that's not all. Under an 'assisted dying' law, once lethal drugs had been authorized, there would be nothing to deter coercion or other pressure being applied in the period before they were ingested. We should not forget that, where 'assisted dying' has been legalized (for example, in the US state of Oregon), there can be weeks, months or occasionally even years between approval to receive lethal drugs and their ingestion. Exchanging post-event for pre-event scrutiny, therefore, has the potential to put the recipient at *increased* risk of encouragement or pressure from others to ingest them.

Advocates of 'assisted dying' tell us not to worry as there would be strict safeguards (see Chapter 11). Suffice it to say here that the proposals that have been put forward to date have included no actual safeguards, only vague qualifying criteria.

A 'right to die'

A common refrain of the campaigning for legal change is that there should be a 'right to die' and that we should have control over our own deaths. In a sense, a 'right to die' already exists (but see Chapter 1). No doctor may lawfully treat us without our consent, and patients are at liberty to refuse or discontinue treatment, including treatment to save or extend their lives. Doctors will tend to discourage such refusal: they have – and, most people would surely agree, should have – a predisposition to preserve life. But the decision to accept or refuse treatment is ours – and ours alone. Neither in law nor in medical ethics does treatment refusal constitute suicide.

It is also open to us to make a legally binding Advance Decision to Refuse Treatment (ADRT). This allows us to specify which treatments we do not wish to have in the event that we are unable to make our wishes known – for example, if we are unconscious and would not wish to have cardiopulmonary resuscitation.

It is also important to understand that, if we refuse life-extending treatment, we are not thereby abandoned. In those circumstances, our doctors have a duty of care to provide what really is assisted dying – not assistance with suicide but assistance with controlling the process of dying. Fifty or so years ago, before the modern hospice movement came of age, this may have been more of an aspiration than a reality. But pain relief is now a sophisticated science and modern hospice and palliative care (see Chapter 17) is able to make pain and other symptom relief a realistic outcome.

But is it really suicide?

In law, 'assisted dying' is assisting suicide. When we think of suicide, we think of a desperate act by someone who for one reason or another feels he or she cannot cope with going on living. We rightly empathize with people in this position and we take steps to try to prevent such irrevocable acts. But there is often a subliminal message that 'assisted dying' is different and that it's about avoiding pain or other physiological distress, and on that account is reasonable and not really suicide.

Let us look, then, at the reasons given by people who have taken their own lives with legally supplied lethal drugs under Oregon's 'Death with Dignity Act'. According to the latest official report, from 1998 to 2023 pain or the fear of it comes well down the list (28.8 per cent). The top two factors were 'losing autonomy' (90.4 per cent) and 'less able to engage in activities making life enjoyable' (89.6 per cent) (Oregon Health Authority 2024: 14). This evidence is consistent with what the Mackay Committee, which examined 'assisted dying' in detail between 2004 and 2005, was told during a visit to Oregon – that the demand for lethal drugs tended to come from people who 'want control of their dying process and want to avert having to be cared for' (House of Lords 2004–5: para. 163). In its report the committee referred to 'terminally ill people who have strong personalities and a history of being in control of their lives and whose suffering derives more from the fact of their terminal illness and from the loss of control which this involves than from the symptoms of their disease' (House of Lords 2004–5: para. 244).

To say this is not in any way to downplay the personal suffering which can accompany any illness. But we have to recognize that physiological pain control is much more effective today than was the case only a few decades ago and that the main issue here is existential distress arising out of a loss of personal control. And it is perhaps worth noting another statistic revealed in the latest official

Oregon Health Authority (2024: 14) report – that 47.1 per cent of those who took their lives via 'assisted dying' from 1998 to 2023 listed being a 'burden on family, friends/caregivers' as one of the reasons for their actions.

Conclusion

For all the above reasons, I am not persuaded that the existing law should be changed. Claims that the law is not working are based on a misunderstanding of why the law exists and how it is applied. The law is not, as campaigners for legal change would have us believe, cruel (see Chapter 12). It combines deterrence of malicious activity with compassion where it is clear that, though there has been a breach of the law, there has been no criminal activity. In this it is no different from other criminal laws.

This is not to say there is no problem. We are living longer. While for many people this can mean a new lease of life, for others it can mean a life of pain, discomfort or frustration as life-limiting illness and immobility overtake them. But reaching blindly for the Statute Book is not the answer.

We can all empathize with someone who breaks the criminal law in highly exceptional circumstances – for example, a man who injures a nocturnal intruder while defending his family and home, or a mother who in desperation steals food to feed her starving children. But we do not advocate legalizing assault or theft in advance and in prescribed circumstances. We look to see the law maintained to protect all of us and for exceptional cases to be dealt with exceptionally. And that is what happens now with the law relating to what is being called 'assisted dying'.

We should perhaps also recognize that advances in medical science have done more than extend average life spans. They have also revolutionized care of the seriously ill and the dying. Britain was the founder of the modern hospice movement and it has been repeatedly ranked in first place in international surveys for the quality of end-of-life care. Hospices are no longer just places where people go to die. Much of their work is now about bringing difficult medical symptoms under control and enabling seriously ill patients to live fulfilling lives in the community. And it is not just hospices. Major hospitals have specialist palliative care teams, and many doctors and nurses in community medicine have relevant training and experience. That is where the campaigning is needed, not in licensing doctors to give lethal drugs to seriously ill people. 'Assisted dying' is, it might be said, yesterday's answer to today's question.

Note

1. The relevant law in Northern Ireland is almost identical with the law in England and Wales.

References

Commission on Assisted Dying (2011) *The Commission on Assisted Dying*. London: Demos. Available at: https://demos.co.uk/wp-content/uploads/2012/01/476_CoAD_FinalReport_158x240_I_web_single-NEW_.pdf (accessed 4 February 2024).

House of Commons (1961) Suicide Bill [Lords] HC Deb 19 July, vol. 644, cc. 1407–26, *Hansard*, Cols. 1425–26. Available at: https://api.parliament.uk/historic-hansard/commons/1961/jul/19/ suicide-bill-lords (accessed 19 February 2024).

House of Lords (2004–5) *Assisted Dying for the Terminally Ill Bill – First Report.* Available at: https://publications.parliament.uk/pa/ld200405/ldselect/ldasdy/86/8602.htm (accessed 4 February 2024).

House of Lords (2014) Assisted Dying Bill [HL], *Hansard*, 18 July, Col. 775. Available at: https:// publications.parliament.uk/pa/ld201415/ldhansrd/text/140718-0001.htm (accessed 4 February 2024).

Oregon Health Authority (2024) *Oregon Death with Dignity Act: 2023 Data Summary.* Available at: https://www.oregon.gov/oha/PH/PROVIDERPARTNERRESOURCES/EVALUATION-RESEARCH/DEATHWITHDIGNITYACT/Documents/year26.pdf (accessed 13 April 2024).

11 Safeguards – what safeguards?

Robert Preston

Introduction

In this chapter, I examine the proposed safeguards in Baroness Meacher's Bill from the 2021–22 session of Parliament (House of Lords 2021), explain why they are hardly worthy of the name and suggest how, if Parliament really feels (despite all the evidence) that it should go down the 'assisted dying' road, they might be revised.

What are the 'safeguards'?

The proposals to date for legalizing 'assisted dying' specify four main conditions which applicants must meet if they are to receive lethal drugs for assisted suicide. They must:

- have been diagnosed as terminally ill and have received a prognosis of 6 months or less;
- have a settled wish to die;
- have mental capacity;
- be free from coercion or pressure.

These proposed conditions are not, however, accompanied by any minimum steps which someone assessing a request for lethal drugs must take to ensure that they are actually met. What we have here, therefore, are not safeguards but simply criteria – broadly worded statements of what should happen in an ideal world rather than mandatory procedures to ensure that it does happen in today's real world.

Advocates of legalization may argue that setting out how safeguards would work is a matter of detail and, as such, can be dealt with by considering amendments at Committee Stage or via secondary legislation. But safeguards are not details. They are of the essence of what is being proposed.

We are not talking here about typical legislation. We are talking about legislation with, literally, life-or-death consequences. The presence of workable and effective safeguards is an integral part of any decision to proceed with such legislation. Before Parliament can responsibly agree to such a Bill proceeding, therefore, it has a duty to do more than take note of a handful of broadly worded eligibility criteria. It must also satisfy itself that those criteria come with sufficiently robust procedures in place to allow a judgement to be made as to their realism.

The decision-making process

It is suggested that the arbiters of whether or not an applicant for lethal drugs meets the above tests should be doctors. They would be expected to assess requests and be 'satisfied' that applicants met all the proposed criteria. The decisions by doctors would then be passed to a judge of the High Court for endorsement. The relationship between these two proposed levels of scrutiny is not made clear. What is clear is that doctors would find themselves not merely confirming that a request for lethal drugs met the medical criteria but also deciding on the request *as a whole*.

The question arises therefore: are doctors qualified to make these decisions? For some of the criteria involved – for example, whether an applicant is terminally ill and has a prognosis of 6 months or less – this may well be so. For other criteria, however, that is unlikely to be the case. Take, for example, the condition that an applicant for lethal drugs must have 'a clear and settled intention to end their own life which has been reached voluntarily, on an informed basis and without coercion or duress' (House of Lords 2021: 3(3)(c)). We are looking here at judgements that go beyond a doctor's professional knowledge.

Judging whether an apparent wish to die is a settled wish and whether or not there has been or might be any pressure, overt or covert, at work in the background are social rather than medical judgements. A doctor who has known a patient well over an extended period of time and has seen the patient regularly, not simply in the consulting room but also in a home setting, might just be able to make a knowledge-based judgement of whether a request for lethal drugs met the requirement. But that is not the usual pattern of clinical care in Britain today. Patients are now registered, not with a doctor, but with a GP practice. They often see a variety of doctors over time and home visits are very much the exception. A doctor faced with a request for lethal drugs is unlikely, therefore, to have any first-hand knowledge of the applicant's family situation or of just how much thought has gone into the request.

But this is not all. A recent membership survey by the British Medical Association revealed that a majority of doctors would refuse to consider requests for lethal drugs (BMA 2020). Those making such requests would therefore in many cases find themselves obliged to find alternative and willing doctors to assess them. Such doctors would have even less first-hand knowledge on which to base a judgement.

Such 'doctor-shopping' is a regular feature of Oregon's 'assisted dying' regime. In 2023, for instance, 167 doctors in Oregon wrote 560 prescriptions for lethal drugs. At least one of these doctors wrote no fewer than 76 such prescriptions (Oregon Health Authority 2024: 9). We could expect to see a similar situation in the UK if 'assisted dying' were to be legalized – of assessments made by doctors who had never met the patient before and had no first-hand knowledge of his or her character, psychology or family situation.

So, if doctors are not qualified to assess requests for lethal drugs, who is? The answer, I suggest, is the High Court. The Court is accustomed to considering requests and giving judgments in this area – for example, where withdrawal of artificial nutrition and hydration or the switching-off of life support is involved. In these cases, however, the Court is the sole decision-maker, having sought and taken into account evidence from a range of parties. In such cases, doctors are simply expert witnesses advising the Court on those aspects of a request that lie within their professional competence. The same arrangements should be adopted for any legalized 'assisted dying' regime. The Court would consider evidence from a range of parties, including doctors, psychiatrists, social workers and, not least, the applicant and members of his or her family. And it would be for the Court to reach a balanced judgement having weighed all the evidence, medical and non-medical. To put it another way, the process would be Court-led rather than just Court-endorsed.

Apart from the inability of most doctors to make knowledge-based judgements on criteria that lie outside their professional competence, embedding 'assisted dying' in health care confers on it a spurious aura of benevolence. From a patient's point of view, a decision by a doctor is, not unreasonably, seen as a best-interests decision. The involvement of doctors in an 'assisted dying' regime, other than in providing the Court with an expert opinion on strictly medical aspects, risks sending the misleading message to the patient that in his or her case taking lethal drugs is a best-interests course of action. This may not matter for a minority of strong-willed and determined applicants. But, as I have argued in Chapter 10, most terminally ill people are not like that. They are dependent on their treating doctor, often hanging on his or her every word and indeed every gesture, and very vulnerable to misinterpreting a doctor's approval of a request as signalling the patient 'would be better off dead'. To avoid this risk, the process should be separated from health care.

The criteria

Terminal illness

Diagnosing terminal illness appears at face value relatively straightforward. However, that word 'relatively' is important. Evidence submitted by the Royal College of Pathologists to the Mackay Committee stated that post-mortem studies revealed that 'significant errors (that is, misdiagnosis of terminal illness resulting in inappropriate treatment) occur in about five per cent of cases' (House of Lords 2004–5: Minutes of Evidence, 3 September). Misdiagnosis may not be common, but it does happen – and more often than is generally thought (Chapter 16).

When we come to prognosis of life remaining, the scope for error is much greater (Chapter 16). Within days or a few weeks, prognosis can be reasonably accurate. But, in the words of a doctor from the Royal College of General Practitioners to the Mackay Committee, 'when this stretches to months, then the scope for error can extend into years'. A doctor from the Royal College of Physicians agreed, describing such prognoses as 'pretty desperately hopeless as an accurate factor' (House of Lords 2004–5: para. 118). And yet, prognosis is important. Patients and their families often ask: 'How long have I got?', to which any answer is little more than guesswork. But guessing is not a viable safeguard.

The rationale of terminal illness as a criterion for supplying lethal drugs is open to challenge. To argue that 'assisted dying' can be justified on grounds of relieving suffering surely invites the question: 'Why is it compassionate to supply lethal drugs to people who are expecting to die shortly of natural causes but not to others with serious chronic illnesses who may have to endure discomfort and immobility for much longer?' In reality, far from being a clear criterion for 'assisted dying', terminal illness is an entirely arbitrary and irrational one.

Baroness Butler-Sloss, a former president of the Family Division of the High Court, has summed the matter up neatly:

> Laws, like nation states, are more secure when their boundaries rest on natural frontiers. The law that we have rests on just such a frontier. It rests on the principle that we do not involve ourselves in deliberately bringing about the deaths of others. Once we start making exceptions based on arbitrary criteria like terminal illness, that frontier becomes just a line in the sand, easily crossed and hard to defend. (Bingham 2013).

A terminal illness criterion may make legalization of 'assisted dying' more palatable to sceptical legislators, but it is entirely arbitrary and it contains within itself the seeds of its own expansion.

Anyone inclined to doubt this danger of legislative drift should read the words of the late Lord Joffe to the Mackay Committee when he was commending his own Private Member Bill on 'assisted dying'. 'I feel we are starting off', he said, 'this is a first stage' (House of Lords 2004–5: para. 92). These words are amply supported by the slackening of criteria seen in jurisdictions that have chosen to go down the 'assisted dying' road.

Settled wish to die

What constitutes a 'settled wish to die'? It is a phrase that could mean different things to different people. Yet a doctor assessing a request for lethal drugs, and in many cases a doctor who has never met the applicant before, would have to make such an assessment. If we are talking about real and effective safeguards, therefore, we have to ask ourselves, how might a 'settled wish to die' be reliably established?

It may be that Advance Decisions to Refuse Treatment (ADRTs) (mentioned in Chapter 10) provide a model here. If an applicant for lethal drugs were able to produce a declaration, made at a suitable interval of time before, that in the event of being diagnosed as terminally ill he or she might wish to consider seeking 'assisted dying', that could perhaps be held to constitute grounds for concluding, in the event that such a request were to be made, that it stemmed from a settled wish. The interval of time during which such a declaration had existed would need to be considered. In my view, it should not be less than 12 months. But simply stating that a request for lethal drugs must stem from a settled wish to die will not do.

Mental capacity

It is proposed that persons seeking 'assisted dying' should have 'the capacity to make the decision to end their own life' (House of Lords 2021: 3(3)(b)) and that decision-making capacity should 'be construed in accordance with the Mental

Capacity Act 2005' (House of Lords 2021: 12). However, the Mental Capacity Act 2005 (MCA) states explicitly in Section 62 that, 'for the avoidance of doubt, it is hereby declared that nothing in this Act is to be taken to affect the law relating to murder or manslaughter or the operation of section 2 of the Suicide Act 1961 (assisting suicide)'. Thus, if mental capacity for 'assisted dying' were to be in accord with the MCA, that Act would also have to be changed.

More substantially, the MCA states in Section 1 that 'a person must be assumed to have capacity unless it is established that he lacks capacity'. In other words, if the MCA were to apply to a request for lethal drugs, the applicant would have to be regarded as having decision-making capacity unless there were evidence to the contrary. Yet capacity is decision-specific. A person may have capacity to make some decisions but not others with more serious consequences. It is difficult to think of a more serious decision than to seek lethal drugs for suicide. Society's view of suicide supports this. A doctor who encounters a potentially suicidal patient is under a duty of care to ensure that patient's safety. Yet it is being suggested that, if we were to have an 'assisted dying' law, there should be an assumption of decision-making capacity unless there were evidence to the contrary. This is yet another crucial issue which has not been thought through (see Chapter 13 for further discussion).

The latest set of proposals shed little light on how decision-making capacity should be assessed. But insofar as they do so, they reveal a laxer approach than the Oregon law on which they are modelled. They say that, if a doctor assessing a request for lethal drugs 'has any doubt as to a person's capacity', the applicant should be referred to 'an appropriate specialist' (whatever that might mean) and that the doctor considering the request should simply 'take account of any opinion provided by the appropriate specialist' (House of Lords. 2021: 3(5)). In other words, under the proposals being put before us, an assessing doctor could overrule an opinion from an 'appropriate specialist' and approve an application for lethal drugs where there was doubt concerning decision-making capacity. Even Oregon's 'assisted dying' law is tighter than this! (Oregon Revised Statutes 1997: 127.825 §3.03).

Freedom from pressure

It is proposed that a request for lethal drugs should have been reached 'voluntarily' and 'without coercion or duress' (House of Lords 2021: 3(3)(c)). Such a requirement is clearly essential. But just how the existence of such freedom from pressure is to be established is not stated. The people who step out of the pages of 'assisted dying' Bills are decisive and self-confident individuals who know their own mind and aren't vulnerable to pressure of any kind. The campaigners who are paraded in front of us in the media are similar. They have been in control all their lives and no-one is going to coerce them. But many seriously ill people are not in that position. While readers would not themselves, I feel sure, dream of pressuring a vulnerable person into seeking lethal drugs for suicide, that does not mean others would not do so (Chapter 25). Proper safeguards must be designed for real life rather than for a perfect world.

Elder abuse is on the rise and has been estimated to affect in one form or another some 500,000 people annually in Britain. It may not always be sustained and deliberate abuse – loss of temper with a demanding elderly relative, for instance. But it can be more calculated, such as a wish to hasten an inheritance or to be rid of a care burden (coercion and carer burden are further discussed in Chapter 26). Whatever form it takes, it can be difficult to uncover. It is essential, therefore, that 'assisted dying' proposals should explain how pressure or abuse is to be detected and it is all the more reason why these non-medical judgements should not be placed on the shoulders of doctors.

Conclusion

I am not persuaded that the existing law is in need of change (Finlay and Preston 2020; and see Chapter 10 in this volume). However, I would urge those who take a different view to take the issue of safeguards seriously and, before they come forward with further proposals for legal change, to think through and to set out the steps that would need to be taken to produce safeguards that are more than just philosophical concepts but safeguards capable of handling the real-world pressures of terminal illness and complex personal and family dynamics. Foremost among these should be the separation of decision-making in 'assisted dying' from health care and the placing of responsibility where it belongs (see Chapters 19 and 20).

We are constantly urged by campaigners for 'assisted dying' to 'catch up' with other jurisdictions that have gone down this road. We should instead, I suggest, be learning from their mistakes. If the UK Parliament (or any other legislature) is to be asked yet again to consider legalizing 'assisted dying', it should be offered a proposal that would set a rigorous international standard for such legislation rather than be just another near-slavish imitation of defective legislation elsewhere.

References

Bingham, J. (2013) 'We tinker with assisted suicide laws at our peril', warns Baroness Butler-Sloss, *The Telegraph*, 15 December. Available at: https://www.telegraph.co.uk/news/uknews/law-and-order/10517189/We-tinker-with-assisted-suicide-laws-at-our-peril-warns-Baroness-Butler-Sloss.html (accessed 5 February 2024).

British Medical Association (BMA) (2020) *BMA Survey on Physician-Assisted Dying*, Kantar, Public Division. Available at: https://www.bma.org.uk/media/3367/bma-physician-assisted-dying-survey-report-oct-2020.pdf (accessed 5 February 2024).

Finlay, I. and Preston, R. (2020) *Death by Appointment: A Rational Guide to the Assisted Dying Debate*. Newcastle upon Tyne: Cambridge Scholars Publishing.

House of Lords (2004–5) *Assisted Dying for the Terminally Ill Bill – First Report*. Available at: https://publications.parliament.uk/pa/ld200405/ldselect/ldasdy/86/8602.htm (accessed 4 February 2024).

House of Lords (2021) *Assisted Dying Bill* [HL 13]. Available at: https://bills.parliament.uk/publications/41676/documents/322 (accessed 5 February 2024).

Oregon Health Authority (2024) *Oregon Death with Dignity Act: 2023 Data Summary*. Available at: https://www.oregon.gov/oha/PH/PROVIDERPARTNERRESOURCES/EVALUATIONRE-SEARCH/DEATHWITHDIGNITYACT/Documents/year26.pdf (accessed 13 April 2024).

Oregon Revised Statutes (1997) *Death with Dignity Act*, ORS 127.800–127.995. Available at: https://www.oregon.gov/oha/PH/PROVIDERPARTNERRESOURCES/EVALUATIONRE-SEARCH/DEATHWITHDIGNITYACT/Pages/ors.aspx (accessed 5 February 2024).

12 Reviewing prosecution policy on assisted suicide and 'mercy killing' in England and Wales[1]

Alexandra Mullock

Introduction

While the term 'assisted dying' is often interpreted to include both assisting a suicide and voluntary euthanasia, this chapter primarily concerns the law on assisted suicide and the relevant offence-specific Crown Prosecution Service (CPS) Policy (the Assisted Suicide Prosecution Policy).[2] This is because most activity within the so-called assisted dying domain within the jurisdiction (England and Wales) relates to the Suicide Act 1961. In cases involving voluntary euthanasia – sometimes described as 'mercy killing' – where the suspect has killed the victim rather than encouraged or assisted their suicide, the law on murder is generally applicable, which has traditionally left little scope for prosecutorial discretion. Recently, however, a more significant role for discretion has been created by CPS prosecution guidance pertaining to the public interest stage in 'mercy killings' (the Mercy Killing Policy).[3] This essentially replicates many of the factors within the Assisted Suicide Policy.

Since the Mercy Killing Policy is a recent development, it remains to be seen how impactful this development will prove. It seems clear, however, that it has opened the door to what might be viewed as a 'mercy killing' de facto defence to murder, where a person who has killed another person at their request will not be prosecuted if they can show that they were only motivated by compassion to kill a person who wanted to die but was unable to achieve their own death. This potential shift might be viewed as following the philosophy of the Assisted Suicide Policy, which this chapter explores by examining its impact and the broader debate about what ought to be permissible.

The policy and data

There is clear evidence of the impact of the Assisted Suicide Policy. We know that although assisted suicide is a serious crime, the chances of being prosecuted after assisting a suicide are extremely slim. The English legal position on assisted suicide has been described as presenting 'a stern face but a kind heart' (Cohen 2009). The *stern face* is evident through the blanket ban on assisting or encouraging a suicide under the Suicide Act 1961, which carries a maximum

14-year sentence upon conviction. The *kind heart* may be discerned from the offence specific prosecution policy, because the deployment of this Policy within the exercise of prosecutorial discretion[4] means that it is extremely rare for anyone to be prosecuted even when they have clearly provided potentially culpable assistance. The Assisted Suicide Policy established a range of factors tending 'for' and 'against' prosecution, which collectively indicate that if a suspect was 'wholly motivated by compassion' to provide a limited (ideally minimal) form of assistance to an adult with capacity who has demonstrated a clear wish to die, prosecution is very unlikely to serve the public interest. Thus, we see kindness in the clear tendency not to prosecute set against the *stern* ban; a ban that is viewed as essential by some, but which others see as problematic; for example, the former president of the Supreme Court, Baroness Hale, described it as a form of 'cruelty'.[5]

The Policy was created as a result of a successful human rights challenge in 2009.[6] Debbie Purdy had multiple sclerosis and when considering whether she might eventually wish to seek an assisted suicide in Switzerland with her husband's help, she argued that they had insufficient information upon which to assess the risk of prosecution. Ms Purdy convinced the House of Lords that Article 8 of the European Convention was violated by the ambiguous and uncertain exercise of prosecutorial discretion.

The Policy established a series of factors to guide police and prosecutors. Some factors concern the victim – whether they were an adult with capacity who had a clear, settled, autonomous wish to die, which tends against prosecution, or whether they were generally vulnerable or perhaps susceptible to coercion by the suspect, which tends towards prosecution. Notably, the victim's health is seemingly irrelevant when considering the wrongness of any assistance, beyond the question of capacity and a factor that refers to their ability to act alone, which indicates that helping a person not able to act alone is less likely to invite prosecution compared to helping an able-bodied person. On this point, Penney Lewis has observed that, '[W]ithout any restriction based on the victim's condition or experience, the policy is more liberal in this respect than most assisted dying regimes' (2011: 126).

Other Policy factors concern the suspect – whether they provided only reluctant and minimal assistance in circumstances suggesting that compassion was their only motivation, which tends against prosecution, or whether they exerted pressure or encouragement, a factor in favour of prosecution. The upshot of the policy is that while 'encouraging' a suicide should always invite prosecution, providing limited assistance that appears to be 'wholly motivated by compassion' is almost certain not to lead to prosecution.

Writing in 2010, I suggested that the Assisted Suicide Policy had effectively decriminalized certain modes of compassionately assisting a suicide because prosecution was very unlikely (Mullock 2010). Similarly, Lewis suggested that the Policy has 'accelerated informal legal change on assisted suicide' (2011:121). The data during the intervening years support this view. CPS data shows that between April 2009 and the end of March 2023, from the 182 cases referred to the CPS, only a small number were referred onwards for prosecution, from which there have been only four successful prosecutions. One prosecution led to an acquittal; while eight other investigations revealed evidence of *killing*, rather than assisting suicide, and so were referred for homicide charges.

Before discussing the social context of this approach, it is worth mentioning that there may be many more cases of assisting or encouraging a suicide that were not investigated during the period in question. Data from the main Swiss assisted suicide organization, *Dignitas*, reveals that between 2009 and 2023, 464 UK citizens died at Dignitas.[7] The Swiss organization, *Exit*, also offers this service for non-Swiss people, so more UK citizens are certain to have died there, while others are likely to have received some assistance to die at home.

The social context

The Assisted Suicide Policy is silent on the possible distinction between assisting within England/Wales or travelling to a more permissive jurisdiction, namely Switzerland. When people go to Switzerland, however, the assistance by the family is likely to be limited to help with travel and other practical arrangements, which is minimal relative to the main assistance provided by the Swiss doctor, who prescribes the drugs, and the volunteers (usually nurses) who assist with ingestion. As the Dignitas data shows, travelling to Switzerland for assisted suicide is a well-established option for those who are sufficiently wealthy to meet the cost (around £10,000) and sufficiently healthy to make the journey. The 2024 House of Commons Health and Social Care Select Committee Report (HC321), on Assisted Dying/Assisted Suicide (House of Commons 2024), includes evidence from family members who had assisted loved ones in this way. These accounts discuss the need to travel while still healthy enough to do so: '[W]e are shortening people's lives as they are choosing to go out early' (House of Commons 2024: 13). Others discussed 'hellish' prosecutorial investigations lasting for 2 years, with family members coming to 'the brink of suicide' (House of Commons 2024: 11). Another witness spoke of the challenges of gathering the necessary medical information to establish eligibility for the Swiss organizations: '… it's the loneliness and the fact that officialdom makes fugitives of you' (House of Commons 2024: 8).

Patients seeking to die at Dignitas or Exit need to justify their wish to die on the grounds of poor health. Although Swiss law does not restrict access to lawful assisted suicide to those with a terminal condition, the involvement of the Swiss doctor and the relevant organization is only lawful if there is a reason, namely a medical condition, to show that such assistance is altruistic. To meet this requirement, medical evidence is needed from a patient's doctor.

Doctors must be cautious to avoid being seen to facilitate a patient's plan to die in this way because a factor tending in favour of prosecution includes *acting in one's capacity as a healthcare professional*. Subsequent guidance issued in 2014 sought to clarify matters by adding that this would be the case if there was a 'relationship of care', within which 'the suspect may have exerted some influence on the victim'. This places doctors in an uncertain, potentially perilous position.

Providing medical records in accordance with the Data Protection Act 1988 is lawful because patients have a right to access their medical records. Merely providing medical records is also unlikely to be viewed as *exerting influence*. Going any further than simply releasing records, however, might be viewed as risky. British Medical Association guidance instructs doctors that they should not write a report specifically for the purposes of an application to have an assisted suicide in Switzerland (BMA 2019).

We see, therefore, that the impact of the policy means the family of the deceased are very unlikely to be prosecuted, although the investigation may have a devastating impact on them. Healthcare professionals are at greater risk of prosecution for simply providing information, although as no such prosecutions have (to my knowledge) occurred, it seems that the policy has deterred doctors from going beyond their obligation to release information. The policy may therefore be seen as 'kind' for rarely prosecuting. However, the social and medical reality faced by people wishing to die, and those who assist such suicides, suggests that while the lenient philosophy softens the stern face of the prohibition, the overall approach is problematic for several reasons.

The ban and the Assisted Suicide Policy strongly discourage healthcare professionals or other support services from engaging with those wishing to seek assisted suicide, and so the opportunity to provide safeguards is diminished. Left to their own devices, if individuals have the funds to travel to Switzerland there is little meaningful scrutiny of their mental or physical health. They might die sooner than they would ideally wish while their health permits them to travel. Any prosecutorial investigation comes too late to save vulnerable individuals from family members whose motives are not compassionate; and if those relatives have realized that performative compassion will avoid prosecution, the policy makes the ban easy to dodge. Consequently, the legal climate means that desperate people considering the option of assisted dying are effectively abandoned. Unsurprisingly, this has led to observations that the Policy provides 'too little, too late' for possible victims of abuse (Biggs 2011). There is, however, little justification for creating a less 'kind' Policy. It would make a bad situation worse for individuals seeking assisted suicide and for relatives who are genuinely motivated by compassion to assist. The recent expansion of the philosophy underpinning Assisted Suicide Policy to the Mercy Killing Policy means that the factors that have shaped the legal climate regarding assisted suicide will now apply to cases of mercy killing. This represents a dramatic development in the approach to prosecuting homicide. It also strengthens the case for considering the merits of formal legal change over informal legal change via prosecution policy.

Conclusion

The lack of prosecutions for assisted suicide reflects a lenient approach which supports the argument that assisting a suicide may be morally blameless because it is potentially altruistic. However, if we look behind the deployment of the policy, we see a tricky compromise between the ban and the policy ethos of not prosecuting when a suspect appears to have been motivated by compassion. While the lenient approach might reflect a recognition that assisting a suicide is not necessarily morally wrong, assessing the motivations and actions of suspects who are wise to the policy may be very challenging. With the promulgation of the Mercy Killing Policy along parallel lines to assisted suicide, we see an expansion of the informal legal shift to excuse what would otherwise be murder. Both policies share a philosophy that compassionate motivation to assist another who is determined to die should not invite criminal prosecution. The exceptionalism that has been created by these policies ought to be considered more carefully within the debate about legalizing assisted dying.

Notes

1. Thanks are due to Professor Sarah Devaney (University of Manchester) for reading a draft of this chapter.
2. See the CPS website, available at: https://www.cps.gov.uk/publication/assisted-suicide (accessed 1 April 2024). Note that this website is updated each year in April.
3. Available at: https://www.cps.gov.uk/legal-guidance/homicide-murder-manslaughter-infanticide-and-causing-or-allowing-death-or-serious (accessed 1 April 2024). See section 'Application of the Public Interest Stage to "mercy killings" and suicide pacts in the context of "mercy killings"', which can be found under 'Public Interest'.
4. See Section 2(4) of the Suicide Act 1961. Available at: https://www.legislation.gov.uk/ukpga/Eliz2/9-10/60/data.pdf (accessed 1 April 2024).
5. See paragraph 313 in: *R (on the application of Nicklinson and another) (Apellants) v Ministry of Justice (Respondent)* [2014] UKSC 38. Available at: https://www.supremecourt.uk/cases/docs/uksc-2013-0235-judgment.pdf (accessed 1 April 2024).
6. *R (On the application of Purdy) v DPP* [2009] UKHL 45. Available at: https://www.bailii.org/uk/cases/UKHL/2009/45.html (accessed 1 April 2024).
7. Dignitas data is available at: http://www.dignitas.ch/index.php?option=com_content&view=article&id=32&Itemid=72&lang=en (accessed 1 April 2024).

References

Biggs, H. (2011) Legitimate compassion or compassionate legitimation? Reflections on the policy for prosecutors in respect of cases of encouraging or assisting suicide, *Feminist Legal Studies*, 19 (1): 83–92.

British Medical Association (BMA) (2019) *Responding to Patient Requests for Assisted Dying: Guidance for Doctors*, BMA 20190390. Available at: https://www.bma.org.uk/advice-and-support/ethics/end-of-life/responding-to-patient-requests-for-assisted-dying (accessed 1 April 2024).

Cohen, D. (2009) BMA meeting: Doctors vote against protecting relatives who accompany people abroad for help with dying, *British Medical Association*, 339: b2699. Available at: https://doi.org/10.1136/bmj.b2699.

House of Commons (2024) *Assisted Dying/Assisted Suicide*, Health and Social Care Committee: Second Report of Session 2023–24, 20 February. Available at: https://publications.parliament.uk/pa/cm5804/cmselect/cmhealth/321/report.html (accessed 1 April 2024).

Lewis, P. (2011) Informal legal change on assisted suicide: the policy for prosecutors, *Legal Studies*, 31 (1): 119–34.

Mullock, A. (2010) Overlooking the criminally compassionate: what are the implications of prosecutorial policy on encouraging or assisting suicide?, *Medical Law Review*, 18 (4): 442–70.

13 Assisted dying – the capacity complexities

Alex Ruck Keene[1]

Introduction

To date, all legislative proposals advanced before the Westminster Parliament (and, indeed, all other legislation either proposed or enacted in comparable jurisdictions) have been predicated upon a requirement that the person in question has the mental capacity to take the decision in question. Subject to one point that I make later in the chapter about the role of the UN Convention on the Rights of Persons with Disabilities, it is difficult to imagine that any future legislation could be advanced on any other basis, as the linkage between capacity and autonomy is seen as so central. However, as set out in this chapter, reliance on capacity is perhaps not as straightforward as sometimes thought (see Chapter 25).[2]

Components of capacity

In England and Wales, capacity is now most usually considered by reference to the terms of the Mental Capacity Act 2005 (MCA). If capacity for purposes of any legislation providing for assisted dying is to be assessed by reference to the MCA, a number of matters would need to be squarely addressed.[3] In any other jurisdiction where similar capacity legislation applies, these issues arise in connection with proposed or enacted laws to allow assisted dying. Whether they are or have been addressed transparently and robustly is perhaps a different matter.

Whether and how the principles relating to capacity apply

There are three key principles in Section 1 MCA relating to capacity (see Box 13.1). Each of these raises issues requiring consideration.

Box 13.1: Relevant principles from Section 1, Mental Capacity Act 2005

- A person must be assumed to have capacity unless it is established that he lacks capacity.
- A person is not to be treated as unable to make a decision unless all practicable steps to help him to do so have been taken without success.
- A person is not to be treated as unable to make a decision merely because he makes an unwise decision.

Source: HMSO (2005).

In relation to the principle of the presumption of capacity, the simple question is whether it is right to rely upon this given the gravity of the decision in question. Linked to this is whether the burden of proof lies upon the person to prove that they have capacity to make the decision, or whether it lies upon the assessor to show that they do not. If the question were being approached from the perspective of the MCA, the burden would clearly lie upon the assessor, but that is because the assessor would – if the person does not have capacity – then be proceeding to take action in the best interests of the person. However, as there is no suggestion in models advanced for assisted dying in the United Kingdom of action being taken by others on a best interests basis, it might be thought that any arguments in favour of it being for the assessor to prove incapacity fall away, and that it should always be for the person seeking assistance to prove capacity.

In relation to the 'support principle', the critical question can be framed as whether the assessor should be required to take steps to support the person to make the decision, or should they simply be taking the person as they find them?

In relation to the 'unwise decisions' principle, there are both ethical and practical issues to consider. The ethical issues are two-fold. First, there is the issue of whether a decision to seek assistance with dying can or should ever be seen, in and of itself, to be unwise. Second, while a doctor must respect an unwise, but capacitous, decision to refuse life-sustaining treatment because otherwise they would be committing assault, is a doctor under an equivalent ethical obligation to respect a patient's request to seek assistance with dying while at the same time making what appear to be unwise decisions about their medical care, for instance refusing effective treatments? The practical issue is what is to happen where an assessor, irrespective of whatever settled high-level position may be recorded in statute, has a personal view that seeking assistance with death is necessarily unwise either in general or for that particular patient.

What is the decision that the person must make, as capacity is decision-specific? (i.e. a person cannot be said simply to have or lack capacity)

Framing this question is important at a practical level, as it will shape how the issue is considered by both those seeking assistance and those assessing capacity, but also because it will frame what information is relevant to the question.

What information is relevant to the decision?

There is a statutory definition in the MCA (Section 3(1)) of what it means to be able to make a decision, namely to be able to understand the relevant information, retain it, use or weigh it, and to be able to communicate the decision. The choice of what information is relevant (and, almost – if not as – important, what information is *not* relevant) is a choice with significant implications. Put crudely, the less information relating to the decision the person needs to be able to understand, retain, use and weigh, the more likely it is that they will have capacity to make the decision (e.g. activities of daily living); conversely, the more that they need to be able to process, the less likely it is that they will have capacity (e.g. decisions with major implications for self and for others). Furthermore, there has been a dearth of research on what information is required to be able to make a decision to seek assisted dying; (unsurprisingly) a dearth of case law considering the question in the English context, and little sustained engagement by legislatures with this issue.

Whether the person can make the decision

Whether a particular person can make a decision (to seek or to consent to assisted dying, or whichever other formulation is chosen) is first and foremost going to be a matter for the assessor to consider. In this regard, however, it is perhaps important to note that 16 years after the MCA came into force, the question (in particular) what it means to 'use or weigh' information is one that still causes considerable challenges in application.

The relevance of any impairment or disturbance in the functioning of the mind or brain

In situations governed by the MCA, a conclusion that a person cannot make the decision in question (i.e. they cannot understand, retain, use or weigh the relevant information, or communicate their decision) can only lead to a conclusion that they lack capacity to take the relevant decision if they cannot do so because of an impairment of, or disturbance in, the functioning of their mind or brain. This is likely to be a particularly complex issue to disentangle in the context of conditions such as depression or side-effects of medication.

The time-specificity of capacity

For purposes of the MCA, capacity is both decision- and time-specific. This gives rise to two issues. The first is the impact of degenerative cognitive conditions such as dementia. Put shortly – does the person have to have capacity to seek assistance at the point of such formal assessment(s) as are likely to form the centrepiece of any legislation *and* at the point when assistance is rendered? Or does it suffice that they have capacity solely at the former point? And if solely the former, would this open the way to advance requests for assistance in dying?

The second is how to address the position of a person with fluctuating capacity, for instance bipolar disorder? For purposes of the MCA, the statutory guidance is, in effect, to take the person at their best, as an aspect of the 'support' principle. Would such be an acceptable approach in this context? And, if not, would it be discriminatory against those with conditions which give rise to fluctuating capacity to exclude them from accessing any legislative scheme that is established?

What level of rigour is required when assessing capacity?

The answer to this question will depend, both systemically, and at an individual level, upon attitudes towards seeking assistance with dying. In other words, if the starting position is that seeking assistance is something unusual and risky, then this would push towards a rigorous assessment of capacity in all circumstances. Conversely, if the starting position is that seeking assistance is always or sometimes (for instance, in the presence of suffering) a reasonable course of action, then this would push towards a much more light touch assessment of capacity. The potential for unspoken or unacknowledged assumptions in this context needs to be recognized.

Linked to this is whether and how steps can be taken to secure against the risk that capacity determinations do not appropriately take account of protected characteristics. There is limited research relating to the impact of race upon capacity assessment, but far less research than, for instance, in relation to the application of the Mental Health Act 1983. There is also very little, if any, research on the effect of gender, age or the assessor's perception of physical disability, or other unconscious or conscious bias upon capacity determination. Some might well consider that these are all areas which require further consideration if (in effect) assisted dying is to be offered as a treatment option.

Who assesses capacity?

The assumption in most proposals for legalizing assisted dying is that capacity assessment is the domain of medical professionals. However, it is of note that the Court of Protection (the court with oversight of the MCA) is clear that capacity is not a purely medical matter, and that it routinely draws upon the expertise of other professionals, including psychologists and social workers. Some might think that – at least in some circumstances – the essentially existential rather than medical issues to which the assessment of capacity to seek assistance with dying give rise, there is no obvious reason why it should be seen as a primarily medical matter (see Chapters 19 and 20).

Sufficiency of capacity

All models make capacity a necessary, but not sufficient, condition, with further requirements including requirements to the effect that the decision is clear and settled, informed, and made without coercion or duress. The interaction between coercion and capacity can be complex, and it is perhaps relevant to note that the High Court has developed a complex and somewhat poorly delineated jurisdiction to deal with the position where a person *has* capacity but is in some way vulnerable to coercion or duress. Such coercion or duress can be overt, but can also be the result of 'enmeshment.'

At a deeper level, some might question whether capacity is, in effect, ethically insufficient. In other words, if a person perceives that they have a choice between seeking assistance in dying and receiving inadequate care, then whether they have capacity applying the test under the MCA (or any equivalent test) might be thought to be a question which is at one level entirely artificial.

Validity of the concept of capacity

It is perhaps important to note that the UN Committee on the Rights of Persons with Disabilities – the treaty body for the UN Convention on the Rights of

Persons with Disabilities (CRPD), which the UK ratified in 2009 – strongly challenges the validity of the concept of mental capacity. In its General Comment 1 on Article 12 (the right to legal capacity), the Committee asserted that mental capacity was not, 'as commonly presented, an objective, scientific and naturally occurring phenomenon. Mental capacity is contingent on social and political contexts, as are the disciplines, professions and practices which play a dominant role in assessing mental capacity' (United Nations 2014: para. 14). Not only did the Committee attack the older models of capacity such as that based on status – that is, that a diagnosis of an impairment automatically meant that the individual's decisions could not be regarded as legally valid – but also the functional model, which is the model used in the MCA and in capacity legislation elsewhere. (The functional model asks whether the person is cognitively able to process the relevant information at the point where they are required to make a specific decision.)

The Committee considered the functional approach to be flawed in part because 'it presumes to be able to accurately assess the inner-workings of the human mind and, when the person does not pass the assessment, it then denies him or her a core human right – the right to equal recognition before the law' (United Nations 2014: para. 15).

I should make clear that I do not consider that the Committee's interpretation of Article 12 CRPD is, in fact, correct, or that the UK is required to abandon reliance upon the concept of mental capacity. But it is striking that one international body would suggest that a fundamental plank of all models adopted or put forward to date is incompatible with international law.

Conclusion

As I hope that I have shown in this chapter, the reliance on capacity as the touchstone for assisted dying is one that gives rise to questions that I strongly suggest need to be debated and answered before, rather than after, any legislation is passed.

Notes

1. I was one of the barristers instructed by the claimant, Noel Conway, in a challenge to the ban on assisted suicide contained in Section 2(1) of the Suicide Act 1961, considered by English courts up to and including the Supreme Court between 2016 and 2018.
2. This chapter draws from a submission to the Health Select Committee's 2023 inquiry into Assisted Dying/Assisted Suicide, which I co-ordinated on behalf of the Complex Life and Death Decisions Research Group. A list of the members of the group, and case-law/academic references for the propositions set out in this chapter, can be found at: HSC-Committee-CLADD-Research-Group-evidence-January-2023.pdf (mentalcapacitylawandpolicy.org.uk). I should emphasize that the views expressed in this chapter are my views, rather than necessarily reflecting the views of the group.
3. If the law were to be changed to allow assisted dying, Section 62 MCA would also need to be considered. This was introduced during the passage of the MCA to confirm that it does not alter the law relating to murder, manslaughter, or the ban on providing assistance with suicide

contained in Section 2(1) of the Suicide Act 1961. I do not address Section 62 further in this chapter, as its focus is on the substantive questions of capacity.

References

Her Majesty's Stationery Office (HMSO) (2005) *The Mental Capacity Act 2005.* Available at: https://www.legislation.gov.uk/ukpga/2005/9/contents (accessed 16 April 2024).

United Nations (2014) *Convention on the Rights of Persons with Disabilities: General Comment No. 1 (19 May 2014), Article 12: Equal recognition before the law.* United Nations Human Rights, Office of the High Commissioner. Reprinted with the permission of the United Nations. Available at: https://www.ohchr.org/en/hrbodies/crpd/pages/gc.aspx (accessed 16 April 2024).

14 A journey through the contested territory of assisted dying: how law can go wrong – and right

Richard Huxtable[1]

Introduction

Whether the law governing some aspect of human behaviour goes wrong or right will depend on what we mean by 'wrong' and 'right'. Rightness and wrongness may be judged from many different perspectives but where assisted dying is concerned, two such perspectives appear especially important.

First, there is the ethical perspective – or, rather, ethical perspectives, plural. We know, in relation to assisted dying, that there are strong ethical arguments on each side (Huxtable 2013). Those who support the practice, and believe the law should reflect this, will claim that *choice matters*, *suffering matters*, and *consistency matters* – we already provide euthanasia to animals and allow (human) patients to refuse life-sustaining treatments, so why not allow requesting humans to have their lives ended? Those who oppose the practice, and think the law should reflect this, argue that *life matters*. They also say that *medicine matters*, such that we should not involve doctors in ending lives. And they further claim that *consequences matter*, pointing to the 'slippery slopes' apparent in those countries that have allowed assisted dying, whether by assisted suicide or by euthanasia, or both.

Most would agree that the law should (only) adopt a position that is ethically correct (assuming that we can identify and agree on what is ethically correct). But the rightness or wrongness of law can be judged, secondly, from a distinctly legal perspective. Law is essentially about using rules to guide human behaviour (Fuller 1969). Understood in this way, there are various ways that the law might fail in its essential mission. The rules may be unclear or contradictory, which means they cannot guide anybody. Or the rules may not be backed up in practice, such that the law-on-the-books says one thing, but the law-in-action behaves differently, creating confusion.

The implementation of the law governing assisted dying in England and Wales has been questioned, despite the Director of Public Prosecutions' guidance on assisted suicide and on manslaughter (see Chapter 12). Some claim that stern pronouncements that euthanasia is murder do not translate into convictions or (in those rare cases where the accused is convicted of some other offence) imprisonment. For example, in 1992, rheumatologist Dr Nigel Cox was prosecuted over the death of Mrs Lillian Boyes, who died minutes after Cox injected her with potassium chloride. Cox was charged with attempted murder, seemingly in order to avoid the mandatory penalty of imprisonment that would follow a conviction for murder. Cox was convicted of this lesser offence but, strikingly, he was issued with (only) a suspended sentence and the General Medical Council also allowed Cox to continue to practise, albeit with supervision and – perhaps tellingly – after receiving further training in palliative medicine (see Ferguson 1997; and further discussions in Huxtable 2007).

The 'rules' nevertheless still insist that assisted dying is unlawful. There are persisting calls to change that legal position to allow assisted dying in some form. Many countries have already taken such a step. As we reflect on whether and how the law in England and Wales might develop, we should think carefully about the ethical and legal dimensions just sketched. We should also heed Goddard's suggestions in *Making Laws That Work* (2022). Goddard suggests that a coherent proposal to change the law requires, as a starting point, a sure grasp of three things: what the law currently says; the problem that a change in the law is designed to fix; and 'what the world would look like' if the law were to be changed.

Informed by these perspectives, I will use an extended walking metaphor to reflect on different ways that the law on assisted dying might go wrong (or right), offering four suggestions for politicians, legal officials, patients, healthcare professionals and citizens to consider.

Check your surroundings – and walk, don't run

Our journey should begin with us looking around, exploring our surroundings, and setting off at a suitably cautious pace. In other words, we start with Goddard's point about identifying the problem(s) to be fixed, then think about his concern – which is shared by opponents of assisted dying – with the effects that a suggested fix might have on the world.

The current law (at least, according to the written rules) provides a clear barrier – no-one should involve themselves in bringing about the death of another. If legal change is being considered, then there are numerous models from other countries to adopt or adapt. However, the chosen rules will need to suit the particular culture and context; studies suggest 'that attributes unique to each culture are instrumental in shaping public attitudes towards euthanasia' (Karumathil and Tripathi 2022). Delving into experiences elsewhere may even suggest different answers to perceived problems at home, short of changing the legal rules. It is striking that, in the Netherlands, some speculate whether assisted dying would have commanded such high support there, had palliative care been more prominent and available earlier (Albaladejo 2019). The UK, of course, pioneered the provision of palliative care – but, even here, access is variable and relies substantially on charitable provision by hospices. If suffering – and more specifically the relief of suffering – matters, then we might query whether enhanced provision of palliative care in the UK could reduce, even remove, the case for assisted dying.

But if legal change is still being considered, then there is now substantial evidence to examine from countries that have made the move. Supporters of assisted dying reject opponents' claims that countries like the Netherlands and Belgium have slid down a slippery slope (Lewis and Black 2013). Some legislatures, like Oregon in the USA, appear only to have slightly extended beyond their original remit. There are, however, conflicting interpretations of the relevant data, both from Oregon and elsewhere (Finlay and Preston 2020). And opponents have a strong case for arguing that jurisdictions like the Netherlands and Belgium, and more recently Canada, have travelled a long way from their starting-points.

The Dutch policy (and subsequent law) began with terminally and incurably ill adults, but has developed over 50 years to encompass people with psychiatric conditions and children, and the incidence of euthanasia has tripled in 10 years (Lerner and Caplan 2015). Canada has also moved swiftly, from a law in 2016 that focused on the terminally ill, to one which now encompasses people who are 'unbearably suffering', whether or not they are dying; assisted dying (principally euthanasia) already accounts for 4.1 per cent of deaths there nationally and there are plans to extend provision to the mentally ill (Lopez Steven 2023). Such developments require voters and lawmakers to think, early, about what is (or is not) to be allowed, where to draw the relevant lines, and how any precedents set or principles adopted might affect the direction of travel.

Signpost rights of way – and offer (informed) choices

Of course, people will want the freedom to choose for themselves which path(s) they will take: they will want to self-rule and have their autonomous (self-determined) choices respected. Supporters of assisted dying accordingly claim that, because both choice and consistency matter, the law should not only allow people to refuse unwanted treatments, but also allow assisted dying for those who want it. This, they say, would show true respect for self-rule and is a change that commands substantial public support, as opinion polls consistently reveal 65–80 per cent support for making this a lawful option. Recognizing that some medical professionals nevertheless resist such a change, supporters further argue that their autonomy can also be respected by affording them a right to conscientiously object to participation in assessment for, or provision of, assisted dying (Huxtable and Mullock 2015). However, there are at least four reasons, to which the law should be alert, why it is not necessarily the case that respect for self-rule means allowing assisted dying.

First, respect for autonomy requires a person's choice to be suitably well-informed, hence our commitment nowadays to 'informed consent'. But we may query whether the aforementioned surveys are sufficiently robust and whether the choices they report are sufficiently informed about the options that are currently available and what a change in the law might look like. Researchers have found that survey responses are influenced by the contexts in which questions are asked, how questions are worded, and how they are ordered (Magelssen et al. 2016). Citizens – and, indeed, some healthcare professionals – also appear to be unaware, not only about what legal options already exist, but also about existing options for treatment and care, including palliative care (Reid et al. 2008). Some surveys have even found that only 43 per cent of people understood that the provision of assistance in dying means giving lethal drugs (see Chapter 2 for further discussion of opinion polls). It is notable that public support for assisted dying reduces, once respondents are better informed about the options, evidence and arguments (Care Not Killing 2014).

Second, respect for self-rule need not be understood in the ways depicted by supporters. Some maintain that respect for self-rule provides only a *shield* against unwanted bodily intrusion – it does not provide a *sword*, which people can brandish to make demands on others to accede to their will (Huxtable 2013). According to such arguments, there is no inconsistency in (only) allowing people to refuse that to which they do not consent. Others suggest that supporters are fundamentally mistaken about autonomy in a different way, as autonomy is not as individualistic as they claim, but is instead relational; to paraphrase John Donne, no person is an island (Chapter 29).

Indeed, however we are to understand 'autonomy', the third point is that the law should be concerned with the autonomy of *everybody*, not only those who support (and seek) assisted dying. Critics of assisted dying say it is perfectly ethical and consistent to constrain some people's choices, if allowing those choices would infringe on the autonomy of others, such as people who are vulnerable. In short, autonomy has its limits, so it may be right to constrain my autonomous choice if respecting it would jeopardize or disrespect the autonomy of other people.

And finally, as assisted dying is premised on a commitment to respecting choice, then this obviously implies that people will have realistic choices available, about which they can be informed and from which they can select. Unfortunately, as things stand, the variable provision of palliative care means too few people have this as a viable choice when approaching their end of life. Mindful of how the Canadian law looks likely to progress, we should also consider whether there is sufficient mental health care. Some also express concerns about whether a conscientious objection clause can and will do enough to respect and protect objecting professionals (Chapter 7), who may feel hindered in their career or even compelled to exit the profession (McDougall et al. 2022).

Walk the talk – and check the perimeters

But suppose assisted dying has been allowed in some form. The rules will need to specify such matters as how assessments are to be undertaken, who is licensed to provide lethal drugs, to whom and subject to what conditions, what is to be reported, and what ongoing monitoring is required at all stages. Crucially, what the law *says* must be reflected in what providers and legal officials actually *do*.

In 1994, the House of Lords Select Committee opposed a change in the law of England and Wales, highlighting 'the human tendency to test the limits of any regulation' (House of Lords 1994: 49). That fear has been borne out and there are periodic reports, for example from the Netherlands, that doctors who have failed to observe the relevant rules have not faced sanctions (Huxtable and Möller 2007). Such mixed messages undermine the law's ability to guide behaviour and may lead it down a dangerously slippery slope. Better, then, to ensure that there are clear rules, which are monitored – and enforced.

Leave no-one behind

Ultimately, whichever rules are adopted on assisted dying – whether permissive or prohibitive – we should work to ensure that no-one is left behind. The different ethical positions on assisted dying endure because they each capture something important. If prohibition remains, then efforts must be made to address the concerns motivating the pleas of those who seek assisted dying. If permission is granted, then we must still invest in helping and protecting people who are distressed, vulnerable or disabled, and protect those who do not want to participate in bringing about the early death of another.

Conclusion

It remains to be seen whether England and Wales are on a journey towards allowing assisted dying in some form. As these debates continue, I have suggested that politicians, legal officials, patients, healthcare professionals and citizens should:

- *Check your surroundings – and walk (not run).* We should be clear about the problems to be fixed and different means of, and models for, fixing them. There will be important lessons to heed from other legal systems, including about how law might develop and, if reform is envisaged, we should ensure that the chosen model best suits our particular context.
- *Signpost rights of way – and offer (informed) choices.* Affording people (informed and realistic) choices certainly matters, but we should also think carefully about any limits that might rightly be placed around people's choices.
- *Walk the talk – and check the perimeters.* If legal change does occur, then the rules must be clear, monitored and enforced.
- *Leave no-one behind.* Everyone's needs and wishes should be considered and addressed, regardless of the direction in which we ultimately travel.

In deciding which path to take, everyone's views matter, not least those of the people most likely to be directly affected (hence the contemporary importance of the slogan 'Nothing about us without us'). Law governs everyone – and must protect everyone, even when empowering some. We should not lose sight of this when considering the contested territory of assisted dying.

Note

1. Richard Huxtable serves on various ethics (and related) committees, and chairs the UK Clinical Ethics Network. His research is funded by (among others) the Wellcome Trust, NIHR and EPSRC. He has provided evidence and advice to various commissions on assisted dying and has undertaken work commissioned by the Jersey Government. The views expressed in this chapter are his, and should not be taken to represent those of any individuals, organizations or groups with and for which he works.

References

Albaladejo, A. (2019) Fear of assisted dying: could it lead to euthanasia on demand or worsen access to palliative care?, *British Medical Journal*, 364: l852. Available at: https://doi.org/10.1136/bmj.l852.

Care Not Killing (2014) 'Assisted dying' and public opinion, *Care Not Killing*, 18 July. Available at: https://www.carenotkilling.org.uk/public-opinion/assisted-dying-public-opinion/ (accessed 20 February 2024).

Ferguson, P.R. (1997) Causing death or allowing to die? Developments in the law, *Journal of Medical Ethics*, 23 (6): 368–72.

Finlay, I. and Preston, R. (2020) *Death by Appointment: A Rational Guide to the Assisted Dying Debate*. Newcastle upon Tyne: Cambridge Scholars Publishing.

Fuller, L.L. (1969) *The Morality of Law*, revised edn. New Haven, CT: Yale University Press (first published 1964).

Goddard, D. (2022) *Making Laws That Work: How Laws Fail and How We Can Do Better*. Oxford: Hart Publishing.

House of Lords (1994) *Report of the Select Committee on Medical Ethics*, HL Paper 21. London: HMSO.

Huxtable, R. (2007) *Euthanasia, Ethics and the Law: From Conflict to Compromise*. London: Routledge-Cavendish.

Huxtable, R. (2013) *Euthanasia: All that Matters*. London: Hodder.

Huxtable, R. and Möller, M. (2007) 'Setting a principled boundary'? Euthanasia as a response to 'life fatigue', *Bioethics*, 21 (3): 117–26.

Huxtable, R. and Mullock, A. (2015) Voices of discontent? Conscience, compromise and assisted dying, *Medical Law Review*, 23 (2): 242–62.

Karumathil, A.A. and Tripathi, R. (2022) Culture and attitudes towards euthanasia: an integrative review, *OMEGA: Journal of Death and Dying*, 86 (2): 688–720.

Lerner, B.H. and Caplan, A.L. (2015) Euthanasia in Belgium and the Netherlands: On a slippery slope?, *JAMA Internal Medicine*, 175 (10): 1640–41.

Lewis, P. and Black, I. (2013) Adherence to the request criterion in jurisdictions where assisted dying is lawful? A review of the criteria and evidence in the Netherlands, Belgium, Oregon, and Switzerland, *Journal of Law, Medicine and Ethics*, 41 (4): 885–98.

Lopez Steven, B. (2023) Number of assisted deaths jumped more than 30 per cent in 2022, report says, *CBC News*, 27 October. Available at: https://www.cbc.ca/news/politics/maid-canada-report-2022-1.7009704 (accessed 20 February 2024).

Magelssen, M., Supphellen, M., Nortvedt, P. and Materstvedt, L.J. (2016) Attitudes towards assisted dying are influenced by question wording and order: a survey experiment, *BMC Medical Ethics*, 17: 24. Available at: https://bmcmedethics.biomedcentral.com/articles/10.1186/s12910-016-0107-3 (accessed 20 February 2024).

McDougall, R.J., White, B.P., Ko, D. et al. (2022) Junior doctors and conscientious objection to voluntary assisted dying: ethical complexity in practice, *Journal of Medical Ethics*, 48 (8): 517–21.

Reid, C.M., Gooberman-Hill, R. and Hanks, G.W. (2008) Opioid analgesics for cancer pain: symptom control for the living or comfort for the dying? A qualitative study to investigate the factors influencing the decision to accept morphine for pain caused by cancer, *Annals of Oncology*, 19 (1): 44–48.

PART 4

Medical and palliative care issues

15 Physician-assisted suicide for psychiatric disorders: pros and cons(equences)

John Maher

Introduction

This chapter is about physician-assisted suicide for psychiatric disorders (PAS-PD). A variety of other terms are used, including 'psychiatric euthanasia', 'physician-assisted death' and 'medical assistance in dying for sole mental illness'. But let's be explicit: we are talking about suicide. Currently, Belgium, Luxembourg, the Netherlands, Spain and Switzerland allow PAS-PD. Canada has plans to follow suit. I shall split my comments, which largely draw on debates in Canada, between consideration of the arguments used to support and to oppose PAS-PD.

Arguments in (putative) support of PAS-PD

1. PAS-PD is not suicide. A specious conceptual distinction is made that PAS-PD is a well thought out, planned, non-violent course of action and that this easily distinguishes it from violent suicide. In reality, 75 per cent of all suicides are thoughtfully planned out and most of those attempts that seem impulsive have in fact been mentally rehearsed for extended periods of time. Suicide is defined as self-killing. Seeking the assistance of a physician to kill you is still overtly suicidal: your aim is that you should be killed. This attempted artificial demarcation amounts to perfidious inducement. I have a patient right now who is demanding physician-assisted suicide precisely because she has internalized the messaging that it is not suicide; she is adamant that if a doctor and the law allow it, then it cannot be suicide and she would never otherwise kill herself.

2. Medical assessors can distinguish between active suicidality and PAS-PD. On what basis? Both the Canadian and American suicide prevention associations assert there is no meaningful distinction.

3. PAS-PD will allow supportive caregivers and family members to participate in the death. The little data we have available (from Switzerland) shows that about 20 per cent of family members and friends who had witnessed death by assisted suicide had full or partial post-traumatic stress disorder (PTSD), and 16 per cent had depressive symptoms about 19 months after the death (Wagner et al. 2012). The romanticized staging of euthanasia in the terminal context is being transposed onto the extremely different and complex family dynamic where the loved one has decades of life still ahead; a dynamic rife with guilt and desperation.

4. Psychological suffering is as severe as physical suffering. No-one on either side of this issue disagrees with this and implying that they do is just a political stratagem used by PAS-PD advocates repeatedly and unfairly to impugn people who object to the practice. It is a red herring.

5. People with physical illnesses who also have psychiatric disorders are being approved for physician-assisted suicide in Canada, therefore excluding people with psychiatric disorders alone is not acceptable. This is a categorical fallacy. The point being made by PAS-PD opponents is that a psychiatric disorder is not a sufficient condition for physician-assisted suicide, not that it is an exclusionary condition. Psychiatric disorders are treatable and potentially reversible; terminal illness is irreversible.

6. Most people with a psychiatric disorder do not lack capacity for medical decision-making. Again, no-one on either side of this issue disagrees with this. Of course, some severely ill people lack capacity, and of course some people in a grey zone will be very difficult to sort out in that regard. We know psychiatrists commonly come to very different conclusions with the same patient in that middle zone. The concern is that some people wrongly found to be capable will choose PAS-PD in circumstances of unrecognized impaired judgement or despair. Furthermore, assessing capacity in persons with developmental delay, autism, dissociative disorders and personality disorders where symptoms and states can fluctuate dramatically can be extremely difficult (the complexities around capacity are discussed in Chapter 13). Persistence of intent may be impossible to ascertain or establish. In particular, eating disorders represent the paradigm case of someone demonstrating normative or legal capacity while simultaneously starving themself to death.

7. PAS-PD is a more dignified death than killing yourself. Nothing can diminish your inherent dignity (see Chapter 28). In any case, it is not altogether clear that the lethal drugs currently being used do necessarily provide a more dignified death (see Chapter 21).

8. PAS-PD is altruistic. The messages that you can avoid burdening others, that you can save scarce healthcare resources, or even that you could give your organs up for transplantation (see Chapter 1), are all ways of saying that PAS-PD is altruistic. PAS-PD undermines the cornerstone of good psychiatric care by loudly proclaiming that the easiest way to relieve suffering is to accept death. Insidiously, it encourages patients to give up and it risks giving permission to psychiatrists to give up too, especially on difficult or demanding patients.

9. PAS-PD takes the worry out of 'botching' your suicide. Of people who attempt suicide, the median rate of repeat attempts is 23 per cent after 4 years, but the median rate of completed suicides is 6.7 per cent after 9 years (Owens et al. 2002). That means over 4,000 people in Canada die by suicide each year and, disturbingly, 90 per cent of those people have mental illness. The fact that approximately only 7 per cent ultimately complete suicide tells us that something important has happened to change the planned course of action. No such existential and decisional crossroads are or will be available to the person receiving PAS-PD.

Arguments in opposition to PAS-PD

1. PAS-PD is facilitated suicide and undermines suicide prevention efforts. As evidenced by recent data from the Benelux countries, physician-assisted suicide seemed to foster suicide contagion in that region through the 2000s. Suicide rates went up in Belgium, Luxembourg and the Netherlands (three countries that allow PAS-PD) while going down in contiguous countries (Jones 2022; see also Chapters 4 and 29). Those three countries allow PAS-PD only after standard treatments have been tried. The problem with their euthanasia process is that it is retrospective, not prospective, and that defining what constitutes a sufficient number of standard psychiatric treatments is arbitrary given the huge number of biopsychosocial treatment options that will always be available prospectively.

2. Mental illnesses are treatable. Unlike terminal illnesses where treatment options to reverse or slow the disease process are clearly exhausted, psychiatric care has endless treatment combinations and modalities (medication, psychotherapy, neuro-modulation, psychosocial activation). Additionally, with support, people often adapt over time to certain continuing symptoms. This is not to say that suffering is never profound and protracted, but with persistence, amelioration is possible.

3. We cannot identify who has suffering that cannot be ameliorated. There are people who will refuse treatments out of exhaustion, despair, or the mistaken belief that 'everything has been tried'. Unfortunately, we cannot identify who will improve substantially and who will not. In my own work as a sub-specialist psychiatrist for the last two decades treating only 'treatment-resistant' psychotic disorders, it has become very clear that most patients referred to me are under-treated. Persistence and hindsight are profoundly advantageous in planning pathways to effective recovery.

4. PAS-PD is not the solution to underfunding of mental health services. In Canada, only one in three adults, and only one in five children, have access to required mental health care. Government underfunding represents sustained systemic stigmatization insofar as economic analyses by the Mental Health Commission of Canada repeatedly show that improved mental healthcare funding will save billions of dollars. The willingness of some prolific PAS physician providers to euthanize people while on waiting lists for treatments likely to be effective is profoundly disturbing. To shrug your shoulders and say that the failure of the social system should not stop people from choosing death (they would otherwise not want) is an abrogation of the physician's duty as an advocate committed to the preservation of life. It is complicity with suicide inducement.

5. The very existence of a PAS-PD legal option is coercive. Vulnerability is just that. Even if unintentional, when a doctor brings up PAS-PD it is an ideological (not evidence-based or clinically founded) declaration that the situation is hopeless. Without sustained hope, recovery efforts fizzle out on both sides of the physician-patient partnership. Inducement or subtle coercion unto death at times of greatest fragility has now profoundly contaminated the clinical encounters in Canada. I have been told repeatedly by some patients that, 'If you really cared about my suffering, you would kill me'.

Meanwhile, the worries about mental illnesses themselves tending the person towards depressive cognitions (around worthlessness, helplessness and hopelessness) are very real (Appelbaum 2016).

Box 15.1: Case history – depression

There is a 17-year-old girl in my hometown with depression whose psychiatrist has already promised her PAS-PD when she turns 18. She has not yet had even standard treatment for depression. Her caseworker came to me for advice, desperately wanting to override the death wish reinforcement that her powerful psychiatrist has given her.

---

6. *A legal system that allows family doctors and nurse practitioners to approve PAS-PD without psychiatrist involvement is errant.* Some healthcare professionals do not know what they do not know. If someone with a psychiatric disorder wants to die because of symptoms of that disorder, then by definition the disorder is inadequately treated and sophisticated psychiatric care should be mandatory before any invitation to death.

Box 15.2: Case histories – schizophrenia

I have a patient with schizophrenia who has a delusional belief that he has terminal cancer. He was approved for physician-assisted suicide by a family doctor who told him that there was no need to speak with me, his treating psychiatrist of many years. That same doctor says she knows enough psychiatry not to require input from any psychiatrist on end-of-life decisions.

One of my other patients was invited by her family doctor to consider physician-assisted suicide while in the middle of a medication trial with me for her schizophrenia. PAS-PD subverts traditional psychiatric care and undermines good professional practice. Of grave concern, the regulatory College of Physicians and Surgeons in Ontario now requires that, if a patient makes a request for physician-assisted suicide, you must make an 'effective referral' to another physician who will assist even if you object for reasons of conscience or hold the very reasonable position that the patient has treatable illness.

The PAS-PD law coming into force in Canada (now delayed to 2027) does not require that standard psychiatric treatments even be tried first, or that someone with mental illness who wants PAS-PD even has to see a psychiatrist.

7. *Substance use disorders will also be eligible.* Substance use disorders are classified as mental disorders and people with addictions will also be eligible for physician-assisted suicide under Canadian law. Addictions that induce despair in so many. We have

an opioid crisis and are now planning to offer death to these addicted souls. The fix to end all fixes.

8. People with mental illness are often poor and endure abject loneliness. Canadian politicians and expansionists of assisted suicide are ignoring the fact-checked newspaper articles about people being approved for physician-assisted suicide primarily for reasons of poverty, inadequate housing or social exclusion.[1] Caseworkers are already suggesting physician-assisted suicide to veterans with PTSD.

In a public survey (*National Post* 2023), a third of Canadians who responded shockingly supported offering physician-assisted suicide to people for reasons of homelessness or poverty alone. It is laughable to say there is no slippery slope and that solid social values and political wisdom will limit abuses. Is our ignorance of history so absolute? As Lerner and Caplan have commented: 'Physicians must primarily remain healers. There are numerous groups that are potentially vulnerable to abuses waiting at the end of the slippery slope …. When a society does poorly in the alleviation of suffering, it should be careful not to slide into trouble. Instead, it should fix its real problems' (2015: 1641).

9. Confidentiality rules mean important collateral medical history from family members is inaccessible. Family members have no say or input and only hear about the physician-assisted death of their loved ones after the fact. They, more than any others, may possess knowledge about transient suicidal ideation and cycles of decompensation that are inevitably followed by periods of wellness. They alone may know a client's deepest wish to stay alive.

Conclusion

To say we are ready for a societal change that normalizes and induces suicide is simply to give up on the people who most need us to not give up on them. The Canadian law is nothing less than collusion with despair masquerading as false liberty. We must not add to the tragic tally of suicides. Because Canadian law lacks even the most obvious safeguards, many who would have recovered from their mental illnesses will now die, not because of their illnesses but because the law allows them to. I hope Canada is a cautionary tale for other countries.

Note

1. See, for example, the case of the Paralympian Christine Gauthier (Edginton 2023).

References

Applebaum, P.S. (2016) Physician-assisted death for patients with mental disorders – reasons for concern, *JAMA Psychiatry*, 73 (4): 325–26.

Edginton, S. (2023) Canadian Paralympian: I asked for a disability ramp – and was offered euthanasia, *The Telegraph*, 2 September. Available at: https://www.telegraph.co.uk/world-news/2023/09/02/canada-paralympian-christine-gauthier-stairlift-euthanasia/ (accessed 8 March 2024).

Jones, D.A. (2022) Euthanasia, assisted-suicide, and suicide rates in Europe, *Journal of Ethics in Mental Health*, 11: 1–35. Available at: https://jemh.ca/issues/open/documents/JEMH%20

article%20EAS%20and%20suicide%20rates%20in%20Europe%20-%20copy-edited%20final.pdf (accessed 8 March 2024).

Lerner, B.H. and Caplan, A.L. (2015) Euthanasia in Belgium and the Netherlands: on a slippery slope?, *JAMA Internal Medicine*, 175 (10): 1640–41.

Owens, D., Horrocks, J. and House, A. (2002) Fatal and non-fatal repetition of self-harm: systematic review, *British Journal of Psychiatry*, 181 (3): 193–99.

Wagner, B., Müller, J. and Maercker, A. (2012) Death by request in Switzerland: posttraumatic stress disorder and complicated grief after witnessing assisted suicide, *European Psychiatry*, 27 (7): 542–46.

16 Challenges in diagnosis and prognosis

Fiona MacCormick

Introduction

Over recent decades, various jurisdictions have proposed, and some have introduced, new legislation for assisted suicide. Eligibility criteria for people wishing to access assisted suicide commonly include the requirement that the applicant must have an incurable condition that is likely to lead to their death within a limited and specified period. Eligibility criteria like these are put forward as safeguards, offering reassurance that only people who are close to the end of life will be offered assisted suicide. They also affirm that it is possible to make a distinction between people who should be allowed life-ending drugs and those who should not. This chapter will consider these eligibility criteria in more detail, exploring the technical aspects of diagnosis and prognosis while also considering the ethical assumptions underlying such criteria.

Eligibility criteria: context and significance

In the UK, former Bills to introduce assisted suicide have all listed eligibility criteria which refer to diagnosis and prognosis. In 2012, Margo Macdonald MSP proposed the Assisted Suicide (Scotland) Bill, offering people with terminal and life-shortening conditions the opportunity to end their lives by being prescribed life-ending medication. In England, the Assisted Dying Bill [HL] 2014–15, introduced by Lord Falconer, specified that eligible people must have a terminal illness which could not be reversed by treatment, and be reasonably expected to die within 6 months. These same criteria were proposed in two subsequent assisted suicide Bills in England in 2015 and 2021. Assisted dying legislation currently under consideration in the Isle of Man and Jersey both limit eligibility to those with terminal or incurable physical conditions.

The requirements for an applicant to have a terminal illness with a limited prognosis are often viewed as safeguards, the concern being that life-ending medication could *wrongly* be given to a person who still has some life worth living. On the contrary, these criteria imply that assisted suicide should *only* be given to those whose lives are no longer worth living, owing to the nature of their diagnosis or prognosis. The assumptions underlying these criteria are critical. First, that the value of a life is not inherent but dependent on certain characteristics; and second, that it is possible to differentiate between the value of people's lives according to characteristics such as their diagnosis and prognosis. The first assumption will be touched upon in other chapters (Chapters 6, 22, 23 and 28) but it is foundational to the second assumption which is the focus of this chapter. It makes little sense to differentiate between people on the basis of human value, if all humans are deemed to have the same inherent value. The conviction that human dignity and value are objective and unchangeable, rather than relative, is the basis for human rights set out by the United Nations (2015) in the Universal Declaration of Human Rights (UDHR). This was first asserted against the background of appalling inhumanity flowing from the belief that some groups of people *did not* have the same value and dignity as others. Therefore, careful consideration must be given, not just to questions around whether it is possible to determine which people have lost human dignity to the point where assisted suicide is permissible (Chapter 28), but whether it is ethical to attempt to draw this line between people in the first place.

Diagnosis of terminal conditions is not always possible

Despite substantial advances in medical diagnostics, making a diagnosis can still be very challenging, and diagnostic error remains a major source of preventable harm across the world (Newman-Toker et al. 2024). In its 2015 report, the US National Academy of Medicine determined that: 'most people will experience at least one diagnostic error in their lifetime, sometimes with devastating consequences' (Balogh et al. 2015: 1, 19 and 355). One might expect that diagnosis would be more obvious and certain in advanced disease compared to disease at an earlier stage, but in post-mortems about 30 per cent of the medically certified causes of death are wrong and in about 5 per cent they are significantly wrong, suggesting 'misdiagnosis of the terminal illness resulting in inappropriate treatment' (House of Lords 2005: 730)[1].

Yet, there are many reasons why an exact diagnosis of terminal disease may not be possible: the person is too frail for a specific investigation, or the site of suspected disease is technically impossible or too high risk to biopsy because of its proximity to large vessels or organs. Sometimes a biopsy could enable an accurate diagnosis, but the person declines further invasive procedures. Of course, sadly many patients do receive exact diagnoses of advanced disease specified in site and tissue type, for which there is no curative treatment. But, even with a precise diagnosis, estimating prognosis is far from an exact science.

Clinical case study: diagnosis[2]

Mrs Z was in her fifties, with multiple chronic conditions including asthma, obesity, chronic pain, diabetes and heart disease when she was admitted to hospital with abdominal pain, nausea and vomiting. A CT scan revealed a probable cancer of the gallbladder with apparent spread to the liver. The oncology multidisciplinary team felt that the cancer could not be cured with surgery, and although chemotherapy would have been an option, Mrs Z's physical condition was such that it was felt she would not be well enough to tolerate and benefit from chemotherapy.

Therefore, a biopsy of the gallbladder was not pursued and the focus of her care became symptom management alone. Mrs Z was told that she had incurable cancer and, although it was difficult to be certain without a biopsy, in such cancers the expected prognosis would usually be less than 1 year. She went home for end-of-life care, with symptom management via a pump delivering medications under the skin. After a few months, her condition had not deteriorated and her medications were gradually weaned down and stopped. Nine months after her first CT scan, a re-staging scan showed a significant improvement and simply suggested a persistent gallbladder polyp. A further CT scan a few months later showed the polyp was stable and probably benign. It is now believed that she never had a cancer.

Challenges in prognosis

It is well recognized that the likely clinical trajectory towards death differs in different categories of condition (such as cancer, non-cancer and dementia) (Murray et al. 2005). Cancers generally tend to run a more predictable course with sudden patterns of decline, whereas in chronic organ failure the trajectory is often fluctuating, longer and less predictable within an overall pattern of decline. People with dementia may deteriorate very slowly over time with moderate fluctuations in their condition.

Yet, the practice of prognosticating for individual people continues to be riddled with inaccuracies. In 2016, a systematic review of studies of prognostic accuracy in palliative care, both for cancer and non-cancer patients, found that clinicians' predictions are frequently inaccurate, with accuracy varying from 23 per cent to 78 per cent. No sub-group of clinicians was consistently shown to be more accurate than any other (White et al. 2016).

Estimates of survival of patients with advanced cancer found that patients' own estimates tend to be over-optimistic and inaccurate. Clinicians' estimates are wrong for almost half the patients, with doctors and nurses being correct in their prognostic estimates in 56.3 per cent and 55.5 per cent respectively, and multidisciplinary teams correct in 57.5 per cent of cases (Gwilliam et al. 2013). Although several prognostic tools have been developed for use in patients with advanced cancer, a study comparing four such tools against clinical predictions of survival found that there was no evidence that the tools assessed were more accurate than clinician estimates alone (Stone et al. 2021). Improvements in cancer treatments, such as the development and use of immunotherapy, also mean that many people are living longer with cancer, making prognostication increasingly challenging. For people with incurable non-malignant conditions, prognosis is considered even more difficult.

This broad and heterogeneous group of conditions includes diseases such as chronic obstructive pulmonary disease, congestive heart failure, dementias, chronic liver and chronic kidney disease, and many types of chronic and progressive neurological disorders. These non-cancer incurable conditions have much less certainty and often longer and fluctuating disease trajectories than many cancers. However, as these conditions are non-malignant, they are often not perceived as being terminal conditions. And even though many chronic non-cancer conditions have a similar symptom burden to advanced cancer, many people with these conditions do not access palliative care services in a timely way (Coventry et al. 2005). The prognostic difficulties in non-cancer incurable disease result in serious delays in care.

In their systematic review, Coventry et al. (2005) looked at 11 studies evaluating the ability of prognostic tools to predict survival in older adults with life-limiting, non-malignant disease. While the review was able to highlight several factors associated with survival, the authors were unable to recommend any specific prognostic model. They suggested that the heterogeneity of the non-cancer patient population and the unpredictable course of non-cancer disease combine to make accurate prognosis in this group extremely challenging. They also highlighted that social and psychological factors, which are often poorly investigated, may well play a part in survival in those with non-cancer chronic disease.

Clinical case study: prognosis

Mrs X was in her fifties with advanced chronic obstructive pulmonary disease and anxiety. She had had multiple hospital admissions with exacerbations of her lung disease and her community palliative care team and primary care team felt that she was approaching the end of her life. She didn't wish to die at home and was admitted to the local hospice. However, after 2 months in the hospice her condition had not deteriorated. She was transferred to a community hospital where she was cared for by a multidisciplinary team. Over the next few months, her condition fluctuated and the team considered her to be close to death on multiple occasions, but she would always rally and stabilize. After 8 months in the community hospital, Mrs X decided that she was determined to get home. She remained very frail, bed-bound and short of breath on minimal exertion, but she was keen to wean down her medications and over time managed to do so. Once appropriate care and support were in place she was discharged home. After 4 months at home, she was hospitalized with an acute exacerbation of her lung disease. She failed to improve with treatment and her family were warned she might die. She subsequently stabilized, was discharged home, but after just a few days she was readmitted to hospital following further deterioration in her condition. She was transferred to the community hospital for end-of-life care and died a few days later.

Discussion and conclusion

As outlined above, even in advanced disease there are many reasons why diagnosis may be uncertain. Even with a firm diagnosis of advanced disease, prognostication remains complex and riddled with uncertainties. Thus, eligibility criteria that assume diagnosis and prognosis are accurate and verifiable concepts are profoundly misleading. But even if there were a tool with 100 per cent accuracy for determining diagnosis and prognosis, would this solve the problem and allay safeguarding fears? Using diagnosis and prognosis as criteria for assisted suicide/assisted dying implies that after a certain point these lives are of less value, less deserving of care.

There is a deeper tension seldom highlighted in discussions about safeguards. While proposals to legalize assisted suicide are often brought with the well-meaning aims of honouring autonomy and ending suffering, they intrinsically strike at the core of the much-esteemed value of the inherent worth of all people, as set out in the UDHR. Article 1 states: 'All human beings are born free and equal in dignity and rights' (United Nations 2015: 4). There are important distinctions to be made here, for instance between inherent and attributed dignity, which are discussed in Chapter 28. And the notion of rights is also complex (see Chapters 1 and 28). However, the UDHR stresses that the starting point is that human beings are *equal in dignity*. Legislative change that undermines this stance should be very carefully considered.

These eligibility criteria determine the value of a life based on the person's diagnosis and prognosis. In any other sphere of life, the characteristics of the person (such as race, sex, disability) would not allow discrimination. Yet the implicit assumption of these eligibility criteria is that it is acceptable to discriminate on the basis of diagnosis and prognosis. This is a sea change in the way society has viewed humanity since the publication of the UDHR.

There is real value in seeking to determine accurate diagnosis and prognosis: not so that life can be prematurely ended, but rather so that the person and their family can be better supported and access timely care and provide true dignity in dying. If all lives have inherent dignity and value, then there can be no dividing line to determine who does or does not have such qualities. If society were to determine that some lives have value and others do not, this should not be done without recognizing the gravity of this change and the impact it will have on the treatment of all people, especially the weak and vulnerable. Rather than advocating to end the lives of those people closest to death, we should instead campaign for the highest quality care for all people regardless of diagnosis or prognosis in order to demonstrate true care and compassion to all, especially when those in despair feel their lives no longer have value. In any case, as things stand, eligibility criteria for assisted suicide/assisted dying which assume diagnosis and prognosis can be regarded as accurate and verifiable should be viewed with considerable caution and scepticism.

Notes

1. This is from the 'Memorandum by The Royal College of Pathologists', which continued: 'Therefore, the procedure of making "a determination that the patient has a terminal illness" is not ... reliable ... Almost all histopathologists (doctors who perform postmortem examinations) have experience of cases deemed to have died from an untreatable terminal illness, but

post mortem examination discloses another condition – that would have been treatable – for the patient's death' (House of Lords 2005: 730; dated 3 September 2004).
2. The case studies draw upon real cases, but are anonymized for the sake of confidentiality.

References

Balogh, E.P., Miller, B.T. and Ball, J.R. (eds) (2015) *Improving Diagnosis in Health Care*. Washington, DC: The National Academies Press. Available at: https://doi.org/10.17226/21794 (accessed 22 February 2024).

Coventry, P.A., Grande, G.E., Richards, D.A. and Todd, C.J. (2005) Prediction of appropriate timing of palliative care for older adults with non-malignant life-threatening disease: a systematic review, *Age and Ageing*, 34 (3): 218–27.

Gwilliam, B., Keeley, V., Todd, C. et al. (2013) Prognosticating in patients with advanced cancer – observational study comparing the accuracy of clinicians' and patients' estimates of survival, *Annals of Oncology*, 24 (2): 482–88.

House of Lords (2005) *Assisted Dying for the Terminally Ill Bill [HL] vol. II: Evidence*. Select Committee on the Assisted Dying for the Terminally Ill Bill. Available at: https://publications.parliament.uk/pa/ld200405/ldselect/ldasdy/86/86ii.pdf (accessed 11 March 2024).

Murray, S.A., Kendall, M., Boyd, K. and Sheikh, A. (2005) Illness trajectories and palliative care. *British Medical Journal*, 330 (7498): 1007–11.

Newman-Toker, D.E., Nassery, N., Schaffer, A.C. et al. (2024) Burden of serious harms from diagnostic error in the USA, *BMJ Quality & Safety*, 33: 109–20. Available at: https://doi.org/10.1136/bmjqs-2021-014130.

Stone, P., Vickerstaff, V., Kalpakidou, A. et al. (2021) Prognostic tools or clinical predictions: which are better in palliative care?, *PLoS ONE*, 16(4): e0249763. Available at: https://doi.org/10.1371/journal.pone.0249763 (accessed 22 February 2024).

United Nations (2015) *Universal Declaration of Human Rights*. First proclaimed and adopted by the United Nations General Assembly in 1948. Available at: https://www.un.org/en/udhrbook/pdf/udhr_booklet_en_web.pdf (accessed 22 February 2024).

White, N., Reid, F., Harris, A. et al. (2016) A systematic review of predictions of survival in palliative care: how accurate are clinicians and who are the experts?, *PLoS ONE*, 11(8): e0161407. Available at: https://doi.org/10.1371/journal.pone.0161407 (accessed 22 February 2024).

17 Palliative care: need, provision and evidence

Katherine E. Sleeman and
Lesley E. Williamson

Introduction: what is palliative care?

The World Health Organization defines palliative care as 'care that is given with the intention of improving the quality of life of people with a life-limiting illness and those close to them, including symptom management, psychological, social and spiritual support' (WHO 2020). Palliative care is therefore a holistic approach for people with life-limiting illnesses that aims to increase the quality rather than quantity of time left to live.

Many health professionals, including GPs and community nurses, deliver palliative care. Specialist palliative care is delivered by professionals with specialist training in this field, working in multidisciplinary teams of doctors, nurses, social workers, chaplains and allied health professionals. Palliative care aims to alleviate not only physical suffering – such as pain or breathlessness – but also social, psychological and spiritual suffering that can be experienced by people approaching the end of life.

The cornerstone of palliative care is effective communication, which is essential for holistic assessment of needs (physical, psychological, social and spiritual), preferences and goals of care for patients and those close to them. Advance care planning is a process that aims to understand the wishes of patients, anticipate future issues and enable person-centred care as people approach the end of life.

What evidence is there that palliative care works?

Over the past decades, palliative care has developed from a new approach to an established clinical specialty. Its development has been guided by high-quality research, which has provided evidence not only about the need for palliative care across conditions, but also approaches to palliative care that are most effective and cost-effective. Put simply, we now have strong evidence that palliative care works.

Specialist palliative care has been shown in randomized controlled trials to improve quality of life, reduce symptoms and alleviate depression for people who are dying from various conditions, including cancer and chronic respiratory disease (Kavalieratos et al. 2016). People who receive palliative care are less likely to visit emergency departments, less likely to be admitted to hospital in the last months of life and more likely to die at home (Gomes et al. 2013; Williamson et al. 2021). Palliative care improves outcomes for carers who are less likely to experience complex bereavement. Randomized controlled trials have also found that people who receive palliative care live longer than those who do not. This is important because there can be a misconception that when people receive palliative care they will die more quickly; this is not the case.

Evidence-based interventions have been successfully incorporated into routine practice with a positive impact on patients, families and staff. For example, the Integrated Palliative care Outcome Scale for Dementia (IPOS-Dem) has been incorporated into standards of care, improving detection of symptoms and concerns not previously identified (Ellis-Smith et al. 2017). The Integrated Breathlessness Support Service model and self-management toolkit were trialled in research and have since been sucessfully implemented in practice (Reilly et al. 2016).

Perhaps not surprisingly, health economic analyses have found that palliative care is a 'high value' intervention, because it provides better care and outcomes for patients and carers, at the same or lower overall cost. From a costs point of view, savings are highest for those with the most complex needs (May et al. 2018).

Put together, the evidence shows that palliative care is both clinically effective and cost-effective. Although historically palliative care was only considered appropriate when people were close to death, more recent evidence shows that palliative care works best when provided early, alongside the care provided by other specialists such as oncologists, cardiologists and respiratory physicians.

How many people need palliative care?

Although palliative care is often thought of in the context of cancer, recent evidence shows that palliative care can be of benefit to people with a variety of long-term and life-limiting conditions, including dementia, frailty, chronic lung disease and heart disease.

It is estimated that 69–82 per cent of people who die in high-income countries would benefit from palliative care (including both 'specialist' palliative care and care provided by 'generalists'). Hospice UK have estimated that over 100,000 people die each year in the UK with unmet palliative care needs; that is, needing palliative care but not receiving it. This means that over 300 people every day die with unnecessary physical, emotional, social and spiritual distress. Partly driven by population ageing, the number of people dying with palliative care needs is projected to increase by 25–40 per cent by 2040 (Etkind et al. 2017). With approximately 600,000 deaths each year across the UK, this means that by 2040 there will be at least an *additional* 100,000 people dying each year with palliative care needs.

Who receives palliative care (and who does not)?

It is difficult to ascertain who receives palliative care before they die, as there is no national database with information on receipt of palliative care. However, there is compelling evidence that palliative care is not distributed equally in society. Groups who are less likely to receive palliative care are older people, people with non-cancer conditions, people from ethnically minoritized communities, and people with lower socio-economic status such as those living in areas of greater deprivation.

Improving delivery of palliative care so that it is equitable across different groups is a priority given the projected future increase in palliative care need, because when services are stretched, inequalities widen. This phenomenon was observed in relation to the Covid-19 pandemic in the UK: the pandemic precipitated a sustained increase in home deaths, which was greatest for people living in the least deprived areas and smallest for those living in areas with greater deprivation (Sleeman et al. 2022). Without an increase in palliative care services to meet the growing needs, it is likely that inequalities will grow.

How is palliative care provided?

Palliative care is provided across many settings, including in hospitals, in people's homes, in care homes and in hospices. Although hospices are often synonymous with palliative care, only 5 per cent of deaths occur in hospices; most people die at home or in hospital or care homes.

Several research studies have identified gaps and variation in provision of palliative care. A study from 2017 found that the amount Clinical Commissioning Groups spent on palliative care varied from £51.83 to £2,329.19 per person who died per annum (Lancaster et al. 2018). A more recent analysis of Integrated Care System strategies found that few prioritized palliative care (Chambers et al. 2022). The 2022 Marie Curie Better End of Life report found gaps and variation in care for people living at home with life-limiting illnesses (Pask et al. 2022). In this study, only one-third of areas across the UK consistently provided access to an out-of-hours palliative care telephone advice line, even though this has been a NICE recommendation since 2004. The 2023 National Audit of Care at the End of Life (NACEL 2023) found that just 60 per cent of hospitals provide 7-day face-to-face palliative care services, even though this has been a NICE recommendation since 2011.

What is the state of the palliative care workforce?

Most palliative and end-of-life care is delivered in community settings, largely provided by unpaid family carers and communities, including volunteers. GPs and community nurses deliver a high proportion of community-based palliative and end-of-life care, though it is projected that the supply of primary care workforce will soon fall short of demand. Social care is especially important for people nearing the end of life, but little researched. Social care practitioners often work in isolation with little formal end-of-life training and support, which contributes to high staff turnover. The need for palliative and end-of-life care in residential or nursing care homes is projected to more than double by 2040 (Bone et al. 2018). Several research studies have shown that care homes may reduce hospitalization among those approaching the end of life, though they are reliant on access to clinical expertise of visiting healthcare professionals. Supporting the 'generalist' workforce to deliver high-quality palliative care may also help to mitigate staff burnout and improve retention.

Statutory guidance for Integrated Care Boards advocates use of the Ambitions for Palliative and End of Life Care to facilitate delivery of a sufficiently staffed and skilled workforce across all settings. This includes building knowledge, skills and confidence among generalist providers, supported by specialist palliative care providers where appropriate. However, the future of the specialist palliative care workforce is also uncertain. One-third of specialist palliative care doctors are due to retire over the next 10 years; at the same time, fill-rates of specialist training posts are falling. In a 2021 Hospice UK survey of clinical staff working in UK hospices, vacancy rates in community- and hospice-based nursing roles were 11 per cent and 7 per cent respectively. As such, although specialist palliative care is available across all settings, there are serious concerns about the ability of the specialist palliative care workforce to address current and future needs for care.

Closing the gap between evidence and delivery of care

In palliative and end-of-life care, as in other areas of health care, to achieve the best outcomes for patients, carers and society, care and services should be guided by evidence. While research in palliative care is growing, it remains a small research field. The UK Health Research Analysis (2022) report found that just 0.23 per cent of UK health research funding in 2022 was allocated to end-of-life care, though this had increased from 0.16 per cent in 2014.

For the growing evidence base to deliver positive outcomes for people and their families, this evidence must be accessed, understood and used by those who have power to influence policy and practice. There is, therefore, an opportunity to improve people's quality of life at the last stage of life, and reduce inequities, by making better decisions informed by evidence and data, and by putting into practice what we know works. This is especially relevant given the new statutory duties on Integrated Care Boards in England to commission palliative and end-of-life care, and in light of constrained budgets in both health and social care, with growing pressure to avoid ineffective and unnecessary hospital admissions. Hospital admissions escalate during the last months of life; improving palliative care through evidence-informed commissioning will relieve hospital pressures and costs. Better supported staff may also minimize burden, burnout and turnover.

By closing the gap between the evidence and the delivery of care and services for people approaching the end of life, it will be possible to deliver improved care and outcomes for patients and those close to them, and better value for the health and care system.

Conclusions

Providing high-quality palliative and end-of-life care is a strategic, economic and moral imperative, as improving palliative and end-of-life care leads to more integrated care, lower costs and improved outcomes for people living with life-limiting illness. However, variation and gaps in care and services mean thousands of people each year do not receive the palliative care they need. In light of the rapidly increasing need for palliative care, continued investment in research to advance knowledge about the most effective methods of addressing complex symptoms, while ensuring this evidence informs changes to policy and practice, is essential.

References

Bone, A.E., Gomes, B., Etkind, S.N. et al. (2018) What is the impact of population ageing on the future provision of end-of-life care? Population-based projections of place of death, *Palliative Medicine*, 32 (2): 329–36.

Chambers, R.L., Pask, S., Higginson, I.J. et al. (2022) Inclusion of palliative and end of life care in health strategies aimed at integrated care: a documentary analysis, *Health Open Research*, 4: 19. Available at: https://healthopenresearch.org/articles/4-19/v2 (accessed 20 March 2024).

Ellis-Smith, C., Evans, C.J., Murtagh, F.E.M. et al. (2017) Development of a caregiver-reported measure to support systematic assessment of people with dementia in long-term care: the Integrated Palliative care Outcome Scale for Dementia, *Palliative Medicine*, 31 (7): 651–60.

Etkind, S.N., Bone, A.E., Gomes, B. et al. (2017) How many people will need palliative care in 2040? Past trends, future projections and implications for services, *BMC Medicine*, 15: 102. Available at: https://doi.org/10.1186/s12916-017-0860-2.

Gomes, B., Calanzani, N., Curiale, et al. (2013) Effectiveness and cost effectiveness of home palliative care services for adults with advanced illness and their caregivers, *Cochrane Database of Systematic Reviews*, 6: CD007760. Available at: https://doi.org/10.1002/14651858.CD007760.pub2 (accessed 20 March 2024).

Kavalieratos, D., Corbelli, J., Zhang, D. et al. (2016) Association between palliative care and patient and caregiver outcomes: a systematic review and meta-analysis, *Journal of the American Medical Association*, 316 (20): 2104-2114.

Lancaster, H., Finlay, I., Downman, M. and Dumas, J. (2018) Commissioning of specialist palliative care services in England, *BMJ Supportive & Palliative Care*, 8 (1): 93–101.

May, P., Normand, C., Cassel, J.B. et al. (2018) Economics of palliative care for hospitalized adults with serious illness: a meta-analysis, *JAMA Internal Medicine*, 178 (6): 820–29.

NACEL (2023) *National Audit of Care at the End of Life. Fourth Round of the Audit (2022/23) Report – England and Wales* [online]. London: Healthcare Quality Improvement Partnership (HQIP). Available at: https://s3.eu-west-2.amazonaws.com/nhsbn-static/NACEL/2023/NACEL%20 2022%20Summary%20Report%20-%20Final.pdf (accessed 20 March 2024).

Pask, S., Davies, J.M., Mohamed, A. et al. (2022) *Better End of Life 2022, Mind the Gaps: Understanding and Improving Out-of-Hours Care for People with Advanced Illness and Their Informal Carers*, Research Report [online]. London: Marie Curie. Available at: https://www.mariecurie.org.uk/globalassets/media/documents/policy/beol-reports-2022/better-end-of-life-report-2022.pdf (accessed 20 March 2024).

Reilly, C.C., Bausewein, C., Pannell, C. et al. (2016) Patients' experiences of a new integrated breathlessness support service for patients with refractory breathlessness: results of a postal survey, *Palliative Medicine*, 30 (3): 313–22.

Sleeman, K.E., Leniz, J., Davies, J.M. et al. (2022) *Fairer Care at Home: The Covid-19 Pandemic: A Stress Test for Palliative and End of Life Care in England*, Better End of Life Research Report [online]. London: Marie Curie. Available at: https://www.mariecurie.org.uk/globalassets/media/documents/research/publications/beol-2022/h903a-beol-england.pdf (accessed 20 March 2024).

UK Health Research Analysis. (2022) *UK Clinical Research Collaboration 2023* [online]. Swindon: Medical Research Council. Available: https://hrcsonline.net/reports/analysis-reports/uk-health-research-analysis-2022/ (accessed 10 February 2024).

World Health Organization (WHO) (2020) *Palliative Care – Key Facts* [online]. Available at: https://www.who.int/news-room/fact-sheets/detail/palliative-care (accessed 10 February 2024).

Williamson, L.E., Evans, C.J., Cripps, R.L. et al. (2021) Factors associated with emergency department visits by people with dementia near the end of life: a systematic review, *Journal of the American Medical Directors Association*, 22 (10): 2046–55.e3.

18 Sedation at the end of life

Katherine Frew and Paul Paes

Introduction

The use of sedative drugs at the end of life has been widely debated in the past 30 years because of its association with hastening death. Many different approaches to using sedation have been described, including the intermittent use of drugs to treat specific symptoms, as well as the continuous use of drugs to render a patient unconscious until death. These approaches have been regarded by some as merely a method of providing symptom control and by others as another form of euthanasia. Much controversy has revolved around this juxtaposition, with many research studies setting out with the aim of investigating whether sedation indeed does hasten death, and whether, if it does, death is intended.

This debate around sedation at the end of life has taken place within the context of an increased awareness, in the perceptions of both the medical community and the UK population, of end-of-life issues. In other parts of Europe, such as the Netherlands and Belgium, the legalization of euthanasia has contributed to and formed the basis of the debate, which has been primarily concerned with establishing a distinction between sedation and euthanasia.

This chapter will describe and define the practices of sedation at the end of life and consider whether they may be distinguished from euthanasia.

Types of sedation

The practice of *ordinary sedation* (Quill et al. 2009) has received the least attention in the literature. It involves the widely accepted practice of using drugs that have sedative properties to provide relief from symptoms such as pain or breathlessness. The intention in their use is to reduce the presence or intensity of symptoms. If consciousness is reduced, this is an unintentional secondary effect, avoided if possible by reducing the dose or changing the drug. This is a practice and concept used across the whole of health care, not limited to palliative care.

Proportionate palliative sedation (PPS) is the use of sedative drugs with the intention of treating symptoms (such as pain or breathlessness) but with an acceptance of a reduction in consciousness as a secondary intent. This occurs when symptoms are so severe that they cannot be controlled while maintaining full consciousness, because the strength of the drug required to control the symptoms causes sedation. Importantly, in the context of fully informed consent, the symptoms drive the need for sedation rather than sedation being the primary aim. Sedative medication is titrated up to achieve symptom relief, is regularly reviewed and, when possible, the dose is reduced – that is, the aim of treatment is symptom

Table 18.1: Types of sedation

Term	Primary intent
Ordinary sedation	Titration of potentially sedative drugs to treat symptoms with avoidance of reduction in consciousness
Proportionate palliative sedation	Titration of potentially sedative drugs to treat symptoms with acceptance of reduction in consciousness
Palliative sedation to unconsciousness	Use of sedative drugs to cause unconsciousness until death
Continuous deep sedation	Use of sedative drugs to cause unconsciousness until death
Continuous sedation until death	**Either** Titration of potentially sedative drugs to treat symptoms with acceptance of reduction in consciousness **Or** Use of sedative drugs to cause unconsciousness until death
Palliative sedation	**Either** Titration of potentially sedative drugs to treat symptoms with acceptance of reduction in consciousness **Or** Use of sedative drugs to cause unconsciousness until death
Terminal sedation	Use of sedative drugs to cause unconsciousness until death

control using the lowest dose of sedation possible, and only for as long as it is required. Where symptoms are severe and inadequately controlled by other measures (i.e. the symptoms are 'refractory'), deep sedation may occasionally be continued until death, which some have termed *palliative sedation to unconsciousness* (PSU).

Many have described both ordinary and proportionate palliative sedation (the use of sedative drugs to treat symptoms without primarily intending a reduction in consciousness) as part of standard medical practice. It is important to understand standard practice in order to interpret studies appropriately that explore the more controversial practices of sedation.

Continuous deep sedation (CDS) is the intentional induction of unconsciousness, with the aim of maintaining unconsciousness until death occurs. The aim is to avoid recovery of consciousness if it may lead to the return of the refractory symptom for which it is being used. CDS became especially controversial in the early 2000s as evidence from studies outside the UK described physicians using CDS with the explicit intention of hastening death (Rietjens et al. 2004) and as a way to avoid the bureaucracy associated with administering euthanasia (Seale et al. 2015). This use of sedation is markedly different to other, more overtly proportional, forms of sedation. PSU may be considered a form of CDS, but the application of CDS in the literature falls beyond PSU, especially concerning the requirement for death to be imminent.

Palliative sedation and palliative sedation therapy are terms which confusingly are applied to all forms of sedation, primary or secondary, light or deep, intermittent or continuous. Clarity about the type of sedation is essential to determine the intent, its effect and the ethical implications (see Table 18.1).

Ethical implications

Central to debates about sedation at the end of life is whether the practice hastens death, but the reduction or removal of consciousness is also an important moral consideration. Ten Have and Welie (2014) considered four principal features to guide an assessment of the moral acceptability of sedation at the end of life, which support its distinction from euthanasia. These factors are: terminality, refractory symptoms, proportionality, and separation of decisions about forgoing treatment.

Terminality

In the 1990s literature, there was a clear assumption that death was hastened by the use of sedatives and opioids at the end of life. Initial descriptions of the practice of 'terminal sedation' indeed asserted this as a feature of its use. 'In a stuporous state the patient can no longer eat and drink, dehydrates to death, if it's taking too long the morphine drip is increased until there is a quicker death' (Billings and Block 1996: 22). This perception of end-of-life care lingers among many in the general public, even now. But there is no evidence from research studies of shortened survival in patients when sedation is titrated to control symptoms.

One of the key features of the use of sedation at the end of life relies on an assessment of prognosis, and an understanding that if a person is not in the final stages of life (the final 2 weeks of life is often referred to in guidelines), there is a much higher risk of hastening death. Moreover, the impact of reducing or removing consciousness (ending the 'biographical life') is accepted only when life is drawing to its natural end.

Thus, the terminality feature requires that a person is dying (in the last days or within the last 2 weeks of life at most) and accepts that the practice of sedation, when used for the indications and in the way described below, does not hasten death.

Refractory symptoms

Distress at the end of life may arise from both physical and psycho/existential roots. In people who are dying, the source of distress may become harder to identify owing to cognitive and communication changes. Pain and breathlessness are more easily detected. It is important to make distinctions between judicious management decisions targeted at different particular symptoms (for example, using opioids rather than sedation for pain). Careful and skilled assessments are crucial to ensure that extreme treatments which reduce consciousness are reserved for extreme symptoms. The term 'refractory' relates to the intractable nature of symptoms, rather than being determined by their source. The severity of symptoms, lack of response to earlier treatments, access to specialists in palliative care, and prognosis (determining the time in which further treatments could reasonably be considered and trialled), are required to determine the point at which a symptom may be deemed refractory.

Proportionality

Ten Have and Welie (2014) consider the rule of proportionality to be applied to sedation in two ways. First is the proportional nature of the response to a refractory symptom: balancing the anticipated benefit with harm. While reducing or removing consciousness must be considered a moral *harm*, the anticipated benefit, namely the relief of symptoms, must be proportional. Sedation is therefore an option of last resort, when all other reasonable measures, preserving consciousness, have been tried. Even if sedation does not hasten death, the *harm* of reducing or removing a person's agency must be appreciated.

The second aspect of proportionality is in direct relation to the depth of sedation used. This is described in the definition of proportionate palliative sedation – the lowest dose of sedation required to bring about the effect of relief of symptoms ought to be used. This approach to considering the moral acceptability of sedation may appear to rule out the use of CDS or PSU, unless the degree of symptoms experienced truly requires unconsciousness until death. Situations which may require this response can arise when an acute terminal event (e.g. obstruction of an airway or a major haemorrhage) generates acute (within seconds or minutes) overwhelming symptoms with death imminently anticipated (i.e. within minutes or hours). In these situations, the use of high doses of sedative drugs to cause unconsciousness until death may be considered proportionate, given the anticipated imminence of death and the overwhelming nature of the symptoms experienced.

Separation of decisions about forgoing treatment

Decisions which take place at the time of sedation are critical to determining the moral nature of the practice. In early papers from the Netherlands, the practices of using CDS and routinely withholding or withdrawing artificial nutrition and hydration (ANH) were described. These caused significant concern, and subsequent guidelines have emphasized the importance of separating decisions about ANH from the decision to use sedation. The importance of this can most clearly be seen in the case of CDS. As the intent of CDS is to maintain unconsciousness, a person's ability to eat and drink is removed by the drugs; if death is not biologically imminent, it is evident that death would be hastened.

This distinction is especially important in countries where euthanasia is legal, where the practice of CDS has been used as an alternative or even as a preferable form of hastening death, since it circumvents the need to follow the euthanasia legislation. This was reported in the UNBIASED study (Seale et al. 2015) in which healthcare professionals in the UK, Belgium and the Netherlands were interviewed concerning their use of sedation for patients at the end of life. One respondent from the Netherlands stated: 'the best part is you do not have to have anything arranged and it's just always possible' (Seale et al. 2015: 350).

The authors reasonably suggested that this revealed the motivation was to use sedation as an acceptable alternative to euthanasia. In contrast, healthcare professionals from the UK described specific concerns about hastening death and expressed either no intent to hasten death or, at most, partial intent.

Conclusion

The terms described above – terminality, refractory symptoms, proportionality, and separation of decisions about forgoing treatment – provide an approach to consider the ethics of different types of sedation and determine the extent to which sedation is or is not being used as a surrogate for euthanasia. Thus, if the person is close to death, if there are symptoms which require sedative medication rather than any other, if the treatment is proportionate to the need arising from the symptoms, and if the sedation is not being used specifically to deprive the person of nutrition and hydration, then it can be said with clarity that sedation is not being used with the intent of hastening death.

Sedation at the end of life remains problematic, primarily because of its persisting association with hastening death and the wide variations in practice. Consideration of hydration is particularly important in the sedated patient. Meticulous attention to the type of sedation, intention and consistent application of language and definitions can support an improved understanding of the distinction between sedation that is an important part of the provision of end-of-life care without hastening death, and the ethically more problematic forms of continuous deep sedation, when the intention is tantamount to euthanasia.

References

Billings, J.A. and Block, S.D. (1996) Slow euthanasia, *Journal of Palliative Care*, 12 (4): 21–30.

Quill, T.E., Lo, B., Brock, D.W. and Meisel, A. (2009) Last-resort options for palliative sedation, *Annals of Internal Medicine*, 151 (6): 421–24.

Rietjens, J.A.C., van der Heide, A., Vrakking, A.M. et al. (2004) Physician reports of terminal sedation without hydration or nutrition for patients nearing death in the Netherlands, *Annals of Internal Medicine*, 141 (3): 178–85.

Seale, C., Raus, K., Bruinsma, S. et al. (2015) The language of sedation in end-of-life care: the ethical reasoning of care providers in three countries, *Health*, 19 (4): 339–54.

ten Have, H. and Welie, J. (2014) Palliative sedation versus euthanasia: an ethical assessment, *Journal of Pain and Symptom Management*, 47 (1): 123–36.

19 Should assisted dying be part of mainstream health care?

Suzanne Ost and Nancy Preston

Introduction

The debate in many countries prior to the introduction of a lawful assisted dying model focused upon whether assisted dying was morally right or wrong. There was less focus on how it impacts healthcare systems and healthcare professionals, or how patients and families navigate these systems. Yet the majority of laws permitting assisted dying are medicalized, with clinical teams being directly involved in the practice. In this chapter, we explore whether a de-medicalized, civic assisted dying model involving third sector organizations (outside of health care) working with an external review panel, rather than a medicalized approach (within the healthcare system), should be considered. We use the term 'assisted dying' to encompasses a patient receiving medication to end their life which is either self-administered (assisted suicide) or administered by someone else (euthanasia).

Medicalized assisted dying: the Oregon example

The approach used in Oregon is assisted suicide only, and often considered as the possible model for the UK. It has been explored by the Health and Social Care Committee and its medicalized approach to assisted dying is reflected in the most recent Bill that sought to reform the law in England and Wales (House of Lords 2021). Other jurisdictions will have different models for how assisted dying is or ought to be provided, but the same question about medical involvement is still relevant. Through the Death With Dignity Act (DWDA), Oregon was the first jurisdiction to permit assisted suicide in 1997 (euthanasia is prohibited by federal law in the USA), for people with a prognosis of less than 6 months. When we talk about an assisted dying model such as Oregon's, the process (involving three sequential requests for a prescription for lethal medication and physician assessment) does not happen within hours or minutes of a death. It needs to be planned for and so may start weeks in advance to ensure the competency and the ability of the person who wants assisted suicide to perform the act.

The attraction of the Oregon system is that the rates of death by assisted suicide have remained low, although there was a 28 per cent increase in rates in 2021 (Riley 2023). Most people accessing assisted suicide in Oregon tend to be well educated and have sufficient access to funds to cover the costs – estimated at about US$5,000. This raises questions of equality of access and the costs alone may limit the numbers using it. The Oregon system also runs into problems with its implementation for two reasons. First, there can be difficulty in identifying a doctor to assess a patient's competency and then prescribe, *and* in identifying a pharmacist willing to dispense the required medicines. Second, reviews of cases are retrospective, meaning there is no oversight by a review panel prior to the occurrence of assisted suicide.

Difficulties in implementing assisted dying into healthcare systems

There is an uneasy relationship between assisted dying and healthcare systems. Research conducted in the Netherlands showed that for healthcare professionals, and doctors in particular who were performing euthanasia, it was 'stressful to kill somebody' (Lewis and Preston 2019). Some doctors needed time off following administering euthanasia, limited the number they carried out, or even moved away from areas of work where these requests were likely to occur. Many doctors who support legal reform in the UK also acknowledge they do not wish to be involved in assisting a death (BMA 2020; Mahase 2023). This is not surprising given that, based on some estimates, only a small proportion of doctors in countries where it is legal to assist a death actually get involved (Gamondi et al. 2019).[1] All healthcare team members are impacted by an assisted death. It stays with you, is never normal, and is potentially an emotional burden (Lewis and Preston 2019). Hospitals are also reluctant to be associated with assisted dying (Digby et al. 2022), so in many cases the death takes place in the home setting. Is there another option which reduces involvement of the healthcare service?

A de-medicalized, civic approach

Perhaps instead we should look to countries which operate assisted dying outside of the healthcare system, such as Switzerland and Austria. Article 115 of the Swiss Penal Code outlaws 'incitement or assistance to suicide from selfish motives'. So you can assist someone to die if you do not personally benefit. In the 1970s, right-to-die associations began to promote this Article to assist someone to die so long as this was not done for selfish purposes. As no role is specifically set out for doctors, when they get involved they do so as people performing a civic rather than medical act (Gamondi et al. 2018). Assisted dying is predominantly conducted by right-to-die associations (Fischer et al. 2008). Volunteer doctors perform assessments of a patient's competence and eligibility and prescribe medications. It is rare for a patient's treating doctor to be involved.

However, difficulties exist with the Swiss approach. Navigation of the assisted dying procedures is heavily reliant on a supportive family member or friend. Research suggests the decision for an assisted death is only shared with a very limited number of people (Gamondi et al. 2019, 2020). Discussing their desire for an assisted death can be exhausting and patients could face challenges by friends and family if shared too widely, resulting in secrecy. This places a burden on those they have disclosed their wishes to and asked for help. They navigate the system together in isolation. This can be made worse as they attempt to enable the death with their own doctors, who in many cases are trying to distance themselves from the assisted death and in some cases delay the process. Indeed, in interviews with palliative care doctors (Gamondi et al. 2019), none had prescribed or even made assessments to demonstrate a patient's capacity. The legal vacuum doctors find themselves in gives them freedom as to when to get involved, but can result in people being lost in the system.

An enhanced de-medicalized, civic model as a potential alternative

Learning from the Swiss experience, an enhanced de-medicalized model (Ost 2010) may be preferable for those countries, like the UK, where a change in the law is being contemplated (see Figure 19.1). It would remove the need to embed assisted dying in the healthcare service, so there would be no loss of trust or confidence in healthcare staff, a fear repeatedly expressed in parliamentary debates and reflected in memories of the Liverpool Care Pathway debacle. This might also offer protection to people who may be potentially vulnerable and could be coerced (Ost and Biggs 2021) through a system of prospective review such as we propose below.

To avoid people being lost when navigating the system, there would need to be clear public messaging about how to access an assisted death. The Austrian assisted dying model might offer a solution, with a review panel requiring reports from specialists including in palliative care. A panel would improve monitoring both before and after the death. In most countries, reviews only happen after assisted dying. This means there is no oversight of the whole process, with estimates that up to 50 per cent of assisted deaths in Belgium are never recorded (Riley 2023). There is growing recognition that some review of applications for assisted dying is required *prior* to its occurrence. A panel process offers greater support for potentially vulnerable people, removes the decision from doctors alone (because besides a healthcare professional, these panels could also include a psychiatrist, palliative care specialist, lawyer and ethicist), and means cases are logged and can be followed up. These panels could be accountable and report to the High Court. Or they could be regulated by a newly constituted assisted dying tribunal, akin to the Law Commission's surrogacy law reform proposal involving the Human Fertilization and Embryology Authority holding regulated surrogacy organizations to account (Law Commission and Scottish Law Commission 2023: 53).

Crucial to all of this would be assessment of mental capacity and assurance that all options, including palliative care, had been explored. As in all jurisdictions where assisted dying is permitted, the person requesting the assisted death must have capacity at the time of death. This would be a crucial feature of the review panel. It would also be necessary to check for any undue influence or pressure through the use of a screening tool (Ost and Biggs 2021: 194). Part of the assessment could be a palliative care specialist's consultation report to demonstrate all options had been explored. These reports would need to be approved by the review panel. And just because a request for an assisted death was approved, this would not mean that it must be acted on. It is unclear how many people prepare the paperwork to gain an assisted death but do not use it. In Canada, of the people who chose not to have an assisted death, for 40 per cent of them it was because palliative care was enough (Government of Canada 2023).

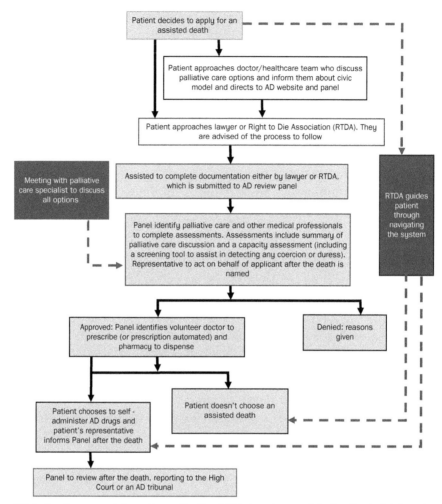

Figure 19.1 Draft proposal for a de-medicalized/third-sector model of self-administered assisted dying (AD).

Family members and friends must also not be forgotten. They need support when going through the procedure and also after the death. Their bereavement experience following an assisted death is potentially as good, if not better, than a natural death (Lowers et al. 2020). This may be, in part, because they know they have respected the person's wishes in helping them, but also because they know when to expect the death. However, they rarely seem to access bereavement services, perhaps to maintain secrecy about the nature of the death (Gamondi et al. 2018, 2019). Concerns may arise after the death when friends or family who were not party to the decision then find out and feel excluded. This can feel like a sudden unexpected death, which we know can result in more complex bereavement. Hence methods to support families both during and after the assisted death are vital.

Public expectations versus reality

When members of the public talk about an assisted death, they may envisage a doctor who has cared for them, sitting at their bedside, administering lethal drugs. This is unlikely to happen in any jurisdiction, with so few doctors willing to be involved. A balance is needed between what the public want and what is best for the health service and the individuals working within it. In some ways, British people have already shown support for a de-medicalized model in seeking an assisted death in Switzerland. If there were a change in the law, rather than travelling to Switzerland, most people could die at home. This would reduce patients' and families' distress at such a difficult time.

Conclusion

An enhanced de-medicalized approach would remove direct involvement from the health service and offer protection to potentially vulnerable patients with safeguards involving stronger regulation and prospective review. We advocate that a de-medicalized approach to assisted dying be carefully considered in the UK and in other jurisdictions contemplating a change in their laws.

Note

1. For Oregon statistics, see: https://www.oregon.gov/oha/ph/providerpartnerresources/ evaluationresearch/deathwithdignityact/pages/ar-index.aspx (accessed 15 February 2024).

References

British Medical Association (BMA) (2020) *BMA Survey on Physician-Assisted Suicide*. London: Kantar. Available at: https://www.bma.org.uk/media/3367/bma-physician-assisted-dying-survey-report-oct-2020.pdf (accessed 15 February 2024).

Digby, R., McDougall, R., Gold, M. et al. (2022) Introducing voluntary assisted dying: staff perspectives in an acute hospital, *International Journal of Health Policy and Management*, 11 (6): 777–85.

Fischer, S., Huber, C.A., Imhof, L. et al. (2008) Suicide assisted by two Swiss right-to-die organisations, *Journal of Medical Ethics*, 34 (11): 810–14.

Gamondi, C., Borasio, G.D., Oliver, P. et al. (2019) Responses to assisted suicide requests: an interview study with Swiss palliative care physicians, *BMJ Supportive & Palliative Care*, 9: e7. Available at: http://dx.doi.org/10.1136/bmjspcare-2016-001291 (accessed 15 February 2024).

Gamondi, C., Pott, M., Preston, N. and Payne, S. (2018) Family caregivers' reflections on experiences of assisted suicide in Switzerland: a qualitative interview study, *Journal of Pain and Symptom Management*, 55 (4): 1085–94.

Gamondi, C., Pott, M., Preston, N. and Payne, S. (2020) Swiss families' experiences of interactions with providers during assisted suicide: a secondary data analysis of an interview study, *Journal of Palliative Medicine*, 23 (4): 506–12.

Government of Canada (2023) *Fourth Annual Report on Medical Assistance in Dying in Canada 2022*. Available at: https://www.canada.ca/en/health-canada/services/publications/

health-system-services/annual-report-medical-assistance-dying-2022.html#a7 (accessed 15 February 2024).

House of Lords (2021) *Assisted Dying Bill* [HL 13]. Available at: https://bills.parliament.uk/publications/41676/documents/322 (accessed 5 February 2024).

Law Commission and Scottish Law Commission (2023) *Building Families Through Surrogacy: A New Law, vol. I: Core Report* [HC 1236]. Available at: https://s3-eu-west-2.amazonaws.com/cloud-platform-e218f50a4812967ba1215eaecede923f/uploads/sites/30/2023/03/1.-Surrogacy-core-report.pdf (accessed 15 February 2024).

Lewis, D. and Preston N. (2019) Dutch healthcare professionals experiences of assisted dying: a constructivist qualitative study conducted in a chronic disease care centre and hospice, *Research Square*, posted 2 August.' Available at: https://doi.org/10.21203/rs.2.11826/v1 (accessed 18 April 2024).

Lowers, J., Scardaville, M., Hughes, S. and Preston, N. (2020) Comparison of the experience of caregiving at end of life or in hastened death: a narrative synthesis review, *BMC Palliative Care*, 19: 154. Available at: https://doi.org/10.1186/s12904-020-00660-8.

Mahase, E. (2023) Royal College of Surgeons of England moves to neutral position on assisted dying, *British Medical Journal*, 381: 1397. Available at: https://doi.org/10.1136/bmj.p1397.

Ost, S. (2010) The de-medicalisation of assisted dying: is a less medicalised model the way forward?, *Medical Law Review*, 18 (4): 497–540.

Ost, S. and Biggs, H. (2021) *Exploitation, Ethics and Law*. Abingdon: Routledge.

Riley, S. (2023) Watching the watchmen: changing tides in the oversight of medical assistance in dying, *Journal of Medical Ethics*, 49 (7): 453–57.

20 De-medicalization: why we should completely separate assisted dying from health care and what this would achieve

H. Lucy Thomas

Introduction

The debate about legalizing assisted dying is highly polarized and dominated by voices at the extremes. Those determined to legalize assisted dying at any cost dismiss, rather than engage with, concerns about significant unintended consequences. At the other end of the spectrum are those who believe that ending one's life is morally wrong in all circumstances. Those of us who believe *both* that there are legitimate reasons why people might want the potential option of an assisted death *and* that there are major flaws in current approaches to assisted dying are rarely heard. This is not the basis for good law-making.

I am not opposed to the principle of legalizing a mechanism for assisting people to end their lives in certain very specific circumstances. However, as a doctor working in both palliative care and public health, I have profound concerns about the implications of the current medicalized approach for individual patients and wider society (Thomas 2020). Yet there is nothing inevitable about embedding assisted dying in health care – ending someone's life is not a medical procedure and giving someone a standard lethal dose of a toxic chemical requires no medical knowledge or skills.

There have been occasional thoughtful proposals for removing aspects of assisted dying from health care – including establishing a multidisciplinary panel to determine eligibility with regulatory oversight from the High Court or an independent tribunal (see Chapter 19), or giving the courts the role of judging applications and licensing non-medical practitioners as providers (Fritz 2019). Unfortunately, such proposals have been almost entirely ignored.

In this chapter, I will go a step further and question the role of medicine at every stage of the assisted death process – challenging not only the role of doctors as arbiters and administrators, but also the use of illness and disability as the criteria for what constitutes an acceptable reason to end one's life. I argue that complete de-medicalization is required not only to avoid the specific highly problematic consequences of locating assisted dying within health care, but to free us to think more critically about the circumstances in which it might be justifiable to assist someone to end their life and how this might safely be achieved.

Why illness and disability as the eligibility criteria?

There is an implicit assumption on both sides of the debate that if assisted dying is legalized the presence of some form of illness or disability should be pivotal criteria determining access. While this shapes all aspects of our thinking on assisted dying, it is almost never explicitly justified or questioned. Even the purpose of legalizing access to assisted dying in the circumstances described by the criteria is unclear.

In some jurisdictions, such as the US states where the practice has been legalized, if an adult has decision-making capacity, then the presence of a terminal illness – with an arbitrary prognosis of less than 6 months to live – is the one and only factor determining eligibility (Oregon Health Authority 2024). The law does not require that such individuals are experiencing any suffering, nor that they have received any alternative support or care. In jurisdictions where assisted dying is available to people whose illness or disability is not thought to be terminal, there is usually a requirement that they are experiencing 'unbearable' or 'intolerable' suffering. Some laws also specify that this suffering 'cannot be relieved under conditions they consider acceptable'. However, as we shall see, this does not mean that attempts must actually have been made to try to achieve this.

The usual societal response to someone expressing the desire to end their life is suicide prevention. In contemporary secular societies, this is not driven by a belief that life is sacred or that people should not have the right to make profound decisions about their lives that others might think are unwise. Instead, we try to prevent someone ending their life because it is a completely irreversible act that precludes any future decision-making – whereas most despair that leads people to want to do so is not irreversible. Rather than providing a rationale for why someone with terminal or incurable illness or disability expressing the desire to end their life should be treated in a fundamentally different way to someone without, advocates try to deflect any comparison between the practice of assisted dying and suicide. Their campaign materials focus on the prospect of unbearable pain and other physical suffering if the practice is not legalized – implying that this is the main motivation for seeking an assisted death and makes it fundamentally different to the desire to end life in all other circumstances. Some even claim that the fact that those with a terminal diagnosis are 'dying anyway' means that they cannot, apparently by definition, be suicidal. However, this supposed distinction misrepresents both the reasons why individuals access assisted dying and what we know about suicidality.

How does the desire for an assisted death differ from suicidality?

Contrary to common myths about suicide, suicidal thoughts are common and not necessarily associated with mental illness, and most people who are suicidal just want to bring an end to their suffering rather than actively want to die (Samaritans 2024). Suicidality is always complex and multifactorial, but suicidal ideation is more likely when people feel defeated or humiliated and believe they are powerless – 'entrapped' in a situation from which there is no way out (O'Connor 2021). This is aggravated by 'perceived burdensomeness' – the feeling many suicidal people have that they are a burden on others. Far from distinguishing people with suicidal ideation from those seeking an assisted death, these feelings and beliefs are common in those with advanced illness and disability (Monforte-Royo et al. 2012) and are key motivations for wanting to access assisted dying. Despite the campaigning focus on unbearable pain, the officially reported 'end-of-life concerns' of the terminally ill patients who have accessed an assisted death in the US state of Oregon show that pain and other physical symptoms have been minority concerns, with 'losing autonomy', 'less able to engage in activities that make life enjoyable', 'loss of dignity' and 'being a burden on family, friends/caregivers' being by far the predominant factors (Oregon Health Authority 2024).

Of particular relevance to how we respond to someone expressing the desire to end their life, a terminal or incurable medical condition does not mean that someone's wish to end their life is fixed or irreversible. Those with advanced and terminal illness and disability are often adapting to rapidly changing circumstances and are situationally vulnerable. Far too often they are struggling to access appropriate treatment, care and enablement services, and feeling marginalized, devalued or even abandoned by society. Unsurprisingly, addressing these issues can radically change how someone feels about whether their remaining life is worth living. Interventions, like a move to a different care setting, can change even 'long-lasting and apparently consolidated wishes to die' (Ohnsorge et al. 2014).

The discriminatory assumptions underlying medical eligibility criteria

As there is no robust justification for using advanced illness and disability to determine access to assisted dying, it is difficult to see these criteria as anything other than discriminatory – reflecting and reinforcing prejudicial attitudes about what makes a life worth living. The fact that this is almost never challenged reflects the depth of unconscious disablism in society. The use of any other protected characteristic – age, sex, race or gender identity – to determine whether to prevent or assist someone ending their life would certainly not go unquestioned.

The role of doctors in suicide prevention and assisted dying

Doctors are at the forefront of suicide prevention. The usual medical response to a patient expressing the desire to end their life includes exploring the reasons why they feel their life is no longer worth living and working alongside others to address issues amenable to intervention. As people considering ending their lives are often experiencing 'cognitive constriction' (O'Connor 2021) – the inability to see there could be any other possible route out of their suffering – helping them to see otherwise takes time and skill. By supporting a patient through this process, a doctor shows they value their patient's life at a time when the patient is struggling to do so themselves. A doctor cannot simultaneously try to prevent a patient from ending their life and assist them to do so – and by assisting they affirm the patient's view that their remaining life is not worth living. Some patients who access assisted dying specifically mention how the involvement of a doctor validates their decision to end their life and prevents them from 'having to take full responsibility' for it (Richards 2017). Given the powerful influence of the doctor–patient relationship, the UK Crown Prosecution Service has formally advised prosecutors that the involvement of a doctor in assisting a patient to end their life would be a public interest factor in favour of prosecution (CPS 2014; see Chapter 12). Similarly, we might expect the medical profession to be specifically prohibited from any involvement in legalized assisted dying. Instead, the medical approach to assisted dying gives doctors the determining role: using the presence or absence of terminal or incurable illness or disability as the pivotal factor to decide who should be supported to find a way through their suffering and who should instead be assisted to end their life, and then actively assisting the latter. This does not enhance patient autonomy. It extends medical power and authority, with doctors enacting societal judgements about which lives are worth living.

The consequences of medicalized assisted dying

In addition to the direct impact of using prejudicial criteria to determine the healthcare response to a patient's suffering, the medical approach to assisted dying has a number of other specific problematic consequences.

Erasing the centuries-old boundary between providing medical care and deliberately ending a patient's life creates risks and uncertainties for both patients and doctors. This is compounded by the euphemistic language used; with ending a life variously termed 'assisted dying', 'assistance in dying', or even providing 'dignity in dying', it is not surprising that the public are unclear about the difference between this and palliative care (Curia Market Research 2017). In my clinical practice, it is not uncommon for patients to be reluctant to come into the hospice for fear of being 'bumped off', and I often have to reassure them we will not be hastening their death. Unfortunately, such concerns might not be completely misplaced in countries where the absolute prohibition on doctors ending their patients' lives is lifted, with doctors in the Netherlands describing the pressure they can come under from relatives to perform euthanasia even when the patient is not clearly requesting it themselves (Snijdewind et al. 2018).

Some of the evolution in the practice of assisted dying that has occurred over time in countries where the practice has been legalized is a direct logical consequence of legalizing assisted dying as a medical procedure.

First, with assisted dying framed as a medical treatment, it is difficult to justify restricting access to an arbitrarily defined group of patients. Canada legalized assisted dying for patients with mental capacity and a terminal illness in 2016. Less than 5 years later, the requirement that a patient's natural death be 'reasonably foreseeable' was dropped following legal challenge (Government of Canada 2024). Given that those who lack mental capacity should receive the same standard of health care as everyone else, the next logical step has been to extend assisted dying to those who lack decision-making capacity. In Canada, someone whose natural death is reasonably foreseeable can now receive an assisted death if they had the capacity to consent when they initially made the request, but they do not need to have retained this capacity when they are 'assisted' to end their lives. In the Netherlands, it is now possible to make a request for euthanasia in anticipation of future circumstances – which would need to be respected even if the individual lacks the capacity to consent when these circumstances arise. This has been upheld by the courts despite examples of patients with dementia having lethal chemicals hidden in their drink and/or being physically restrained so they can receive an 'assisted death' (BBC 2020a). In recent years, Belgium and the Netherlands have extended eligibility for euthanasia to children of any age (BBC 2020b).

Secondly, if assisted dying is a medical procedure, to ensure equity of access it would have to be actively offered to eligible individuals, not only made available to those who know they can request it. In addition, as budget-holders are required to make the best use of scarce resources, it is inevitable that its 'cost-effectiveness' will come to be compared with other healthcare options. Canada provides a salutary lesson on how rapidly these changes can occur and quite how far this logic can lead. Within months of passing their initial legalization in 2016, health economists had estimated the tens of millions of dollars that the healthcare budget would save by providing assisted dying instead of meeting treatment and care costs (Trachtenberg and Manns 2017). Although the current iteration of their legislation supposedly limits assisted dying to those whose illness or disability is leading to 'unbearable mental or physical suffering' that 'cannot be relieved under conditions they consider acceptable', there are increasing examples of individuals being offered an assisted death at the point of receiving a terminal diagnosis despite expressing no desire to end their lives (Gardner et al. 2024), and of disabled people being actively offered the same route when they express distress that their essential care needs are not being met (CBC 2022).

De-medicalizing assisted dying

Given the damaging implications of the medical approach to assisted dying, those of us who are not opposed to it in principle should be actively exploring alternative approaches.

The practical aspects of administering an assisted death outside the healthcare system are relatively straightforward – and there are clear precedents. Despite common misconceptions, assisted dying has not been legalized in Switzerland, it is just that assisting a suicide is not illegal and private organizations like Dignitas have set themselves up to do so outside the healthcare system. In the absence of any regulatory framework, doctors are involved in prescribing the standard doses of the lethal chemical used – although its administration is usually left to lay volunteers. However, as with all other chemicals used for non-healthcare purposes, there is no reason why a chemical used for the non-therapeutic purpose of ending someone's life should require a medical prescription. Instead, a regulatory framework could be set up to provide the required chemical and train and oversee non-clinical practitioners completely outside the healthcare system.

Deciding who should have access to an assisted death is more complex, and would require us to be very clear about what legalizing assisted dying aims to achieve. If the aim is to provide an adult with mental capacity experiencing truly irremediable suffering with the means to end their life safely, then surely eligibility should be based on an assessment that everything possible had been done to address their suffering and to support them to feel valued – and that despite this they have continued with a consistent and unambiguous desire to end their life. When assessing the intractability of someone's suffering, the underlying factors would only be relevant insofar as they impact on options for intervention – there would be no justification for treating suffering related to illness or disability differently to that related to all other circumstances. Relevant professionals, including healthcare staff, would be required to provide evidence of what had been done to address the individual's suffering and any additional options that might exist. The role of assessing and weighing up that evidence and making a final judgement would best be given to the courts, who have the relevant expertise in such matters.

Under such an approach AD would be an option of absolutely last resort, only for consideration when all other options have been exhausted. There would still be a risk that in a resource-constrained environment it might, in practice, come to be considered before other more resource-intensive interventions. Formally acknowledging this risk and locating decision-making within the courts would help to prevent this from happening, but any law would need to be carefully drafted and monitored to ensure that this did not occur.

Alternatively, if the aim is, as many advocates state, to promote autonomy – providing adults with mental capacity the 'right to choose how and when to die' – then serious work would need to be done to elaborate what this would mean in practice. While the concept of a 'rational suicide' has deep philosophical roots (Mayo 1986), this has not been operationalized into a practical means of distinguishing an individual with a 'rational' desire to end their life that should be facilitated from someone whose desire is 'irrational' and should be prevented (see Chapter 29). If this were to be truly about self-determination and autonomous decision-making, an assessment of the rationality of an individual's decision to end their life should not be based on whether it aligns with external judgements about what makes a life worth living, again precluding the use of illness and disability as eligibility criteria. There are a number of significant social, ethical and practical hurdles to developing and implementing such an approach – not least the existence of a strong societal consensus in favour of suicide prevention – which those who genuinely believe in providing this autonomous 'right to choose' would need to address.

Conclusion

There is an almost entirely unquestioned assumption that if assisted dying is legalized, it should be completely embedded within health care, with medical criteria for what constitutes an acceptable reason for ending one's life and doctors as both arbiters and administrators. This medicalized approach has a number of specific highly problematic consequences. De-medicalizing assisted dying – completely separating every aspect of the practice from health care – would avoid these particular repercussions and free us to think more critically about the circumstances in which it might be justifiable to assist someone to end their life and how this might safely be achieved.

References

British Broadcasting Corporation (BBC) (2020a) Euthanasia: Dutch court expands law on dementia cases, *BBC News*, 21 April. Available at: https://www.bbc.co.uk/news/world-europe-52367644 (accessed 14 April 2024).

British Broadcasting Corporation (BBC) (2020b) Netherlands backs euthanasia for terminally ill children under-12, *BBC News*, 14 October. Available at: https://www.bbc.co.uk/news/world-europe-54538288 (accessed 17 April 2024).

Canadian Broadcasting Corporation (CBC) (2022) RCMP called to investigate multiple cases of veterans being offered medically assisted death, *CBC News*, 24 November Available at: https://www.cbc.ca/news/politics/veterans-maid-rcmp-investigation-1.6663885 (accessed 14 April 2024).

Crown Prosecution Service (CPS) (2014) *Suicide: Policy for Prosecutors in Respect of Cases of Encouraging or Assisting Suicide*. Available at: https://www.cps.gov.uk/legal-guidance/suicide-policy-prosecutors-respect-cases-encouraging-or-assisting-suicide (accessed 11 July 2024).

Curia Market Research (2017) *Euthanasia Issues Poll*. Available at: https://euthanasiadebate.org.nz/wp-content/uploads/2018/06/Euthanasia-Poll-Results-November-2017.pdf (accessed 17 April 2024).

Fritz, Z. (2019) The courts should judge applications for assisted suicide, sparing the doctor-patient relationship, *The BMJ Opinion*, 30 January. Available at: https://blogs.bmj.com/bmj/2019/01/30/the-courts-should-judge-applications-for-assisted-suicide-sparing-the-doctor-patient-relationship/ (accessed 18 April 2024).

Gardner, B., Herx, L. and Gaind, S. (2024) What is going on with MAID in Canada?, *Geripal Podcast*, 11 January. Available at: https://geripal.org/what-is-going-on-with-maid-in-canada-bill-gardner-leonie-herx-sonu-gaind/ (accessed 14 April 2024).

Government of Canada (2024) *Medical Assistance in Dying: Legislation in Canada*. Available at: https://www.canada.ca/en/health-canada/services/health-services-benefits/medical-assistance-dying/legislation-canada.html (accessed 17 April 2024).

Mayo, D.J. (1986) The concept of rational suicide, *Journal of Medicine and Philosophy*, 11 (2): 143–55.

Monforte-Royo, C., Villavicencio-Chávez, C., Tomás-Sábado, J. et al. (2012) What lies behind the wish to hasten death? A systematic review and meta-ethnography from the perspective of patients, *PLoS ONE*, 7(5): e37117. Available at: https://doi.org/10.1371/journal.pone.0037117 (accessed 18 April 2024).

O'Connor, R. (2021) *When It is Darkest: Why People Die by Suicide and What We Can Do to Prevent It*. London: Vermilion.

Ohnsorge, K., Gudat, H. and Rehmann-Sutter, C. (2014) Intentions in wishes to die: analysis and a typology – a report of 30 qualitative case studies of terminally ill cancer patients in palliative care, *Psycho-Oncology*, 23 (9): 1021–26.

Oregon Health Authority (2024) *Death with Dignity Act*. Available at: https://www.oregon.gov/oha/PH/PROVIDERPARTNERRESOURCES/EVALUATIONRESEARCH/DEATHWITHDIGNITYACT/Pages/index.aspx (accessed 17 April 2024).

Richards, N. (2017) Assisted suicide as a remedy for suffering? The end-of-life references of British 'suicide tourists', *Medical Anthropology: Cross Cultural Studies in Health and Illness*, 36 (4): 348–62.

Samaritans (2024) *Myths about Suicide*. Available at: https://www.samaritans.org/how-we-can-help/if-youre-worried-about-someone-else/myths-about-suicide/ (accessed 14 April 2024).

Snijdewind, M.C., van Tol, D.G., Onwuteaka-Philipsen, B.D. and Willems, D.L. (2018) Developments in the practice of physician-assisted dying: perceptions of physicians who had experience with complex cases, *Journal of Medical Ethics*, 44 (5): 292–96.

Thomas, H.L. (2020) Demedicalisation: radically reframing the assisted dying debate – an essay by Lucy Thomas, *British Medical Journal*, 371: m2919. Available at: https://doi.org/10.1136/bmj.m2919 (accessed 18 April 2024).

Trachtenberg, A.J. and Manns, B. (2017) Cost analysis of medical assistance in dying in Canada, *Canadian Medical Association Journal*, 189: E101–5. Available at: https://doi.org/10.1503/cmaj.160650 (accessed 18 April 2024).

21 The enigma of lethal drugs

Claud Regnard[1]

Introduction

The process of introducing new medication is detailed, prolonged and exhaustive. It starts with three stages of clinical trials that provide evidence of safety and efficacy and can take a decade or more. It must then be authorized by a drug regulatory authority, taking a further 1–2 years. Even when approved, new drugs are closely monitored for unexpected problems, often over several years. This last stage is crucial and has uncovered serious problems with drugs that later had to be withdrawn. Even when drugs are re-licensed for a completely different use, scrutiny is required. It is therefore remarkable that lethal combinations of drugs used in assisted suicide and euthanasia (AS&E) have never gone through any of these stages anywhere in the world. Despite the decades of use of AS&E drugs, there is a dearth of published, objective research. All this contrasts with a plethora of anecdotal claims of their efficacy and safety. At the very least, one would expect close monitoring, particularly in the early years of use, and for this to be transparently published, with monitoring of key parameters after administration and blood levels at death. In reality, most AS&E services produce no data, and AS&E jurisdictions either produce scant data or have large gaps in their data (Worthington et al. 2022).

Are palliative care drugs lethal?

Sadly, it is too common a belief that opioids such as morphine have a life-shortening risk when used for pain relief. If this were true, opioids would be a major component of drugs used in assisted suicide/euthanasia, but in fact they play little or no role in these procedures. Many studies have shown that the use of strong analgesics does not hasten death when used by specialists for severe and complex pain and even when used for refractory breathlessness (McPherson et al. 2019; Schofield et al. 2020; Hamatani et al. 2023). Careful use of sedatives has also been shown not to hasten death (Yokomichi et al. 2022). It is a myth that specialist palliative medicine doctors are regularly faced with the dilemma of risking the patient's death to treat severe pain or distress. This 'double effect' concept is not seen in specialist palliative care for several reasons (Regnard et al. 2018). Specialists always adjust drugs to the individual, start with low doses, use routes that allow slow absorption to avoid sudden peaks in blood levels, and allow time for side-effects to wear off or become apparent. If side-effects occur, alternative drugs are used, often in combination with other drugs and treatments. The perception that this is an unacceptably slow process is incorrect. With close monitoring it can take as little as a few hours or days, during which time the patient and family are helped to feel supported and listened to, such that their distress has already reduced while medications are taking effect. Using the defence of 'double effect' in the death of a terminal patient indicates ignorance, negligence or criminal behaviour (Regnard et al. 2018).

Assisted suicide and euthanasia drugs and doses

The variety and number of drugs used in assisted suicide/euthanasia is surprising (Table 21.1); they are usually given in combinations of four or five drugs.

Different AS&E jurisdictions and services use different drugs. Jurisdictions such as Oregon use oral drug mixtures for assisted suicide, combining two to three sedatives, an analgesic and a cardiotoxic drug (Oregon Health Authority, undated). Antiemetics are given before ingestion to reduce the risk of vomiting after swallowing the 100–150 ml bitter-tasting mixture. Oregon has tried four different combinations over 8 years. Despite having the option of using the oral route, jurisdictions such as Canada principally give drugs intravenously, using a combination of two sedatives and a neuromuscular agent given sequentially (analgesics are not used) (CAMAP 2020). Many AS&E services, such as Dignitas in Switzerland, publish no details of the drugs or routes used.

Doses of drugs used vary between jurisdictions, but they are all several orders of magnitude higher than standard therapeutic doses. Lethal oral doses can be 30 to 300 times accepted therapeutic doses; lethal intravenous doses vary from five

Table 21.1: List of drugs used in assisted suicide and euthanasia

Drugs prescribed for assisted suicide *(usually oral administration)*	Drugs prescribed for euthanasia *(usually intravenous administration)*
Sedatives Amitriptyline Barbiturates (5 types) Benzodiazepines (3 types) Chloral hydrate	*Sedatives* Barbiturates (5 types) Benzodiazepines (3 types) Choral hydrate Propofol
Analgesics Morphine Dextropropoxyphene	*Analgesics* Fentanyl Morphine
Cardiotoxic agents Digoxin Propranolol	*Cardiotoxic agents* Potassium chloride Bupivacaine
Antiemetics Metoclopramide Ondansetron Haloperidol	*Neuromuscular blockers (8 types)* Pancuronium and similar drugs

Adapted from Worthington et al. (2022).

to 24 times accepted therapeutic doses. However, doses and combinations vary greatly between jurisdictions and there is no universally agreed standard or protocol.

Overview of the research and evaluation of lethal drugs

It is an understandable assumption that each AS&E jurisdiction must have based their decisions on published research, thorough evaluation and close monitoring of the lethal drugs they were authorizing in law. This is incorrect. Several sources list the changes in drugs used but these are invariably retrospective, using data based on official data, questionnaires or interviews. There are very few prospective studies and those that exist were completed up to five decades ago. There are no studies looking at the chemical and physical reactions with high doses of AS&E drugs in oral or intravenous mixtures, a key issue since mixing can inactivate drugs or create new, active chemicals with unknown effects.

The lack of evaluative studies may be the reason for a remarkable fact. Not a single drug regulatory authority anywhere in the world has approved a lethal AS&E drug. Supporters of assisted suicide/euthanasia have claimed this is unnecessary since all lethal drugs have already been evaluated and approved for therapeutic purposes. Their view is that AS&E drugs are simply being used 'off-label'. Such use allows drugs to be used in doses and purposes outside regulatory approval. However, although approval exists for therapeutic doses, it does not exist for AS&E drug doses. For example, while a 1g dose of paracetamol is approved, a 300g dose is not and would never be accepted for off-label use. This is because off-label prescribing comes with responsibilities. Prescribers of off-label drugs must be satisfied by the evidence base of safety and efficacy. In addition, they must provide the patient with all available information – including that these are unapproved drugs – monitor and report any effects or complications. This happens infrequently or not at all in AS&E jurisdictions.

In view of this dearth of evidence, it would be expected that there would be close monitoring of current AS&E drug use. This is also incorrect. Official data is either absent or contains large gaps in the data. As stated above, Oregon has experimented with four different drug combinations in the last 8 years (Oregon Health Authority, undated), but this has not been studied under any patient safety study protocols. Canadian AS&E practitioners have produced recommendations for drug use but these are based in part on studies of fatal poisonings, not on prospective evaluations of assisted deaths (Harty et al. 2018). Other jurisdictions have changed their lethal drug protocols, again without study protocols. This lack of patient safeguards is concerning.

Evidence of efficacy and safety of lethal drugs

One of the earliest studies to look at the efficacy of AS&E drugs was approved by the Dutch Ministry of Health, the Dutch Ministry of Justice and the Royal Dutch Medical Association (Groenwoud et al. 2000). Despite the complication rate being up to 31 per cent, the study has never been repeated to assess if there has been any change. Oregon publishes the most detailed and regular updates on complications in their annual reports (Regnard et al. 2023). This shows complications with oral lethal drugs affecting one in nine patients on average. A peak complication rate of 14.8 per cent in 2015 coincided with some clinicians switching from barbiturates to lethal drug combinations. However, the true incidence of Oregon's complications is unknown for two reasons. First, in 2022, data on complications were missing in 74 per cent of assisted deaths; secondly, the complication rate does not include prolonged or failed deaths. Oregon's 2019 official report acknowledges that oral drug combinations have coincided with more prolonged deaths than when barbiturates were available. In 2020, Washington State Department of Health reported that 19 per cent took more than 2 hours to die, but this data is missing from subsequent reports.[2] Canadian AS&E guidance (Bakewell and Naik 2019) recognizes that complications can occur, although one of their key references (Groenwoud et al. 2000) is a study whose data are now over 30 years old.

Recent data about intravenous AS&E drugs are scarce. There is some information on this route for executions in the US, which use drug mixtures very similar to those used for euthanasia. A major problem arose when muscle paralysing agents were administered before sedatives had caused unconsciousness (Bogel-Burroughs 2022). Post-mortem blood levels of sedative in executed prisoners were found to be so low that some may have regained consciousness but been unable to express distress as they were paralysed with curare-like drugs (Zimmers et al. 2005).[3] Anecdotes from AS&E practitioners state that death is faster and more reliable, but there is no published data to support these claims and no study looking at the process leading to death.

Prescribers and pharmacists

The number of doctors willing to prescribe lethal drugs has been very low. Approximately 2 per cent of Canadian and Oregon physicians prescribe, with a smaller percentage in Australian states. Much of the prescribing is by a handful of physicians; for example, in Oregon one doctor wrote 12 per cent of AS&E prescriptions in 2022, with 78 per cent writing only one or two prescriptions. This means that most doctors practising AS&E do so with little experience.

The role of pharmacists is too often ignored (Flood 2020). It is an assumption that they would be willing to prepare and dispense unapproved lethal drugs, but their views have not been considered. As they would not be directly involved in an assisted death, it is unlikely they would have a right to conscientiously object.

Conclusions

Evaluations of the adverse effects and efficacy of lethal drug doses do not exist and monitoring is poor or non-existent. Unsurprisingly, there is no single route, protocol or method of ending life and there is no evidence that AS&E practitioners are systematically collating their experience to improve outcomes. The use of death as the only measure of success assumes the end justifies the means, regardless of the journey for the patient and family. This is akin to continuing the use of thalidomide because it was a successful antiemetic, while disregarding the tragedy that befell one group of vulnerable individuals. Thalidomide was initially approved by 17 countries and had considerably more evidence than currently exists for lethal drugs used in assisted suicide and euthanasia. What is clear with AS&E lethal drugs is that the data are insufficient and of too unacceptable quality to claim they are effective and safe. No therapeutic process requiring fundamental changes in practice and law would be accepted with such poor evidence.

Notes

1. Claud Regnard provides content for the website 'Keep Assisted Dying Out of Healthcare' (www.kadoh.uk). He is a member of the Association of Palliative Medicine of Great Britain and Ireland. From January to April 2024, he was a member of the content group for the Nuffield Council on Bioethics project on assisted dying. He is not a member of, or funded by, any advocacy group related to assisted dying. He is an agnostic.
2. Washington State Department of Health Annual Reports are available via: https://doh.wa.gov/data-and-statistical-reports/health-statistics/death-dignity-act/death-dignity-data (accessed 19 February 2024).
3. Zimmers et al., in connection with executions in the USA, concluded: 'Our evidence clearly indicates the potential for awareness during the unnecessarily complicated and error-prone process of lethal injection' (2005: 1075).

References

Bakewell, F. and Naik, V.N. (2019) *Complications with Medical Assistance in Dying (MAID) in the Community in Canada: Review and Recommendations.* Available at: https://camapcanada.ca/wp-content/uploads/2022/02/Failed-MAID-in-Community-FINAL-CAMAP-Revised.pdf (accessed 2 February 2024).
Bogel-Burroughs, N. (2022) Death penalty researchers call 2022 'Year of the Botched Execution', *New York Times*, 16 December. Available at: https://www.nytimes.com/2022/12/16/us/death-penalty-botched-executions.html (accessed 19 April 2024).
Canadian Association of MAiD Assessors and Providers (CAMAP) (2020) *Intravenous Maid Medication Protocols in Canada: Review and Recommendations.* Available at: https://camap-canada.ca/wp-content/uploads/2022/02/IV-protocol-final.pdf (accessed 1 February 2024).
Flood, B. (2020) Pharmacists and assisted dying, *British Medical Journal*, 368: m1139. Available at: https://doi.org/10.1136/bmj.m1139.
Groenwoud, J.H., van der Heide, A., Onwuteaka, B.D. et al. (2000) Clinical problems with the performance of euthanasia and physician-assisted suicide in the Netherlands, *New England Journal of Medicine*, 342 (8): 551–56.
Hamatani, Y., Iguchi, M., Moriuchi, K. et al. (2023) Effectiveness and safety of morphine administration for refractory dyspnoea among hospitalised patients with advanced heart failure: the Morphine-HF study, *BMJ Supportive & Palliative Care*, 13: e1300–7. Available at: https://doi.org/10.1136/spcare-2023-004247 (accessed 16 February 2024).
Harty, C., Chaput, A.J., Buna, D. et al. (2018) *The Oral MAiD Option in Canada. Part 1: Medication Protocols. Review and Recommendations*, Canadian Association of MAiD Assessors and Providers (CAMAP) White Paper. Available at: https://camapcanada.ca/wp-content/uploads/2022/02/OralMAiD-Med.pdf (accessed 1 February 2024).

McPherson, M.L., Walker, K.A., Davis, M.P. et al. (2019) Safe and appropriate use of methadone in hospice and palliative care: expert consensus white paper, *Journal of Pain and Symptom Management*, 57 (3): 635–45.

Oregon Health Authority (undated) *Death with Dignity Annual Reports*. Available at: https://www.oregon.gov/oha/ph/providerpartnerresources/evaluationresearch/deathwithdignityact/pages/ar-index.aspx (accessed 1 February 2024).

Regnard, C., George, R. and Profitt, A. (2018) Editorial: Dangerous opioids or dangerous prescribers?, *Palliative Medicine*, 32 (10): 1537–38.

Regnard, C., Worthington, A. and Finlay, I. (2023) Oregon Death with Dignity Act access: 25 year analysis, *BMJ Supportive & Palliative Care*. Available at: https://doi.org/10.1136/spcare-2023-004292 (accessed 1 February 2024).

Schofield, G., Baker, I., Bullock, R. et al. (2020) Palliative opioid use, palliative sedation and euthanasia: reaffirming the distinction, *Journal of Medical Ethics*, 46 (1): 48–50.

Worthington, A., Finlay, I. and Regnard, C. (2022) Efficacy and safety of drugs used for 'assisted dying', *British Medical Bulletin*, 142 (1): 15–22.

Yokomichi, N., Yamaguchi, T., Maeda, I. et al. (2022) Effect of continuous deep sedation on survival in the last days of life of cancer patients: a multicenter prospective cohort study, *Palliative Medicine*, 36 (1): 189–99.

Zimmers, T.A., Lubarsky, D.A., Sheldon, J.P. and Koniaris, L.G. (2005) Inadequate anaesthesia in lethal injection for execution – authors' reply, *Lancet*, 366 (9468): 1074–76.

PART 5

Safety and vulnerable groups

22 Disability – a duty to die?

Tanni Grey-Thompson and Flora Klintworth

Introduction: legislating for the everyday citizen

The saying 'no legislation is ever created within a vacuum' is highly relevant to the case of assisted suicide/euthanasia. The personal experience of one of the authors of this chapter (T.G-T.) as a legislator and disabled person has informed her deep reservations about any law in Britain on assisted suicide/euthanasia – even if solely focused on the 'terminally' ill. Since legislators must consider how a law would affect every member of society, this includes not just the terminally ill celebrities of Britain, but also the everyday citizens. Disabled people have a nuanced experience because legislating for assisted suicide/euthanasia has a practical and psychological effect on their lives. This chapter will discuss these effects but oriented around a central idea. Namely, that to condone the death of people who possess certain characteristics or symptoms of pain – such as the safeguard of a 'terminal' or 'irremediable' medical condition – creates a value judgement on those who resolve to live with these same traits. In other words, the positive discrimination required for safeguarding laws on assisted suicide/euthanasia creates unintended consequences for disabled people, and the risk of these adverse effects should outweigh any demand for a contrived interpretation of autonomy (see Chapter 27).

The muffled voices of people with disabilities

It is important to acknowledge the surprising under-representation of disabled people's voices in the debate on assisted suicide/euthanasia. First, there is a clear need for the disabled voice. Statistics from 2021 reveal that 16 million people in the UK have a disability – 18.7 per cent of women and 16.5 per cent of men (Department for Work and Pensions 2023; ONS 2023). A recent United Nations Special Rapporteur on the rights of persons with disabilities described UK policy and practice as a 'pervasive framework and rhetoric that devalues Disabled people's lives', which 'tells Disabled people that they're underserving citizens' (Disability Rights UK 2024). Within the context in which disabled people live in the UK, a policy on assisted suicide/euthanasia could have devaluing ramifications on their lives.

Secondly, no organization *of*, or *for*, disabled people supports a change in the law on assisted suicide/euthanasia. Meanwhile, various disability groups oppose it, such as Not Dead Yet UK (2024), who argue it is the disabled who would be most affected by any change in legislation. The group was founded in response to an increasing number of 'well co-ordinated campaigns aimed at legitimising the killing of terminally ill and disabled people' (Not Dead Yet UK 2024) – which leads to a final point.

Thirdly, the toll of taking a public stance on assisted suicide/euthanasia is not easy. Many disability rights campaigners opposed to assisted suicide/euthanasia simply do not have the same resources as multi-million-pound, celebrity-endorsed organizations, which means that facing accusations of 'wanting people to die badly' or 'denying choice' is extremely costly to these individuals.[1] Ultimately, many disabled people fight to get through each day, in spite of their disabilities, but using their capacity to take on high-level policy battles at the same time can be exhausting. Faced with a glamorous, celebrity-endorsed campaign for a change in the law, the already struggling disabled voice fails to make an impression.

Disabled discrimination in health care

The practice of assisted suicide/euthanasia in medicine should raise concerns on behalf of the disabled community. This is because the experience of disabled people – as demonstrated by the UN Special Rapporteur (Disability Rights UK 2024) – serves as a shocking reminder that the UK is still far from achieving equitable treatment for all. The inequitable treatment of disabled people is extremely relevant in health care.[2] For example, legislation during the Covid-19 pandemic was grossly inadequate, especially when blanket 'Do Not Resuscitate' (DNR) orders were imposed on people with disabilities (Ann Craft Trust 2024). T.G-T.'s personal experience of health care has been disappointing despite, as an elite-level athlete and parliamentarian, experiencing far greater 'privilege' than the everyday disabled person.[3] Furthermore, at a time when the NHS is under significant pressure, individuals who work in the healthcare system are fundamentally unequipped to serve people with disabilities. The evidence is overwhelming: from simple training on mental competency for those in the care sector, to more complicated issues of identifying vulnerability or abuse, British health care is lacking (Hollins 2018; Campbell 2021; Shepperd 2021). With legal mechanisms such as mental competency and settled choice being key requirements of most laws on assisted suicide/euthanasia, disabled people would likely be extremely vulnerable to a lack of safeguarding. This is the reality for many disabled people in Canada.

Upon her visit, the UN Special Rapporteur for the Rights of Disabled People was extremely concerned about the implications of Canada's Medical Assistance in Dying (MAiD) law on people with disabilities, hearing multiple complaints (United Nations 2019). She urged Canada to reform to ensure 'persons with disabilities do not request assisted dying simply because of the absence of community-based alternatives and palliative care' (Quinn et al. 2021). Clearly, disabled people 'slip through the cracks' of Canadian health care and, rather than reach a natural wall of safeguarding, now fall through the window of MAiD (see Chapters 4, 7 and 15). Even though the UK fails to protect its disabled citizens, how much more could it do so if assisted suicide/euthanasia were legalized?

'Better off dead': the psychological effect of assisted suicide/euthanasia on disabled people

The effect assisted suicide/euthanasia would have on societal attitudes towards disability is concerning. Allowing legislation on assisted suicide/euthanasia in any case introduces a value judgement that some people – disabled people – are 'better off dead'. For example, dignity can be lost, argues Dignity in Dying (2024), when a dying person experiences certain symptoms – such as pain, incontinence and dependence on others (see Chapter 28 for fuller discussion of dignity). But what does this mean for the disabled people who resolve to live with these symptoms, not just for the final few months or years, but every day of their lives? The internal feeling of being a burden is inevitable, especially since the NHS is under strain and assisted suicide/euthanasia has been proven by Canada to save money (Office of the Parliamentary Budget Officer 2020). But consider the external pressure that disabled people would feel from others to decide what value their life, or death, has. It is difficult to conceive of such a draconian phenomenon, but this already happens. For example, societal attitudes towards a partner killing their disabled loved one view it as an act of kindness or mercy. Are the victim's wishes ever considered? Or is it presumed that those with disabilities, particular cognitive disabilities, are 'obviously better off dead'? (Luterman 2020). Such an example reflects the increasing narrative that disabled and dying lives are fundamentally unliveable (Campbell 2019).

For a state to offer suicide prevention to some, and euthanasia to others, is the highest degree of cognitive dissonance. Many disabled people fear that to show any signs of melancholy, struggle with their disability, or frustration with their suffering, would be to affirm a wish to die (Hale 2018). But much like Britain's robust legal assumption of 'innocent until proven guilty', we must re-enforce the medical assumption of 'preserve life rather than end it', the focus on which would inevitably shift if assisted suicide/euthanasia were permitted (Campbell 2019).

Conclusion: a very real fear

This chapter illustrates the very real danger that assisted suicide/euthanasia poses to the lives of 16 million disabled people in the UK. Objections may be raised that terminal illness and old age differ from disability, but we challenge the reader to draw tangible symptomatic differences between these two groups. This makes some commentators' chilling words regarding the elderly and infirm's 'duty to die' far more real for disabled people (Parris 2024). Therefore, disabled people cannot avoid social prejudice that is 'institutionalised in the very fabric of our society'

(Barnes 1992). Perhaps the next time the notion of autonomy arises in debate, readers should spare a thought for disabled people's autonomy. Their fear is existential in nature: 'not just about losing the ability to do things for [themselves], but loss of control over both the details and direction of [their] everyday li[ves]' (Pulrang 2022). Assisted suicide/euthanasia would have a profound effect on disabled people; and it is about time their voices were taken seriously.

Notes

1. Such accusations are a common campaign strategy used by organizations campaigning for a law on assisted suicide/euthanasia (Riley and Hehir 2019).
2. There are a myriad of examples of people with disabilities experiencing discrimination, or a lack of reasonable accommodation. Though space does not allow for a full discussion of these factors, train accessibility is one such area where it will take roughly 100 years to make the entirety of the station estate step-free to new-build standards (Disabled Persons Transport Advisory Committee 2022).
3. Tanni Grey-Thompson writes: Being born with spina bifida, my parents were told that had I been born a few years earlier, I would have been taken away, not fed and left to die. My parents and I were put under great pressure to have various operations through my childhood that were unnecessary, like leg lengthening and bladder rebuilds. There was even discussion around the choice of whether to die or live.

References

Ann Craft Trust (2024) *How has covid-19 impacted adults with learning disabilities, physical disabilities, and visual and auditory impairments*. Available at: https://www.anncrafttrust.org/resources/how-has-covid-19-impacted-adults-with-learning-disabilities-physical-disabilities-and-visual-and-auditory-impairments/ (accessed 1 April 2024).

Barnes, C. (1992) *Disabling Imagery and the Media*. The British Council of Organizations of Disabled People. Halifax: Ryburn Publishing. Available at: https://disability-studies.leeds.ac.uk/wp-content/uploads/sites/40/library/Barnes-disabling-imagery.pdf (accessed 12 April 2024).

Campbell, J. (2019) Disabled people like me fear legal assisted suicide: it suggests that some lives are less worth living, *The BMJ Opinion*, 6 February. Available at: https://blogs.bmj.com/bmj/2019/02/06/disabled-people-like-me-fear-legal-assisted-suicide-it-suggests-that-some-lives-are-less-worth-living/ (accessed 2 April 2024).

Campbell, J. (2021) Debate on Domestic Abuse Bill, *Hansard*, vol. 811, Col. 1865. Available at: https://hansard.parliament.uk/Lords/2021-04-21/debates/99B0FAAA-A5C5-41A1-94CC-F1F-B0299C9C3/details#contribution-5A5009CD-AB74-4561-913F-92ACC2814EAB (accessed 16 April 2024).

Department for Work and Pensions (2023) *Family Resources Survey: Financial Year 2021 to 2022*. Available at: https://www.gov.uk/government/statistics/family-resources-survey-financial-year-2021-to-2022 (accessed 2 April 2024).

Dignity in Dying (2024) *Our Position*. Available at: https://www.dignityindying.org.uk/assisted-dying/our-position/ (accessed 2 April 2024).

Disability Rights UK (2024) *UN Rapporteurs Question UK Government Over Benefits Deaths and Austerity*, Press Release. Available at: https://www.disabilityrightsuk.org/news/un-rapporteurs-question-uk-government-over-benefits-deaths-and-austerity-press-release (accessed 16 April 2024).

Disabled Persons Transport Advisory Committee (2022) *DPTAC Reference Frame: Working Towards a Fully Accessible Railway*. Independent Report, 14 February. Available at: https://www.gov.uk/government/publications/dptac-reference-frame-working-towards-a-fully-accessible-railway/dptac-reference-frame-working-towards-a-fully-accessible-railway (accessed 2 April 2024).

Hale, J. (2018) We're told we are a burden. No wonder disabled people fear assisted suicide, *The Guardian*, 1 June. Available at: https://www.theguardian.com/commentisfree/2018/jun/01/disabled-people-assisted-dying-safeguards-pressure (accessed 3 April 2024).

Hollins, S. (2018) Debate on Mental Capacity (Amendment) Bill, *Hansard*, vol. 793, Col. 353. Available at: https://hansard.parliament.uk/Lords/2018-10-15/debates/CA98607A-04F2-4D74-B30E-3C22BC49E928/details#contribution-FA8F7F03-D9A0-4FD5-87C9-F4624F1D46F8 (accessed 16 April 2024).

Luterman, S. (2020) There is nothing loving about killing disabled people, *The Washington Post*, 1 January. Available at: https://www.washingtonpost.com/outlook/2020/01/01/there-is-nothing-loving-about-killing-disabled-people/ (accessed 2 April 2024).

Not Dead Yet UK (2024) *About*. Available at: https://notdeadyetuk.org/about/ (accessed 2 April 2024).

Office for National Statistics (ONS) (2023) *Disability by Age, Sex and Deprivation, England and Wales: Census 2021*. Available at: https://www.ons.gov.uk/peoplepopulationandcommunity/healthandsocialcare/disability/articles/disabilitybyagesexanddeprivationenglandandwales/census2021#cite-this-article (accessed 16 April 2024).

Office of the Parliamentary Budget Officer (2020) *Cost Estimate for Bill C-7 'Medical Assistance in Dying'*, 20 October. Available at: https://distribution-a617274656661637473.pbo-dpb.ca/241708b353e7782a9e5e713c2e281fc5ed932d3d07e9f5dd212e73604762bbc5 accessed (12 March 2024).

Parris, M. (2024) We can't afford a taboo on assisted dying, *The Times*, 29 March. Available at: https://www.thetimes.co.uk/article/we-cant-afford-a-taboo-on-assisted-dying-n6p8bfg9k (accessed 9 April 2024).

Pulrang, A. (2022) Understanding fear in the disability community, *Forbes*, 28 May. Available at: https://www.forbes.com/sites/andrewpulrang/2022/05/28/understanding-fear-in-the-disability-community/ (accessed 3 April 2024).

Quinn, G., Mahler, C. and de Schutter, O. (2021) *Mandates of the Special Rapporteur on the Rights of Persons with Disabilities; the Independent Expert on the Enjoyment of All Human Rights by Older Persons; and the Special Rapporteur on Extreme Poverty and Human Rights*, Reference OL CAN 2/2021, 3 February. Available at: https://spcommreports.ohchr.org/TMResultsBase/DownLoadPublicCommunicationFile?gId=26002 (accessed 12 April 2024).

Riley, L. and Hehir, D. (2019) *The Inescapable Truth: How seventeen people a day will suffer as they die*, Campaign for Dignity in Dying, September. Available at: https://www.dignityindying.org.uk/wp-content/uploads/DiD_Inescapable_Truth_WEB.pdf (accessed 2 April 2024).

Shepperd, L. (2021) Domestic abuse of older people, *In Focus*, House of Lords Library, 9 July. Available at: https://lordslibrary.parliament.uk/domestic-abuse-of-older-people/ (accessed 16 April 2024).

United Nations (2019) *End of Mission Statement by the United Nations Special Rapporteur on the Rights of Persons with Disabilities, Ms. Catalina Devendas-Aguilar, on Her Visit to Canada*. United Nations Human Rights, Office of the High Commission, 12 April. Available at: https://www.ohchr.org/en/statements/2019/04/end-mission-statement-united-nations-special-rapporteur-rights-persons#:~:text=I%20would%20like%20to%20begin,the%20transparency%2C%20openness%20and%20excellent (accessed 17 April 2024).

23 People with intellectual disabilities and autistic people

Sheila Hollins and Alice Firth

Introduction

A number of groups are considered to be particularly vulnerable when it comes to assisted suicide and euthanasia. For people with intellectual disabilities and/or autistic spectrum disorder (ASD), there is concern that others might make decisions for them or that society's, or the assessor's, unconscious bias towards people with intellectual disabilities/ASD may reinforce feelings of inadequacy, with its subtle coercive pressure on individuals to seek assisted suicide or euthanasia. The ability of people with intellectual disabilities/ASD to advocate for themselves is often under threat as they rarely have adequate support for living, let alone for independent decision-making. These difficulties can create significant barriers, preventing a person with intellectual disabilities or an autistic person from having free choices in relation to their own dying.

It's already happening!

It seems unbelievable that euthanasia or physician-assisted suicide would be offered to people with intellectual disabilities/ASD. The proponents of a change in the law say that safeguards would prevent this from happening.

But it is already happening! There is good evidence that this is happening in the Netherlands, although the extent is not fully known (Chapter 6). It is thought that similar practices in Canada and in Belgium are happening, but those countries have less rigorous reporting requirements than the Netherlands. There is a risk of this practice growing in size and being extended to other jurisdictions because of the 'death-making' instincts described by Wolfensberger (1987), who noted the legalization of abortion in the US in 1973 quickly led to calls to legalize infanticide.

In the Netherlands, euthanasia can only be performed at the patient's explicit request and must be reported to the Euthanasia Review Committees, which are charged with ensuring the criteria are followed correctly. But it is difficult to ascertain whether the assessment of mental capacity, or of co-existing mental illness, or the possibility of coercion by others, have been adequately addressed. For instance, many autistic people struggle with depression and are easily influenced, which could compromise their ability to make a lawful request to die.

An unconscious bias against intellectually disabled people introduces a risk that the assessor inadvertently reinforces the patient's feelings of inferiority or of being rejected by society and thus constitutes a coercive pressure towards euthanasia or assisted suicide.

Dutch data

A sample of 900 case descriptions recorded in the Netherlands' Euthanasia Review Committee reports was selected for detailed review. In 39 of the 900 published 'cases', intellectual disabilities or ASD was given as the main or a significant reason for performing euthanasia. Five of these 39 people were younger than 30, with autism listed as the sole underlying reason for seeking death by euthanasia.

The findings have been described in three publications (e.g. Tuffrey Wijne et al. 2018, 2019, 2023). The most recent paper found that characteristics directly associated with intellectual disabilities or ASD were the main (indeed the only) cause of suffering described in eight cases (21 per cent), including seven people with ASD and two people with intellectual disabilities (one person had both). 'Typically, these patients were unable to live with the characteristics of ASD/[intellectual disabilities] and could not cope with the world' (Tuffrey-Wijne et al. 2023). As one case report illustrated:

> As he had never been able to keep up with society, he had become insecure, with recurring depression. Due to his intellectual disability, he felt a great pressure of the world on him which he could not handle. His autistic traits made it increasingly difficult for him to cope with changes around him (2020–27, male, 70s, intellectual disability and ASD).

In eight cases (21 per cent), people with intellectual disabilities/ASD found it difficult to cope with non-life-threatening somatic symptoms or their physical decline because of age-related conditions or symptoms (n = 5), tinnitus (n = 2) or curable cancer (n = 1).

> The routine that she had introduced into her life also gave the patient something to hold on to when dealing with a world that was complex for her … The progressive physical deterioration and the lifelong inability to deal with her environment other than in fixed patterns caused unbearable suffering (2018–14, female, 80s, ASD).

There were a further eight cases (21 per cent) where intellectual disabilities/ASD was a major contributing factor to the person's inability to cope with his or her psychiatric condition.

Discussion

Remorse for being

Societal failures to accept those with intellectual disabilities/ASD and provide adequate support for them to manage their lives have played a part in requests for euthanasia or assisted suicide. In many cases, the suffering was described as feeling excluded from society, depression, sadness, distress at not being the person they would like to be, and they described finding it difficult to cope with changing circumstances. These cases raise the ethical and political issue, namely that society must face its duty to care for its citizens; and 'care' does not entail – except in some sort of corrupted sense – the intentional killing of those citizens.

In trying to understand why this practice has developed in the Netherlands – seemingly unquestioned – we need to go back to the diagnosis of intellectual disabilities/ASD for a person, and to their life trajectory and life opportunities, which are fairly typical across the western world. Hollins's book on remorse explored the impact of feeling unwanted as a person born with an intellectual disability, something that she called 'remorse for being' (Hollins 1998). Typically, people will experience multiple rejections and exclusions during their childhood – they learn that they are not truly welcome. They hear the pity in other voices and the different ways they are treated compared to their brothers and sisters. They do not really belong. And their siblings may perceive them as a burden that they dread inheriting from their parents. All of these factors could tend the person towards the (wrong) feeling that their lives are not worth living. Hence, there is a form of societal coercion towards euthanasia and assisted suicide (Chapter 26).

Comparative mortality

People with disabilities experience stark inequities in health and social care provision (Heslop et al. 2013). Adults with intellectual disabilities are 58 times more likely to die before the age of 50 than their non-disabled peers (looking at age and cause of death), probably as a consequence of discriminatory practices in health care (Hollins et al. 1998). These findings led to the development of the National Mortality Review, known as LeDeR (Learning Disability Mortality Review), which was commissioned to improve the standard and quality of care for people with a learning disability. But levels of premature and avoidable mortality have not improved.[1] The evidence is that people with intellectual disabilities receive fewer tests and less treatment than other people presenting with similar conditions.

Fewer than 6 per cent of adults with an intellectual disability are in paid employment. Few have meaningful activities – people are under-occupied when they cannot participate if they need support and/or transport to get to the place where an activity is being held. When other community members know how to welcome and include people with intellectual disabilities/ASD in local community activities, the need for social care support and transport lessens. If they are known by other local people, then there are people to stand up for them when something goes wrong, when they are next threatened with exclusion.

This is what happened in Romania when high school students spent a few hours every week learning alongside disabled students in special schools. At the end of their schooling, the only option for the students with intellectual disabilities was life in an institution. Their high school friends became their most powerful advocates (Frost 2019).

We suggest that it is our relationships and human connections that work for all of us in the end. Euthanasia is an easy way out and assumes that some people with intellectual disabilities/ASD have a lesser entitlement to an ordinary life. Where are the advocates who recognize their human worth and who are standing against eugenic discrimination?

Against the tide of discrimination, the innovative Oliver McGowan Mandatory Training Programme on learning disability,[2] co-designed and delivered by experts by experience, aims to increase the confidence of health and social care staff to make the necessary reasonable adjustments required under equality legislation and achieve more equal outcomes for people.

The introduction of physician-assisted dying legislation would push back these hard-fought-for changes, which are slowly improving the life chances for people with learning disabilities and autistic people.

The pandemic

More evidence of the fragility of progress towards more equal lives was found during the pandemic, when the risk of dying from Covid-19 was six times higher for people with intellectual disabilities overall. One reason was the routine use of Do Not Resuscitate orders (DNRs). Their lives were not prioritized for scarce health resources. And they remain one of the least-well vaccinated groups in the community.

Sinason (2024) expresses serious concerns about near-death issues for people with intellectual disabilities during the pandemic, who experienced some of the highest death rates in the UK; younger adults with an intellectual disability had a mortality rate 30 times higher than the general population. These young adults with intellectual disabilities experienced external societal trauma, unconscious and explicit societal eugenic death-wishes. These stresses impact on identity and life, making even their sexuality tinged with threat. All this reinforces devaluation of their lives. This is seen, for instance, in concerns about the use of DNR decisions. Sinason describes how several she has known of her age, being over 70, '… have experienced family doctors and psychiatrists encouraging us to accept a … DNR … for ourselves or our disabled partners. We must carefully consider the unconscious impact on all minorities of the notion that their life is not, or may be not, worth living' (Sinason 2024: 134).

If people living with intellectual disabilities and/or autism are already experiencing pressure to view their lives as less worthy of living, how much worse this will be if euthanasia and assisted suicide were legal.

Conclusion

Our mantra for supporting people with intellectual disabilities/ASD in health and social care settings is simply to treat people equally, to listen carefully and treat them with respect. But this needs to be in the knowledge that people with intellectual disabilities/ASD will have had more adverse childhood experiences. Before the early 1980s, post-traumatic stress disorder (PTSD) was not recognized or understood in any way. It is still hugely under-diagnosed in people with intellectual disabilities/ASD, with the result that their reactions to others and to their personal boundaries remain misunderstood by their families, their neighbours and those who support them.

It is easy to see how the loss of hope caused by repeated rejections and by social care failures can result in a request for help in ending a perceived 'worthless life'. Those with intellectual disabilities/ASD are often easily influenced by others. This makes them particularly vulnerable to perceiving early death as the solution to their difficulties, as they struggle to adjust to a society around them that does not make the necessary adjustments to support them finding meaning and purpose in life. Compassion and understanding are called for, not agreement to a request for help to end a life.

Notes

1. See https://www.england.nhs.uk/wp-content/uploads/2019/05/action-from-learning.pdf (accessed 21 February 2024).
2. See https://www.hee.nhs.uk/our-work/learning-disability/current-projects/oliver-mcgowan-mandatory-training-learning-disability-autism (accessed 19 April 2024).

References

Frost, C. (2019) *Community Action in Romania – A Report From Transylvania*, 22 October. Available at: https://www.linkedin.com/pulse/community-action-romania-report-from-transylvania-chris-frost (accessed 6 February 2024).

Heslop, P., Blair, P., Fleming, P. et al. (2013) *Confidential Inquiry into Premature Deaths of People with Learning Disabilities (CIPOLD): Final Report*. Bristol: University of Bristol, Norah Fry Research Centre. Available at: https://www.bristol.ac.uk/media-library/sites/cipold/migrated/documents/fullfinalreport.pdf (accessed 19 April 2024).

Hollins, S. (1998) Remorse for being: through the lens of learning disability, in M. Cox (ed.) *Remorse and Reparation*. London: Jessica Kingsley.

Hollins, S., Attard, M.T., Von Fraunhofer, N. et al. (1998) Mortality in people with learning disability: risks, causes, and death certification findings in London, *Developmental Medicine and Child Neurology*, 40 (1): 50–56.

Sinason, V. (2024) Near-death issues and the impact on the sexuality of people with intellectual disabilities during the pandemic, in S. Earle and M. Blackburn (eds) *Sex, Intimacy and Living with Life-Shortening Conditions*. Abingdon: Routledge.

Tuffrey-Wijne, I., Curfs, L., Finlay, I. and Hollins, S. (2018) Euthanasia and assisted suicide for people with an intellectual disability and/or autism spectrum disorder: an examination of nine relevant euthanasia cases in the Netherlands (2012–2016), *BMC Medical Ethics*, 19: 17. Available at: https://doi.org/10.1186/s12910-018-0257-6 (accessed 5 February 2024).

Tuffrey-Wijne, I., Curfs, L., Finlay, I. and Hollins, S. (2019) 'Because of his intellectual disability, he couldn't cope.' Is euthanasia the answer?, *Journal of Policy and Practice in Intellectual Disabilities*, 16 (2): 113–16. Available at: https://doi.org/10.1111/jppi.12307 (accessed 5 February 2024).

Tuffrey-Wijne, I., Curfs, L., Finlay, I. and Hollins, S. (2023) Euthanasia and physician-assisted suicide in people with intellectual disabilities and/or autism spectrum disorders: an investigation of 39 Dutch case reports (2012–2021), *BJPsych Open*, 9: e87. Available at: https://doi.org/10.1192/bjo.2023.69 (accessed 5 February 2024).

Wolfensberger, W. (1987) *The New Genocide of Handicapped and Afflicted People*. Syracuse, NY: Syracuse University (3rd revised edn., 2002). Available at: https://wolfwolfensberger.com/wp-content/uploads/2023/07/WW-2002-New-Genocide-Handicapped-Afflicted.pdf.

24 Vulnerable lives – euthanasia in the newborn and paediatric populations

John Wyatt

Introduction

In 1901, Dr Charles Goddard, a prominent supporter of both eugenics and voluntary euthanasia and Medical Officer of Health in London, delivered a medical paper entitled 'Suggestions in favour of terminating absolutely hopeless cases of injury or disease' (Goddard 1901). In it he proposed offering euthanasia both to 'those poor creatures with inaccessible and therefore inoperable malignancy' but also to mental defectives, referring to the large number of impaired individuals resident in the asylums: 'for example idiots, beings having only semblance to human form, incapable of improvement in education, and able to feed themselves, or perceiving when the natural functions are performed, unable to enjoy life or of serving any useful purpose in nature' (Goddard 1901).

There is undoubtedly a close connection between the prominence of eugenics in public discourse in early twentieth-century England and rising interest in euthanasia. The new 'scientific' eugenics sought to prevent racial degeneration by restricting the reproduction of those who were called the 'unfit', those with identifiable hereditary abnormalities who 'cluster to the extreme left of the distribution curve, and whose powers of reason and memory were even below those of dogs and other intelligent animals' (Soloway 1990: 20).

In his textbook of 1920, the eminent neurologist Dr Tredgold proposed a lethal chamber for those with a severe mental defect. He suggested that society would 'not necessarily be unjustified' in adopting mercy-killing as 'a self-defence mechanism for ridding itself of its antisocial constituents' (Tredgold 1920: 495). In 1930, Professor Richard Berry, another prominent expert in the field of mental deficiency, supported the use of a state-controlled 'lethal chamber', designed painlessly to exterminate low-grade defectives.[1]

Professor Berry's proposals were, of course, very similar to those put forward in Germany by Karl Binding and Alfred Hoche whose 1920 book, *Permitting the Destruction of Life Unworthy of Life: Its Measure and Form* (see Binding and Hoche 2012), was an inspiration for the hideous Nazi Aktion T4 euthanasia programme.

Selective infanticide

The most obvious and efficient way for society to rid itself of 'worthless lives' is, however, not to focus on children and adults with disability but rather the newborn. The practice of assessing newborn babies after birth and killing or exposing those who are deemed not worthy of existence has been recognized since the dawn of humanity. So-called 'selective infanticide' was well recognized in the classical Graeco-Roman era. In Plato's *Republic*, infanticide was presented as essential to maintain the quality of the citizens. Aristotle supported a law to ensure the compulsory exposure of all malformed babies. Seneca, in his treatise *On Anger* wrote, 'Mad dogs we knock on the head; the fierce and savage ox we slay; unnatural progeny we destroy; we drown even children who at birth are weakly and abnormal. Yet it is not anger, but reason that separates the harmful from the sound' (Wyatt 2009).

Soranus of Ephesus, a Roman physician practising in the first quarter of the second century, wrote the earliest known treatise on gynaecology (Temkin 1956). He included a chapter entitled 'How to recognise the newborn that is worth rearing', providing detailed instruction for midwives on clinical assessment of newborn babies to determine their fitness to survive.

We can identify several underlying assumptions which supported the practice and approval of selective infanticide in the ancient world. First was the belief that the value of a life lay primarily in its usefulness, partly to the parents, but especially to the state as a future citizen. The healthy newborn baby was a future farmer, soldier or mother and so their value resided in their potential to make a future worthwhile contribution. Second was the belief that the value of an individual human life was not inherent, but was acquired at some time after birth, when the child was accepted by the family and society in general. Third, there was the widespread assumption that health and physical wholeness were essential not only to survival but also to human dignity. In a culture that gloried in the so-called 'masculine virtues', the weak, the disabled and the malformed were always likely to be seen as less than fully human.

It is interesting that whereas abortion was criticized by philosophers and statesmen from time to time, the morality of killing sickly or deformed newborns was hardly questioned in the Graeco-Roman world. But although infanticide was widely accepted in the ancient world, Jewish teaching and culture were resolutely opposed to the process. Philo, a well-known Jewish apologist, confirmed the orthodox Jewish view of child exposure when he stated that 'infanticide undoubtedly is murder, since the displeasure of the law is not concerned with ages but with a breach to the human race'. The Roman historian Tacitus, who frequently commented on the strange and exotic practices of foreigners, felt that the unusual attitude of the Jews to newborn infants was worthy of comment. He wrote, with an unmistakable air of astonishment, that infant exposure was unknown among Jews; in fact, 'they regard it as a crime to kill any recently born child' (Wyatt 2009).

The early Christian Church adopted the prohibition of infanticide and the rescue of orphans and abandoned babies was regarded by early Christians as a particular duty. Foundlings were frequently adopted into families, as shown by inscriptions on tombs, and as the numbers grew, Christian orphanages were set up in the third and fourth centuries. Infanticide and child exposure were made punishable by law in the Roman Empire in AD 374, and legal opposition to infanticide and child murder has continued to the present day.

To fast-forward to the present, although the foetus has no independent legal status in the UK, once the baby is born, whatever the gestational age, he or she is covered by a panoply of legal protections and international statutes including the Homicide Act, the Children Act, the Human Rights Act and the UN Convention on the Rights of the Child. Working as a neonatologist in central London, I have sometimes reflected on the fact that if I were intentionally to destroy the life of a tiny premature infant in my care, I would be guilty in English law of exactly the same crime as if I were to destroy the life of the prime minister. This legal equivalence would surely be incomprehensible to any ancient Roman jurist, but reflects the abiding influence of the Judaeo-Christian ethical tradition on contemporary western law.

The last 50 years has seen a remarkable extension of intensive care for critically ill and vulnerable babies. Advanced life support techniques have led to complex ethical dilemmas about when it might be appropriate to withdraw or withhold life-sustaining treatment when it is futile or burdensome. In the UK, as in most developed healthcare systems, it has been recognized that it may be appropriate to withdraw life-sustaining treatment where death is inevitable or invasive treatments are excessively burdensome relative to very limited benefits. In the UK, all treatment decisions must be made in the best interests of the child, and there are agreed procedures requiring agreement between parents and treating clinicians about treatment decisions. In cases where death does not result from withdrawal of treatment, palliative care of the newborn is provided, with the aim being to relieve pain and distressing symptoms, and provide psychological and emotional support for parents, while allowing death to occur through natural processes. In most countries, a clear distinction is drawn between withdrawal of life support treatment, which is legally permissible under controlled circumstances, and intentional hastening of death using lethal medication, which is prohibited.

The Netherlands and the Groningen Protocol

At the time of writing, the Netherlands and Belgium are the only two major jurisdictions where intentional medical killing of infants and children is legally permitted. In the 1990s, nationwide surveys in the Netherlands showed that 62 per cent of infant deaths within the first year after birth were preceded by a physician's end-of-life decision. The majority of deaths were the result of withdrawing or withholding treatment, but a lethal drug was given with the intention to cause death in 15–20 cases every year.

In 2005, the Groningen Protocol was introduced to regularize the practice of neonatal euthanasia (Verhagen and Sauer 2005). The Protocol introduced five criteria:

1. the diagnosis and prognosis must be certain;
2. hopeless and unbearable suffering must be present;
3. diagnosis, prognosis, and unbearable suffering must be confirmed by at least one independent doctor;
4. both parents must give informed consent; and
5. the procedure must be performed in accordance with the accepted medical standard.

In 2016, the Dutch authorities extended use of the Protocol to infants up to the age of one year.

Euthanasia in children and 'mature minors'

The Netherlands

The Dutch Termination of Life on Request and Assisted Suicide Act 2002 enabled euthanasia to be carried out in children who were 12 years and older, merely stipulating that the consent of the parents was required if the patient was between 12 and 16 years. In April 2023, the Dutch Government issued a press release stating that euthanasia would be allowed in children aged 1–12 years: 'The new rules would apply to an estimated group of around 5 to 10 children per year, who suffer unbearably from their disease, have no hope of improvement and for whom palliative care cannot bring relief' (Reuters 2023).

Belgium

A study of 250 children aged 1–17 years who died in Flanders, Belgium, between 2007 and 2008 found that lethal drugs were administered in 13 cases, all without the patient's explicit request (Pousset et al. 2010). Although the legal representatives of the minors were involved in most end-of-life decisions, the children themselves were involved very rarely, even when life ending was intended. At the time of decision-making, patients were often comatose or the physicians deemed them incompetent or too young to be involved.

In 2014, the existing euthanasia law in Belgium was amended to remove any age restriction. However, the amended law does impose some restrictions on minors who request euthanasia. The child must have a terminal or incurable disease, or be near death, or suffering from chronic pain, and must have the consent of the parents and healthcare professionals. The child must also undergo an evaluation by a paediatric psychiatrist to certify that the he or she possesses 'capacity of discernment'.

Canada

In Canada, medical assistance in dying (MAiD) for adults was legalized in 2016 and almost immediately public discussion commenced on extending the law to so-called 'mature minors' – those below the age of 18 who had demonstrated legal capacity. A survey of Canadian paediatricians in 2018 found that 46 per cent of respondents were in favour of extending the option of MAiD to mature minors experiencing progressive or terminal illness or intractable pain (Davies 2018). Twenty-nine per cent of paediatricians believed access should be extended to children or youth with an intolerable disability.

In 2023, the Special Joint Committee on Medical Assistance in Dying recommended expanding MAiD to minors whose death was 'reasonably foreseeable'. They specified that parents could be involved in this process but, ultimately, the decision should rest with the child, provided they were deemed to have legal capacity by an independent assessor.

Dr Ramona Coelho, a family physician in London, Ontario, points out that the document also states that a person may meet the 'reasonably foreseeable death' criterion if they have shown, clearly and seriously, their intention to ensure that death occurs soon or predictably (Coelho 2024). This could result from a refusal to take antibiotics for an infection, stopping oxygen therapy, or a refusal to eat and drink. If legalized, a disabled minor who states their intention to refuse care, or who makes themselves sick enough, could qualify as having a reasonably foreseeable natural death under this provision. This currently happens with adults who are not dying and yet are having their lives ended within days of their first MAiD assessment.

Dr Coelho is bewildered by the thought of 'living in a country where the government has the power to assist in the suicides of my children without my consent … [where] parents' knowledge of their children's maturity and emotional drivers could be ignored … Parents will be devastated if their child's request for MAiD is granted against their wishes' (Coelho 2024).

It is well known that brain development continues into the twenties and pre-teens and teenagers often act impulsively, engaging in risky behaviours without foreseeing the likely consequences. It is possible that children with underlying serious health issues may choose MAiD for misguided reasons – for example, to avoid bullying at school or to be reunited with a deceased loved one. Rates of depression in teens continue to rise and the phenomenon of teenage suicide contagion is well recognized.

There is also the very real possibility that children who appear to have the ability to make decisions for themselves, where the appearance of maturity may have been developed as a defensive measure in the face of abuse, will now be at risk of MAiD, or may see it as a means of escaping an abusive situation. Dr Coelho also points out the risks to indigenous people whose youth have a higher relative suicide rate and a very real concern about suicide contagion. Similarly, children with disabilities can feel they are a burden to their family and to others, particularly when excluded by peers and by society. Rather than pursue death, a different perspective is required on their situation to allow them to be supported in society. The priority, according to Dr Coelho, should be to build up paediatric, palliative care and mental health services, rather than recommend the politically expedient strategy of MAiD (Coelho 2024).

Conclusion

The extension of euthanasia from competent adults to adolescents, children and newborn infants is, of course, a development which was long predicted. Once it becomes accepted that 'unbearable suffering' provides rational justification for active termination of life on the grounds of compassion, then it is logically indefensible to withhold this from babies and children who are deemed to be suffering, even though they clearly are incapable of giving valid consent. In addition, many will argue that just because natural death may not be imminent, and indeed may be many years hence, this does not preclude justification for euthanasia on the grounds of compassion. But the subjectivity of the criteria for life termination, and the obvious possibilities of error and abuse cannot be concealed. Destroying a young life on the grounds of a poor outlook is the ultimate example of the self-fulfilling prophecy!

The prospect of life-termination for 'mature minors' raises many new and complex issues, as eloquently described by Dr Coelho (2024). The physical, emotional and cognitive immaturity of adolescents, coupled with traumatizing experiences of life-threatening disease or severe disability, renders them uniquely vulnerable to impulsive decision-making and inappropriate and sometimes malign influences from others. It is better to seek treatments that might prevent suffering and to try to understand its underlying causes. To end a life is to prevent the possibility of that life ever improving, which is tragic in circumstances where that might be possible in a variety of ways. Offering children the ultimate choice to destroy their own lives, under the guise of compassion, is a betrayal of the solidarity and protection we owe to the most vulnerable in our midst.

Note

1. See Berry (1930: 155), where, in a letter to *The Eugenics Review*, 'on the question of a National Lethal Chamber for the grosser types of our mental defectives', he wrote: 'I have never, at any time or anywhere, "seriously suggested" such a procedure, though I did say in *The Times* that I thought, *when all had seen what I have*, that there would be many who would agree with me that such an act of extinction would be the kindest, wisest, and best thing we could do for all concerned.'

References

Berry, R.J.A. (1930) The lethal chamber proposal, *The Eugenics Review*, 22: 155–56. Available at: https://www.ncbi.nlm.nih.gov/pmc/articles/PMC2984950/pdf/eugenrev00307-0071b.pdf (accessed 1 April 2024).

Binding, K. and Hoche, A. (2012) *Permitting the Destruction of Life Unworthy of Life: Its Measure and Form*, trans. C. Modak. Greenwood, WI: Suzeteo Enterprises (first published 1920).

Coelho, R. (2024) Canada's assisted dying regime should not be expanded to include children, *Al Jazeera*, 16 February. Available at: https://www.aljazeera.com/opinions/2024/2/16/canadas-assisted-dying-regime-should-not-be-expanded-to-include-children (accessed 24 February 2024).

Davies, D. (2018) Medical assistance in dying: a paediatric perspective, *Paediatrics and Child Health*, 23 (2): 125–30.

Goddard, C.E. (1901) *Suggestions in Favour of Terminating Absolutely Hopeless Cases of Injury or Disease*, 17 May. Wellcome Institute for the History of Medicine CMAC/SA/VES/c.4.

Pousset, G., Bilsen, J., Cohen, J. et al. (2010) Medical end-of-life decisions in children in Flanders, Belgium: a population-based postmortem survey, *Archives of Pediatrics and Adolescent Medicine*, 164 (6): 547–53.

Reuters (2023) Dutch to widen 'right-to-die' to include terminally ill children, *Reuters*, 14 April. Available at: https://www.reuters.com/world/europe/dutch-widen-right-to-die-include-terminally-ill-children-2023-04-14/ (accessed 1 April 2024).

Soloway, R.A. (1990) *Demography and Degeneration: Eugenics and the Declining Birthrate in Twentieth-Century Britain*, 2nd edn. Chapel Hill, NC: University of North Carolina Press.

Temkin, O. (1956) *Soranus' Gynaecology*. Baltimore, MD: Johns Hopkins University Press.

Tredgold, A.F. (1920) *Mental Deficiency (Amentia)*, 3rd edn. New York: William Wood. Available at: https://babel.hathitrust.org/cgi/pt?id=uc2.ark:/13960/t7vm4651d&seq=9 (accessed 1 April 2024).

Verhagen, E. and Sauer, P.J. (2005) The Groningen Protocol – euthanasia in severely ill newborns, *New England Journal of Medicine*, 352 (10): 959–62.

Wyatt, J.S. (2009) *Matters of Life and Death*, 2nd edn. London: InterVarsity Press.

25 Older people and those living with dementia

Julian C. Hughes

Introduction

Almost 50 years ago, writing about euthanasia, the philosopher Philippa Foot (1920–2010) said this: '... it may be of the very greatest importance to keep a psychological barrier up against killing ... As things are, people do, by and large, expect to be looked after if they are old or ill. This is one of the good things that we have, but we might lose it ...' (Foot 1977: 112).

We know that most people who die by assisted suicide or euthanasia, in countries where it is permitted, are older. In Oregon, in 2023, 82 per cent of assisted suicides were 65 years or older and the median age was 75 years (Oregon Health Authority 2024: 11). In the same year in the Netherlands, 78.5 per cent of euthanasia deaths were in their sixties to eighties; one person was 104 years old (Regional Euthanasia Review Committees 2023: 13). The question is whether we are at risk of losing something important in society by introducing assisted suicide or euthanasia.

Stigma and discrimination

The origins of the word 'stigma' suggest a mark made by pricking or branding. Older people, including people living with dementia, are in a real sense branded. It is often simply assumed that older people will be incapable in one way or another. In 2019, Francine Prose wrote a piece suggesting that cruel jokes about older people are everywhere and she asked, 'When will we face our ageism epidemic?'.

The stigma surrounding age and dementia are rife (Hughes 2023: 45–52), leading to discrimination and abuse. Remember that there can be *self*-stigmatization. The older person can be infected by the prevailing attitude: 'Maybe I'm not worth the bother, or the cost, or the inconvenience.' So, once it is legal, people accept the prospect of assisted suicide/euthanasia because they accept that their lives are spent; their lives are less worthy of living, which calls to mind the Nazi expression *Lebensunwetes Leben*: 'life unworthy of life'. The worry is that this attitude insinuates its way into our thinking.

Is this an outrageous suggestion? It is not long since Dan Brock (1937–2020) wrote that people with severe dementia were more like animals than normal adults (Brock 1988). The philosophical argument was that, since being a person requires memory, people with severe dementia (lacking all memory) are not persons (Hughes 2011). The work of Tom Kitwood (1937–1998) and Steven Sabat should have persuaded us that there is much more to a person than 'memory' or even cognitive function (Kitwood 1997; Sabat 2001). We are, instead, situated embodied agents (Hughes 2001). It is our situatedness, our embeddedness in multifarious contexts (psychological, cultural, historical, familial, ethical, legal, social and so on) that is key.

It is key for three reasons. First, any discrimination should be eschewed, because we interconnect and are interdependent. Second, this is how our personhood is maintained: by attention to the many different ways in which we engage with the world. Third, it is why *how* we die is not simply a personal matter. It matters for everyone else and, in particular, the law must be applied to everyone equally. So, we must think about protecting those who are dependent on us and vulnerable to discrimination, including by self-stigmatization. To place this protection in jeopardy, to undermine the basis of such protection, is indeed a loss for society.

Evaluative judgements and capacity assessments

Decision-making capacity is critical in discussions about assisted suicide and euthanasia. With others I undertook a study to look at capacity assessments in connection with older people making decisions about going home from a general hospital (Emmett et al. 2013). Our conclusion was that, although the professionals said they were familiar with the legal standards required, the standards were not routinely applied. The complexities, highlighted in Chapter 13, suggest there is no reason to presume that capacity assessments are now better. Can we be sure that assessors for assisted suicide/euthanasia will not tend to deem that people have capacity even where this is questionable? And it will often be questionable when people are frail. These assessments are not straightforward (Kim et al. 2021). They involve value judgements which, with the best will in the world, will inevitably tend to reflect the inclinations of the assessor.

The slippery slope in action: advance euthanasia directives

Even if capacity assessments can be performed so that the person is fully informed – for instance, of the possibility that the (unlicensed) lethal medication might cause unpleasant side-effects or not work (see Chapter 21) – there is the issue of people with more advanced dementia who can no longer consent to euthanasia. The advance euthanasia directive is intended as a means to get around this problem.

However, as discussed with clarity by Cees Hertogh in Chapter 5, it subverts the possibility that the practice of euthanasia forms part of an ongoing caring communication in the context of the doctor–patient relationship (see also Hughes 2023: 220–21). It might even require (as we've heard in Chapters 4 and 5) that the person with advanced dementia needs to be covertly sedated and then held down in order to be killed (Wall 2019).

Elsewhere, Cees Hertogh has asked why more people with mild-to-moderate dementia are not euthanized or provided with assisted suicide to avoid the problem of the doubtful interactions that arise in the later stages (Hertogh et al. 2007).

Perhaps this is because the life instinct is too great. Nevertheless, in the Netherlands in 2022, there were 282 reported cases of euthanasia for people with dementia who were deemed to have decisional capacity; and six cases of people 'in an advanced or very advanced stage of dementia' who lacked capacity but who were euthanized in accordance with their advance euthanasia directive (Regional Euthanasia Review Committees 2023: 11). This reminds me that, in 2005, I attended a conference in which a senior ethicist from the Netherlands reassured me there would never be euthanasia for people with dementia because of worries about genuine consent. Yet here we see the 'slippery slope' in action.

Coercion: the good, the bad and the ugly

The loss of attention to genuine capacity and consent are real losses, partly on account of the utilitarian tendency in society that accompanies the legalization of assisted suicide/euthanasia. But coercion is perhaps of greater concern. It comes in several guises: overt/covert, conscious/subconscious, benign/malign.

The good are those many people I have met who are family carers struggling to support an older parent, while at the same time holding down a job and bringing up a family. They do not want their parents to die. But their fatigue shows and the older person senses it. At present, in the UK, all have the certainty that intentional killing is prohibited. But a change in the law takes away this certainty. It raises a question in the carers' minds and in the minds of the older people. They are a burden. What is the quality of their lives? (but see Chapter 28).

Although she had once been certain about the prohibition on intentional killing, Mary Warnock (1924–2019), the philosopher and member of the House of Lords, became an advocate for a change in the law. She suggested that people with dementia should be seeking euthanasia or assisted suicide in order to decrease the strain on their families and on healthcare resources: 'If you're demented, you're wasting people's lives – your family's lives – and you're wasting the resources of the National Health Service' (Graham 2021: 307). This kind of attitude, once assisted suicide/euthanasia is legal, can work its way into the fabric of society leading to coercion of one sort or another by people whose motivation is otherwise good.

The bad are seen in the extensive evidence of abuse of older people: over 1 in 6 (15.7 per cent) of people aged 60 years and over have suffered some form of abuse (Yon et al. 2017). This is also evident in those many legal cases around testamentary capacity. Typically, someone starts to experience cognitive impairment and an acquaintance or hitherto distant relative appears on the scene. The person then visits a solicitor to make the acquaintance or distant relative the main beneficiary of his or her will. Other family members, shocked when the will is read, try to contest it. How easily would frail and vulnerable elders be subtly coerced to seek assisted suicide/euthanasia for financial gain? And how many clinicians have found themselves unaware of elder abuse, often financial, hidden behind the closed doors of an ostensibly loving family?

The ugly are represented by the son in a medico-legal case in which I was involved. Already with convictions and imprisonment for assault and burglary, he was defrauding his mother (who had moderate-to-severe dementia), trying to control where she lived and even drugging her for his benefit. Who would deny that such a man would be quite capable of arranging that his mother should receive assisted suicide/euthanasia? He would even claim that he was doing this for compassionate reasons. And would the brave social workers in such a case, who withstood his intimidation and abuse, have the resolve to oppose her ostensibly legal wish to seek death once assisted suicide/euthanasia was normalized?

Loneliness and depression

In 2022, in Canada, 17.1 per cent of those who received medical assistance in dying (MAiD) cited isolation or loneliness as the suffering that caused them to seek MAiD (Health Canada 2023: 31). Briggs et al. (2021) investigated the 'wish to die' in a study of 8,174 community-dwelling older people in Ireland. In the preceding month, 279 of them had wished to die, 60 per cent of whom were depressed and 64 per cent lonely. Overall, of those who reported a wish to die either at the start of the study or 2 years later, 72 per cent no longer reported a wish to die when subsequently followed up; in addition, they were less depressed and lonely. Hence, the wish to die fluctuates and can depend on social and mental health support.

Conclusion

In short, older people, including those with dementia, require (at least) basic care and support in a compassionate society, with a legal framework that protects them from coercion and exploitation. And the worry is that assisted suicide/ euthanasia leads to losses in terms of solicitude and to a subtle coarsening of the moral fabric of society, which becomes more individualistic and utilitarian, with the potential for various levels of coercion for convenience. Palliative care for people living with dementia (Hughes et al. 2020) and communities that genuinely care for older people are aims preferable to those that include intentional killing.

References

Briggs, R., Ward, M. and Kenny, R.A. (2021) The 'Wish to Die' in later life: prevalence, longitudinal course and mortality. Data from TILDA, *Age and Ageing*, 50 (4): 1321–28.

Brock, D.W. (1988) Justice and the severely demented elderly, *Journal of Medicine and Philosophy*, 13 (1): 73–99.

Emmett, C., Poole, M., Bond, J. and Hughes, J.C. (2013) Homeward bound or bound for a home? Assessing the capacity of dementia patients to make decisions about hospital discharge: comparing practice with legal standards, *International Journal of Law and Psychiatry*, 36 (1): 73–82.

Foot, P. (1977) Euthanasia, *Philosophy and Public Affairs*, 6 (2): 85–112.

Graham, P. (2021) *Mary Warnock: Ethics, Education and Public Policy in Post-War Britain.* Cambridge: Open Book Publishers. Available at: https://doi.org/10.11647/OBP.0278 (accessed 14 March 2024).

Health Canada (2023) *Fourth Annual Report on Medical Assistance in Dying in Canada 2022.* Ottawa: Health Canada. Available at: https://www.canada.ca/content/dam/hc-sc/documents/

services/medical-assistance-dying/annual-report-2022/annual-report-2022.pdf (accessed 18 March 2024).

Hertogh, C.M.P.M., de Boer, M.E., Dröes, R-M. and Eefsting, J.A. (2007) Would we rather lose our life than lose our self? Lessons from the Dutch debate on euthanasia for patients with dementia, *American Journal of Bioethics*, 7 (4): 48–56.

Hughes, J.C. (2001) Views of the person with dementia, *Journal of Medical Ethics*, 27 (2): 86–91.

Hughes, J.C. (2011) *Thinking Through Dementia*. Oxford: Oxford University Press.

Hughes, J.C. (2023) *Dementia and Ethics Reconsidered*. Maidenhead: Open University Press.

Hughes, J.C., Jolley, D., Jordan, A. and Sampson, E.L. (2020) Palliative care in dementia: issues and evidence, in P. Lilford and J.C. Hughes (eds) *Clinical Topics in Old Age Psychiatry*. Cambridge: Cambridge University Press.

Kim, S.Y.H., Mangino, D. and Nicolini, M. (2021) Is this person with dementia (currently) competent to request euthanasia? A complicated and underexplored question, *Journal of Medical Ethics*, 47: e41. Available at: https://doi.org/10.1136/medethics-2020-106091 (accessed 13 March 2024).

Kitwood, T. (1997) *Dementia Reconsidered: The Person Comes First*. Buckingham: Open University Press.

Oregon Health Authority (2024) *Oregon Death with Dignity Act: 2023 Data Summary*. Available at: https://www.oregon.gov/oha/PH/PROVIDERPARTNERRESOURCES/EVALUATIONRESEARCH/DEATHWITHDIGNITYACT/Documents/year26.pdf (accessed 23 March 2024).

Prose, F. (2019) Cruel jokes about the old are everywhere: when will we face our ageism epidemic?, *The Guardian*, 10 November. Available at: https://www.theguardian.com/commentisfree/2019/nov/10/ok-boomer-jokes-ageism-francine-prose (accessed 14 March 2024).

Regional Euthanasia Review Committees (2023) *Annual Report 2022*, euthanasiecommissie.nl. Available at: https://english.euthanasiecommissie.nl/the-committees/documents/publications/annual-reports/2002/annual-reports/annual-reports (accessed 14 March 2024).

Sabat, S.R. (2001) *The Experience of Alzheimer's Disease: Life Through a Tangled Veil*. Oxford: Blackwell.

Wall, J. (2019) 'Mrs A': a controversial or extreme case?, *Journal of Medical Ethics*, 45 (2): 77–78.

Yon, Y., Mikton, C.R., Gassoumis, Z.D. and Wilber, K.H. (2017) Elder abuse prevalence in community settings: a systematic review and meta-analysis, *Lancet Global Health*, 5: e147–56. Available at: https://doi.org/10.1016/S2214-109X(17)30006-2 (accessed 18 March 2024).

26 The euthanasia paradox – free choice or coercion?

John Maher

Introduction: The Canadian background[1]

In 2016, Canada's parliament introduced an exemption to the federal homicide law and thereby allowed 100,000 doctors and nurse practitioners actively to end the lives of patients whose deaths are 'reasonably foreseeable', whose suffering is subjectively 'grievous', and whose medical condition is objectively 'irremediable'. In 2021, the scope of the law was expanded to include anyone who has a physical medical condition or disability, and their death need not be reasonably foreseeable. Canada's rate of active euthanasia in 2022 was over 4 per cent of all deaths – one of the highest rates in the world – with these deaths coming at the hands of healers.

In surveys, the clear majority of Canadians support euthanasia in the context of terminal illness. The argument that uncontrolled pain must be relieved through death is an easy sell, but it is a selective message promulgated without the general populace fully understanding that palliative care is remarkably effective at mitigating physical and emotional suffering, and that access to palliative care across Canada is relatively inadequate or limited. The palliative care medical community has railed against government insistence that euthanasia should fall under the purview of palliative services. The province of Quebec has explicitly mandated its delivery in palliative centres; that violation of both conscience rights and standards of good palliative care is presently being challenged in the courts.

Outraged disability organizations are shocked by the ableism and discrimination that expansion of access beyond the terminal context represents. Multiple media reports detail veterans and disabled persons being offered euthanasia unsolicited (Brooks 2023). This is particularly disturbing against the background of inadequate funding of social supports to maintain even a basic quality of life. For some, death is being chosen because of poverty, inadequate disability services, or the absence of a basic living allowance. Long-standing stigmatization is now a legislative fiat.

The aim of this chapter is to consider coercion, which immediately brings to mind the avaricious and malign relative who seeks the death of a family member for personal gain. This may occasionally be a reality. But I also wish to emphasize that coercion occurs at a societal level. Stigmatization is itself coercive; so too is the language we use.

Social engineering through language

Social engineering begins with language engineering. The euphemism for euthanasia actively espoused by the well-organized euthanasia lobby in Canada is 'medical assistance in dying' (MAiD). It is framed as a compassionate, benevolent medical act, although it can be cogently argued that killing a person falls outside the domain of traditional medicine in all possible instances. The words 'euthanasia' and 'assisted suicide' are actively eschewed by advocates, government ministers and biased media reporting. The inversion of social taboos against unnecessary mercy killing and inducement to suicide is conscious and systematic. It represents staged, long-term government policy to solve the 'problems of ageing', expensive end-of-life care and the tax burden of the disabled. It is insidious disregard for human life under the guise of compassionate care.

Broad support from within the medical community for euthanasia for the terminally ill has resulted in rapid adoption of the normalization of the practice. In medical student and resident education sessions, there seems to be little active debate about the ethics of assisted suicide or euthanasia, as though the matter is forever settled because the horse is out of the barn. There is also fear of speaking up or countering senior professors who are advocates of euthanasia. Yet the conscience rights of physicians deserve to be safeguarded. Within the hierarchical power structures of medical training, it is often necessary to 'go along to get along' and thereby limit the risk of punitive exclusion or career consequences. Ideologically driven colleagues can be powerful drivers of medical cultures within hospitals and care teams. Coercion can occur at many levels.

The problem of power, conscious and unconscious influence

From the family doctor's office to the hospital bedside, we see the spectrum of vulnerability play out in a relationship where the power and knowledge differentials between doctor and patient range from controllingly paternalistic to the respectfully empowered partnership. Doctors, as bringers of hope or messengers of futility, shape the dialogue and influence decision-making in profoundly conscious and unconscious ways. They also have life stories of their own that shape their values and attitudes towards euthanasia and their projections of the tolerability of suffering for the individual before them. Disability research has long shown that most doctors presume poorer quality of life than disabled people actually enjoy. Transference by doctors who have watched their own family members suffer through a protracted death makes them liable to extrapolate unjustifiably. Such memories, sometimes tinged by guilt at having been ignorant of possible options to relieve some distress, become the lens through which predictions are made (and conveyed). Yet each patient has a life story, resilience, values and family support that are unique and engender myriad ways of coping in adversity or restoring meaning and purpose to life.

What constitutes a good death? What end-of-life business is awaiting attempted resolution? When the social messaging is that all suffering can be avoided at end of life through a euthanasia short-cut, it disrespectfully vitiates the potential positive dynamic of the death scene tableau. Making peace, healing fractured family relationships, honest time with cherished friends, and existential insights can be critical elements of the dying montage. If you are made to feel selfish, or that you are a burden, or that your family members or your medical team cannot bear to work to relieve your suffering, then your choice will to some extent be pressured or even coerced.

You're a burden!

Watching family members fatigued by caring for you can obviously add to your distress. Is the proper social response euthanasia or better medical and home care supports? If you don't want to die yet, then the latter approach is clearly better. If your quality of life is satisfactory but you face external pressures to get on with dying, how truly free are you? What if your personal care costs are eating away at an anticipated inheritance? What if family members are chomping at the bit awaiting granny's millions? What if hospital staff remind you of the bed short-age? What if the social messaging is that you shouldn't be using up healthcare dollars better spent on someone else? What if the encouragement to move along is framed altruistically: reduce the burden on your family and the 'system', and/or – as we are seeing in Canada – give up your organs for transplant and save lives?

Dying is a process, not an event, often fraught with periods of fragility, vulner-ability, possibly variable decision-making confidence (if not incapacity even), and it is a time when you may be in need of protection from aggressive or insen-sitive caregivers. If our physical and emotional suffering are adequately managed, would any of us choose euthanasia without external pressure?

Box 26.1: Case vignette – subliminal messaging

Disturbingly, external pressure can be wholly inadvertent. I was asked to consult on a case where a 72-year-old man with early Parkinson's, now living in a retire-ment/nursing home, asked his only daughter if he should choose euthanasia. He still had many years of life ahead otherwise. In his loneliness, what he wanted more than anything was for her to invite him to live with her and her husband and granddaughter. He had the means to pay for home care supports. Her response broke his spirit. She said, 'I will support whatever decision you want to make.' One hopes that response represents intentional validation rather than unspoken exhaustion or indifference, or an unconscious death wish. What he desperately wanted was for her to be shocked and to beg him to stay alive. Instead, he expe-rienced extreme rejection. He has since scheduled and cancelled (at the last minute) three euthanasia dates over a period of a year.

The temptation of open access

The easy availability of euthanasia in Canada for the non-terminally ill has cre-ated this new phenomenon of anxiety over whether one should avail oneself of the easy mortal exit. As we all know, one of the cornerstones of successful suicide prevention is the limiting of access to easy means. What Canada has done is post a large neon sign over the exit ramp. Euthanasia temptation can be inevitable on the hard, tiring or lonely days. Despair is the great deceiver that abridges your decision horizon and steers you towards easy solutions, even against your own best interests or deepest desire to live longer. Again, it is the social acceptance and availability of assisted suicide and euthanasia that acts as a coercing force.

A therapist colleague has been providing psychotherapy and counselling support to people nearing end of life, and their loved ones, in a hospice setting for decades. She has spoken with me about the profound shift in her work since the advent of euthanasia in Canada in 2016. People who are dying now seek her counsel on whether they should die by euthanasia, rather than naturally, in order to make it easier on loved ones. Loved ones in their turn are expressing their fear that they are pressuring the dying person to live longer because they want every minute possible. This complicated dance of mutual pretence often plays itself out awkwardly. Euthanasia hangs over their time together as invitation, threat or duty.

Box 26.2: Case vignette – fears about lack of social support

I am involved with supporting a 52-year-old patient with a chronic manageable physical illness who lives with his ageing parents. As in other cases, his story shows how the possibility of a 'simple' solution and concerns about social care nudge the decision-making in the direction of assisted suicide or euthanasia. The nudge can be a form of unrecognized coercion. To my surprise, his parents have supported their son's wish for euthanasia. Under Canadian law, he is eligible because he is only required to make the subjective claim that his suffering is 'grievous'. Objectively, he is not suffering physically and his medical condition responds well to a simple medication regimen. His parents fear him living in poverty after their deaths, and they believe no-one else will care for him properly. There is mutual reinforcement for a euthanasia choice despite repeated reassurances to all that the patient will be well supported and cared for, especially given that there is a substantial inheritance that will subsidize his care. Despite that, euthanasia is the planned pathway.

Systemic pressures

On the point of good care, or care within a system of limited resources, you have hospital administrators pressuring doctors not to waste resources, and doctors in turn (consciously or unconsciously) pressuring patients and family members, and patients internalizing the media, doctor and family member messaging that they should be altruistic and self-sacrificing. There are areas of Canada where euthanasia rates now top 7 per cent, showing that when you have prolific euthanasia providers and so-called 'champions of change', the public's trust in medical messaging becomes coercive. If my caring doctor suggests this, then the future is so bleak that this is a good choice and any hope for a better future is misplaced. Importantly and perversely, euthanasia gives doctors permission to give up trying with the hard or difficult patients.

Dignity

Euthanasia is often framed as a better way to die because it is 'more dignified'. The best definition I have heard of what dignity is (but also see Chapter 28) was from a woman with quadriplegia who relied on daily care attendants to wipe her bottom. She said some carers treated her as nothing but an object and did the necessary job. She said others treated her as a person and she felt their gentleness, respect and human connection. She said no-one could take away her dignity because that was exclusively about how she viewed her own self-worth. How often do advocates for euthanasia, like the indifferent caregivers, diminish themselves with a message that devalues life and personhood? Dying surrounded by family who love me and maintain my sense of dignity may make it far less likely that I want to rush off the mortal coil. Are any countries with strong traditions of village life and extended families clamouring for a medical euthanasia option? Those who support and encourage assisted suicide and euthanasia will often point to dignity as the thing to be sought. In doing so, the threat of a loss of dignity hangs as a coercive psychosocial reality over the person facing death, ignoring the possibility that attributed dignity might be maintained and that our inherent dignity is never lost (see Chapter 28).

Conclusion

Euthanasia is no longer the rare exception that legislators in Canada foretold. Are we moving to a time where you will be viewed as selfish if you do not choose euthanasia? Where the social norm will have been validated under the weight of its own expression? That is to say, by normalizing euthanasia we normalize suicide; a culture of death then prevails for the elderly, the disabled, the sick, or those just tired of life. Disturbingly, a recent survey in Canada showed that a third of respondents also supported offering euthanasia to the poor and homeless. Is this our dystopian future?

Coercion can be conscious or unconscious, it can be overt or covert, it can be benignly intended or malign. What I have stressed here is that once euthanasia and assisted suicide are accepted, the social and political culture itself has a coercive force that is insidious and invidious. It also allows medical arrogance and ignorance to masquerade as benevolence. This coercive *zeitgeist* represents a coarsening of our relationships, our institutions and our culture.

Note

1. See Chapter 7 for further description of the Canadian experience.

Reference

Brooks, D. (2023) The outer limits of liberalism, *The Atlantic*, 4 May. Available at: https://www.theatlantic.com/magazine/archive/2023/06/canada-legalized-medical-assisted-suicide-euthanasia-death-maid/673790/ (accessed 25 February 2024).

PART 6

Philosophical and ethical concepts

27 | Autonomy and assisted suicide

Onora O'Neill

Introduction

The central problem for any attempt to legalize assisted suicide is that of drafting legislation which reliably ensures that those who do not seek to die, and in particular do not seek assistance with suicide, are not killed. Without a very clear distinction, legislation could endanger those who do not wish to die and could provide a cover for unlawful killing: that is what is at stake.

The most popular way of trying to draw the necessary distinction is to restrict the lawful assistance of suicide to cases in which an individual's choice to die, and specifically to seek assistance with dying, reflects *individual autonomy*. The other popular argument for assisted suicide appeals to the idea that in difficult cases a person might be 'better off dead' — however, this judgement may be hard to substantiate and, unless linked to some account of individual autonomy, would also permit involuntary euthanasia. Very few, if any, other arguments for legalizing assisted suicide are promoted, although a few people think that assisted suicide would reduce the world population, or save NHS costs, or preserve the size of inheritances. By themselves, all of these lines of thought support involuntary euthanasia, and are seen as suspect.

To find out whether appeals to respect individual autonomy provide good reasons for legalizing assisted dying, we need to understand what is meant by individual autonomy. This is much harder than one might imagine. Conceptions of autonomy have a long history, but the conceptions of individual autonomy that current discussions invoke are surprisingly different from earlier accounts of autonomy, and relatively new. So I begin with a potted history.

A potted history of autonomy

Jurisprudential autonomy

The original use of the term 'autonomy' was *jurisprudential*. The ancient Greeks contrasted colonies, whose laws were made for them by their mother cities, with *self-legislating* or *autonomous* cities that were not colonies, but rather made their own laws. Autonomous cities were politically independent. This political or constitutional use of the term 'autonomy' is still current. It is quite different from contemporary understandings of individual autonomy, and the Greeks would not have spoken of individuals (who do not make laws at all) either as autonomous or as lacking autonomy.

Kantian autonomy

The term 'autonomy' famously acquired a quite different and more abstract sense in the writings of Immanuel Kant in the eighteenth century, which remain much respected – and much misunderstood. Kant classifies principles, not individuals, as autonomous – or otherwise.

Kant characterizes principles as autonomous if they and the reasons for them could be adopted by all, rather than assuming deference to some supposed authority of limited scope, whether Church or State, ideology or preference. Kant, too, does not speak of individuals (who do not make laws at all) as autonomous, or as more or less autonomous. Rather, he describes law-like principles that could be adopted by all for reasons that all could follow as autonomous, and other principles that can be adopted only by those who defer to some other supposed authoritative power or standard as heteronomous (that is, reflecting the law of another).

As Kant sees it, human beings can choose to act on autonomous principles, even if they do not always do so. Reasons for acting on autonomous principles can be given to each and to all. By contrast, reasons for acting on heteronomous principles will carry weight only for those who defer to some preferred authority or standard.

Kant's account of *principled autonomy* is in my view relevant to current debates only because his authority is often, but spuriously, invoked by contemporary liberal advocates of the quite different twentieth-century conceptions of *individual autonomy*.

Individual autonomy

Individual autonomy became prominent in public discussion following the Second World War, first in psychological and philosophical literature. It became a staple component of the revival of liberal political thinking in the 1980s and has now penetrated far and wide into popular culture. Individual autonomy is generally seen as some form of individual independence, which is often, but not always, thought of as desirable.

Questions about individual autonomy

Appeals to the importance of developing, respecting and securing individual autonomy are ubiquitous in contemporary life. For present purposes, we need to focus on *normative* or *practical* questions about individual autonomy, and there are lots of them. When and why should we respect individual autonomy? Does respect for individual autonomy demand a minimal state that legislates sparingly in order not to infringe individual autonomy, and in particular does not regulate action 'between consenting adults'? What might we lose sight of by asking which laws are needed to respect individual autonomy, rather than asking more broadly which laws would be effective, or just, or socially valuable?

For example, we might think – many do – that an autonomous decision to die by suicide should be respected. And we might think – some do – that, if we should respect such suicide decisions, we should also make it lawful for others to assist in the suicide, provided those whom they help to die choose to do so autonomously. Yet we might also think that the influence that one person can have over another would make legislation permitting assisted suicide very risky.

We cannot address practical questions about assisted suicide, or frame adequate legislation, unless we are clear about which forms of individual autonomy should be required for assistance with suicide to be permissible and would have to be embodied in any legislation making it lawful. Unfortunately, there is very little agreement about what individual autonomy amounts to, and even less about the way in which respect for individual autonomy should be embodied in legislation that bears on assisted suicide. The problems are not peculiar to decisions about assisted suicide.

Autonomy in contemporary ethics

There is unfortunately radical disagreement about what individual autonomy amounts to, which has remained unresolved for over two decades. Consider two standard accounts summarizing the range of views taken of individual autonomy in the late 1980s. First, it has been seen as:

> ... an equivalent of liberty (positive or negative ...) ... dignity, integrity, individuality, independence, responsibility and self-knowledge ... self-assertion ... critical reflection ... freedom from obligation ... absence of external causation ... and knowledge of one's own interests ... About the only features that are held constant from one author to another are that autonomy is a feature of persons and that is a desirable quality to have. (Dworkin 1988: 6)

A second list, with little overlap with Dworkin's, can be found in a standard work on informed consent, which claims that autonomy is variously 'associated' with:

> ... privacy, voluntariness, self-mastery, choosing freely, the freedom to choose, choosing one's own moral position and accepting responsibility for one's choices. (Faden and Beauchamp 1986: 7)

This variety was noted over 20 years ago and remains a feature of current public and popular debate about individual autonomy.

Mere sheer choice vs. reflective or reasoned choice

It seems virtually impossible to provide a systematic taxonomy of conceptions of individual autonomy, but it is possible to identify a minimalistic conception. *Minimalist* views of individual autonomy equate it with mere sheer choice, implying all choosing is autonomous choosing (O'Neill 2002).

Non-minimalist views see autonomous choice as choice that meets one or more additional, more demanding standards. As such, the choice must be *informed*, or *fully informed*, or *reasoned*, or *reflective*, or *endorsed* by other choices or *authentic* – or meets some of a gamut of other standards. Non-minimalist views of individual autonomy do not count any old uncoerced choice as autonomous. Only choosing which meets the favoured additional standard or standards counts as autonomous.

The gap between the thought that *mere sheer choice* counts as an exercise of individual autonomy and other more demanding conceptions of individual autonomy has produced endless intractable problems for medical practice.

On minimalist views of individual autonomy, respect for it is simply respect for patient choice — including choices based on lack of understanding or irrational fears, and choices that will endanger health and life. Anything else is seen as unacceptable paternalism. (In practice, professionals can mitigate the possibly disastrous effects of blanket respect for patient choice both by restricting the choice set to professionally approved options and by deeming some patients incompetent to consent.)

Nevertheless, even those who deploy a minimal conception of individual autonomy do not argue for respecting *all* choices, but mostly think that autonomous choice may be restricted to prevent harm or risk of harm to others. Even those who ostensibly think we should respect even minimally autonomous choices often think we *should* legislate against *certain* activities between consenting adults, such as duelling or cannibalism, even where such activities are (at least) minimally autonomous for both parties.

Non-minimal autonomy in medical ethics

In non-minimalist views of individual autonomy, patient choice is to be respected only where it meets the favoured *additional* standards. Here endless debates about those *additional* standards begin. Should we respect patient choices only if they are informed? If so, how much relevant information must be given? And must that information be understood? What if the information is cognitively demanding? Is it acceptable to require very ill patients to make cognitively taxing judgements and exercise non-minimal forms of individual autonomy? Is rejection of medical paternalism perhaps a mask for callous treatment of vulnerable patients? Are demands for patient autonomy a sad consequence of a need to avoid liability for medical injury by seeking pretence of detailed consent, even when patients are not genuinely competent to provide it (Manson and O'Neill 2007)? I mention these debates because they are pertinent to any attempt to reach a view on legislation on assisted suicide on the basis of appeals to individual autonomy.

Individual autonomy and assisted suicide

If autonomy is taken minimally as a matter of mere sheer choice, then a claim that assisted suicide should be legalized to respect individual autonomy would mean that any choice to die – even one that reflects momentary whim, clinical depression, false beliefs or deference to others – should be respected. I doubt whether such positions have serious supporters.

But, if autonomy is *not* taken minimally – is not mere sheer choice – then assisted suicide legislation can only be justified by showing *why some specific non-minimal conception of individual autonomy requires attention and respect, and to be enshrined in legislation.*

Bills to legalize assisted suicide which have come before Parliament have described apparent 'safeguards' to ensure that a choice to die reflects more than a minimal conception of individual autonomy, such as momentary desire, lack of comprehension or lack of information. The difficulties lie in specifying clearly the form or degree of individual autonomy that should be required for this irrevocable choice to be lawful.

A period of delay between an initial decision to request help with suicide and being helped in the suicide is one safeguard for those with fluctuating or momentary desires to die: they are protected from the implementation of a choice which they might have rescinded, but if dead could not rescind. Involving more than one doctor also attempts some protection against its being based on misinformation or reflecting undue influence. But it is doubtful whether legislation can specify all the criteria that may be important.

Exercising or donating autonomy

In suicide, the final act is that of the person, who exercises autonomy through control of his or her actions. But when the patient surrenders control to another for euthanasia – to be injected with lethal drugs – they give all control to the other and trust that their wishes will be complied with. This raises the question whether euthanasia requests (which are the main mode of assisted dying in Canada and the Benelux countries) are a true expression of exercised individual autonomy or the desire for a cloak of medical benevolence by handing responsibility for administering death to the person injecting lethal drugs.

The nub of the question

Incorporating a few 'safeguards' into legislation cannot address the real difficulty of protecting patients (or others) against the consequences of choices that are not well grounded being visited upon them. A convincing non-minimalist account of individual autonomy must take account of the *many* ways in which individual autonomy may be limited. And here our debates remain wholly inadequate.

Much popular coverage of assisted suicide has been marred by relying on two assumptions that obstruct clear thinking. The first is a tendency to think about individual cases that are so miserable that we are tempted to feel that anything must be an improvement. But, of course, legislation has to be safe for all citizens, not tailored for hard cases while risking the lives of others. Unless we can reliably specify the cases for which the legislation is intended, it will not be feasible to legislate. We can only legislate safely if we can reliably pick out the adequately autonomous patient (whatever that may mean) from patients whose choice is not adequately autonomous. Thinking about hard cases is not enough unless we can find clear distinctions between those cases and others.

A second assumption which mars these debates is that the favoured image of the autonomous patient is often coupled with another stereotypical figure, namely the *wholly compassionate* relative, friend, carer or physician. But realities are more complex. Even the most loving families and friends may be greatly burdened by caring for a very ill person, not to mention impoverished. Even compassionate professionals are unlikely to be wholly or solely compassionate. Compassion is often, and understandably, mixed with frustration, anger – even with hopes and interests in another's death.

How can we tell which requests for help with suicide express robust individual autonomy and which do not? How can we tell which choices express compliance with the (spoken or unspoken) desires of burdened carers and relatives, or of expectant heirs, whose compassion may be limited? How do we know which families and professionals are 'wholly compassionate'?

If we are to draft safe legislation to make assisted suicide lawful, we would need to find a way of ensuring that requests for help do not reflect either momentary despair, clinical depression or weary compliance with, or deference to, the desires of relatives, carers and professionals. Even deferential and frightened choices are choices, so minimally autonomous.

In a world of idealized wholly autonomous patients, and of wholly selfless and compassionate families and professionals, legislation providing for assisted dying might, if ethically acceptable, not be risky. But we do not live in that world, and I doubt whether we can draft legislation that is safe for human beings with their full variety of situations and dependence on one another. The philosopher Bernard Williams was, I think, right to suggest that we should not put too much weight on the fragile structure of the voluntary (Williams 2006: 194).

References

Dworkin, G. (1988) *The Theory and Practice of Autonomy*. Cambridge: Cambridge University Press.

Faden, R.F. and Beauchamp, T.L. (1986) *A History and Theory of Informed Consent*. New York: Oxford University Press.

Manson, N.C. and O'Neill, O. (2007) *Rethinking Informed Consent in Bioethics*. Cambridge: Cambridge University Press.

O'Neill, O. (2002) *Autonomy and Trust in Bioethics*. Cambridge: Cambridge University Press.

Williams, B. (2006) *Ethics and the Limits of Philosophy*. Abingdon: Routledge (first published by Fontana in 1985).

28 Dignity, quality of life and the care of the dying

Daniel P. Sulmasy

Introduction

The word 'dignity' arises repeatedly in debates over euthanasia and assisted suicide, both in Europe and in North America. Unlike the phrases 'autonomy' and 'slippery slope', 'dignity' is used by advocates on *both* sides of the question. Consider, for instance, that the most prominent pro-assisted suicide organization in the UK is called 'The Campaign for Dignity in Dying', and refers on its website to the Swiss assisted suicide organization called Dignitas as a model. Yet the disabled community objects to the legalization of assisted suicide because it is understood as an assault on the dignity of those whose lives depend on the assistance of others (Campbell 2006). Or, consider that assisted suicide was legalized in the US state of Oregon by the 'Death with Dignity Act'. Yet opponents of assisted suicide in the United States, such as the Family Research Council, have declared that, 'The idea of assisted suicide is a poison pill that kills the *dignity* of a precious human life' (Knickerbocker 2001: 3; added emphasis). The word 'dignity' cannot mean the same thing in all these instances. A better understanding of this word can therefore bring clarity and insight to the arguments about euthanasia and assisted suicide in Europe, North America and elsewhere in the world.

The importance of dignity

Dignity is an important word in ethics (Sulmasy 2002). It occurs five times in the Universal Declaration of Human Rights of the United Nations. The European Convention on Human Rights and Biomedicine also uses it five times. The liberal rights theorist, Ronald Dworkin, writes that, underlying the conception of human rights is '... this vague but powerful idea of human dignity ... associated with Kant but defended by philosophers of different schools ... recognizing [each person] as a full member of the human community' (Dworkin 1977: 198–99). However, the word 'dignity' is vague, and is used variably, making some conceptual clarification of the word essential in discussions about assisted suicide, euthanasia, or anything else.

Three meanings of dignity

All living things have value. This notion is at the heart of any serious account of environmental ethics (Rolston 1988). We use the word 'dignity', however, to refer to the special value of human beings (or, arguably, the special value of other complex forms of life with highly developed capacities for language, reason, memory, affect, love, imagination, aesthetic experience, humour, and for grasping the finite and the infinite). I have argued that there are three different basic meanings of dignity: intrinsic, attributed and inflorescent dignity (Sulmasy 2008, 2013).

> *Intrinsic dignity*, the meaning most closely associated with the philosopher Immanuel Kant (1724–1804), indicates the worth or value a human being has simply because of being human. This value is, as Dworkin suggests, the basis of human rights. Everyone has intrinsic human dignity. It is truly inalienable – it cannot be taken away or given away – and is radically equal among all human beings. It does not admit of degrees. The leader of the US civil rights movement, the Reverend Dr Martin Luther King Jr (1929–1968), said he learned this meaning of dignity from his grandmother who told him: 'Martin, don't ever let anybody ever tell you that you're not a somebody' (Baker-Fletcher 1993: 23). The conviction that everybody is a somebody is at the heart of *intrinsic* dignity.
>
> *Attributed dignity*, by contrast, is a value we confer upon others, or even upon ourselves. We may describe a certain task as beneath our dignity, or describe an important visitor as a 'dignitary'. It does admit of degrees — people can have variable esteem in our eyes, or even in their own eyes.
>
> *Inflorescent dignity* provides a third basic meaning of dignity, to describe how someone acted virtuously, often in the face of adversity. This meaning has roots in Stoic philosophy. A person of dignity, in this sense, does not engage in crude behaviour or vulgar activities such as denigrating persons who are socially marginalized or promoting vices such as pornography. This value, like attributed dignity, does admit of degrees – people lead more or less dignified lives in this meaning of the word. Yet, like intrinsic dignity, it is not conferred by human attribution or ascribed to someone. It is recognized as objectively good when encountered.

These three meanings are interrelated. Importantly, the intrinsic sense is the fundamental sense. Human beings are considered to be set apart from other life forms and to have intrinsic dignity. And inflorescent dignity is the fruit of intrinsic dignity – the blossoming of human excellence in a life well-lived. Thus, there is no attributed or inflorescent dignity without intrinsic dignity.

Dignity and care at the end of life

With this understanding, we can explain how it is that the word 'dignity' functions in debates about physician-assisted suicide. Proponents use the word in its attributed meaning, arguing that dependence, loss of control, and being a burden on others diminish the esteem of dying persons, and that this can progress to the point at which they consider their lives no longer worth living.

Opponents use the word primarily in its intrinsic meaning (although they also sometimes invoke inflorescent dignity). They acknowledge that illness and the dying process mount an assault on the attributed dignity of patients, but argue that we care about their intrinsic dignity. This creates a moral obligation to enhance the attributed dignity of dying persons and nurture their capacity for inflorescent dignity. Chochinov (2002) has shown how effective dignity-conserving care can be when clinicians recognize this is part of their overall duty.

We have an obligation to eliminate their suffering, but not to eliminate the sufferer. That is because their attributed dignity has no ethical basis except in that it is rooted in their intrinsic dignity. Assisted suicide and euthanasia turn a somebody into a nobody. Once we accept that it can be morally justifiable to aim at eliminating anyone with their intrinsic dignity, solely because we are concerned about the state of their attributed dignity, we have undermined not only the basis for palliative care, but the entire basis for respecting human rights – respect for the intrinsic dignity and worth of human beings.

The philosophy of palliative and hospice care, from the time of Dame Cicely Saunders to the present, is based on a proper understanding of the relationship between attributed and intrinsic dignity. We all know that illness and dying mount a relentless assault upon our individual humanity. The dying look different. They lose control of certain bodily functions; of their freedom of movement and of choice. They often are shunned. The dying need to be reminded of their intrinsic dignity at a time when their diminished attributed dignity can call their own sense of self-worth into fierce doubt. Hospice and palliative care thus work to be present to the dying, to accompany them, to treat their pain and other symptoms, and assure them of their worth and of our care even as the bonds that keep them and us together are slowly dissolving. Dying persons deserve this because of their intrinsic dignity. Assisted suicide and euthanasia ratify the false idea that their intrinsic value somehow has been erased, and that we can dispose of their life rather than acknowledge the inevitability of death while supporting them to live as well as possible until that time. They deserve dignity-enhancing care, not physician-assisted early death.

Quality of life and care for the dying

Both proponents and opponents of assisted suicide are similarly concerned about quality of life. I once heard the US bioethicist Eric Cassell (1928–2021) remark, cogently, that, 'Quality of life is not a variable. It is where we live.'

In a manner that parallels the debate about dignity and care at the end of life, proponents of assisted suicide sometimes argue that the quality of some dying persons' lives can become so diminished that they are better off dead – that the quality of their lives can actually be enhanced by prescribing death. This is commonly parsed as, 'There are states worse than death', and this phrase is then proposed as a justification for euthanasia or assisted suicide. Some investigators have conducted a statistical decision analysis study that allowed persons to assign death a higher numerical quality than being alive (Patrick et al. 1994).

But this sort of thinking is deeply confused. Life has many qualities, such as degrees of pleasure or pain, the quality of being loved, one's relationship with nature, the joy of intellectual discovery or aesthetic appreciation, and so on. But to speak of the quality of someone's life presupposes that this someone is alive for life to have that quality. Talk of 'states worse than death' is, literally, nonsense. To be dead is to cease existing. And there is no quality of what does not exist. The meaning of such a phrase, therefore, can only be figurative, and is used to express great suffering.

Such expression of terrible suffering is a cry for help. This should lead to inquiries about the cause of that suffering without delay, and every effort made to ameliorate the person's suffering.

Hospice and palliative care professionals are centrally concerned with improving, sustaining or slowing the loss of quality in a dying person's life, neither hastening nor delaying death as they accompany patients in the final phases of their lives.

The quality of a person's life is often thought of as if it were one thing but, of course, it is multidimensional and it is not at all clear that there is a common currency by which to make commensurate all these disparate qualities. For example, when dying patients rate the quality of their lives on scales such as the McGill Quality of Life Scale, they may report moderate pain and significant limitations in their activities of daily living such as dressing and bathing, yet rate the overall quality of their lives as outstanding because of the love they are being shown (Cohen et al. 1997).

The task of true care for dying persons is to evaluate each of the dimensions of their quality of life and to assist them to the best of our ability in navigating these challenges. Being incurable does not render a person uncareable. Health professionals must use drugs and other interventions proportionately, parsimoniously and discreetly, always with a restorative intent, aiming at making patients, holistically, as fully themselves as possible, cognisant of the limits imposed by the conditions of human finitude (Sulmasy 2018). Importantly, proportionate care includes using the right intervention for the right dimension of quality in life. One uses morphine for pain. One uses fluoxetine for depression. One uses chaplaincy or other humanistic interventions for spiritual and existential distress. A cocktail of toxic doses of morphine, diazepam and digoxin is simply not 'indicated' – not appropriately responsive care – for a patient who says that he is suffering and would be better off dead.

Importantly, in decisions to forgo life-sustaining treatments, one is always making judgements about the quality of life (Sulmasy 2011). The benefits and burdens associated with life-sustaining treatment are qualities of existence, qualities of life. One can (must) weigh the values of one set of qualities against another in making decisions such as whether, for example, to discontinue chemotherapy or ventilation, or to initiate dialysis. The burdens and benefits of treatment are qualities uniquely relevant to each patient. It is *this* particular patient who is benefitted or burdened by the ventilator. A judgement about the net sum of the burdens and benefits of continuing treatment for each patient is a judgement about the efficacy of the intervention in relation to the quality of life of a particular person. If one were to eschew all judgements of the quality of life, one could never discontinue any life-sustaining therapy.

This is not to say, however, that a weighing of the burdens and benefits associated with continuing treatment exhausts our assessment of the value of life; it is not a judgement about the value of the patient, but about the qualities of the state in which that particular person now finds him or herself.

Conclusion: dignity, quality of life and care for the dying

This brings us to the connection between dignity and quality of life. Diminished quality of life concerns diminutions in the attributed dignity of the patient. But it is critical to understand that diminution in the quality of life of dying patients does not remove their value as human beings; it does not eliminate their intrinsic dignity, which is never exhausted, even by terminal illness. The intrinsic value of a person's life is not a quality of that life, but the condition for the possibility of that life having quality. Life itself, and its value (intrinsic dignity), is completely *unqualified*. When we speak of the quality of a patient's life, we can only be speaking of the attributed value of that life, not the intrinsic value of that life.

And so, we are led once again to considerations about the value of hospice and palliative care as alternatives to assisted suicide and euthanasia. These services promote the quality of life of dying persons while never aiming deliberately to eliminate the condition for the possibility of that quality, the lives of the patients themselves, marked by intrinsic dignity. A commitment to enhancing the quality of life of a dying person requires respect for the intrinsic value of that life – the intrinsic dignity of the dying person. This means that assisted suicide and euthanasia are simply incompatible with genuine care for the dying.

References

Baker-Fletcher, G. (1993) *Somebodyness: Martin Luther King, Jr. and the Theory of Dignity*, Harvard Dissertations in Divinity, No. 31. Minneapolis, MN: Fortress Press.

Campbell, J. (2006) *Assisted dying: a question of choice?* Centre for Disability Studies, School of Sociology and Social Policy, University of Leeds, 15 November. Available at: https://disability-studies.leeds.ac.uk/wp-content/uploads/sites/40/library/Campbell-Leeds-Uni-15-Nov-2006.doc (accessed 27 February 2024).

Chochinov, H.M. (2002) Dignity-conserving care – a new model for palliative care: helping the patient feel valued, *Journal of the American Medical Association*, 287 (17): 2253–60.

Cohen, S.R., Mount, B.M., Bruera, E. et al. (1997) Validity of the McGill Quality Of Life Questionnaire in the palliative care setting: a multi-centre Canadian study demonstrating the importance of the existential domain, *Palliative Medicine*, 11 (1): 3–20.

Dworkin, R. (1977) *Taking Rights Seriously*. Cambridge, MA: Harvard University Press.

Knickerbocker, B. (2001) Latest showdown over assisted suicide, *Christian Science Monitor*, 15 November. Available at: https://www.csmonitor.com/2001/1115/p3s1-usju.html.

Patrick D.L., Starks, H.E., Cain, K.C. et al. (1994) Measuring preferences for health states worse than death, *Medical Decision Making*, 14 (1): 9–18.

Rolston, H. (1988) *Environmental Ethics*. Philadelphia, PA: Temple University Press.

Sulmasy, D.P. (2002) Death, dignity, and the theory of value, *Ethical Perspectives*, 9 (2/3): 103–18.

Sulmasy, D.P. (2008) Dignity and bioethics: history, theory, and selected applications, in E.D. Pellegrino (ed.) *Human Dignity and Bioethics*. Washington, DC: The President's Council on Bioethics.

Sulmasy, D.P. (2011) Speaking of the value of life, *Kennedy Institute of Ethics Journal*, 21 (2): 181–99.

Sulmasy, D.P. (2013) The varieties of human dignity: a logical and conceptual analysis, *Medicine, Health Care and Philosophy*, 16 (4): 937–44.

Sulmasy, D.P. (2018) The last low whispers of our dead: when is it ethically justifiable to render a patient unconscious until death?, *Theoretical Medicine and Bioethics*, 39 (3): 233–63.

29 | The imperative to prevent suicide and not to encourage or assist it

David Albert Jones

Introduction

The word 'suicide' means to kill (-cide) oneself (sui-). The core meaning of suicide is death caused by an action by which a person intentionally ends his or her own life. Sometimes the word is used loosely for some rash or dangerous action: 'you cannot attempt to jump over that waterfall, it would be suicide!'. More subtly there are actions that we fully expect will lead to our deaths but this is not our aim. Consider the soldier who jumps onto a grenade to save others; if by some miracle the grenade does not go off, then the soldier's plan is not thwarted. The soldier acted with the expectation of death but not *in order to* die. This would not be suicide.

Difference between suicide and murder

Suicide intentionally takes the life of a human being. Hence, it is a kind of homicide, and indeed was once termed 'self-murder'. Nevertheless, suicide is clearly very different from what we normally understand by 'murder'. Murder, the intentional killing of an innocent person (that is, of a person outside the context of just war or lawful policing), is wrong because it is unjust. If I commit murder, I rob someone of something that cannot be restored to that person. I exercise the power of life and death over someone as though I were judge, jury and executioner. I commit a grave injustice.

'Rational suicide'

In contrast, the person who kills him- or herself is not being unjust to the person who is killed. You cannot be unjust to yourself (except perhaps in a metaphorical sense). As suicide is not unjust, some people have argued that it is a private matter and not something that is anyone else's business. If I kill myself when overcome by emotion, then my suicide is irrational, but if I calmly decide that my life is no longer enjoyable or meaningful, then, according to some, suicide would be rational. This view is expressed by the name of a group set up a few years ago: the 'Society for Old Age Rational Suicide'. That name, of course, raises the question of why suicide is supposed to be rational only in old age. This seems to imply, and thereby reinforce, a common and very bleak view of growing older. In any case, the group has recently changed its name to 'My Death, My Decision'. No more mention of 'rational suicide'.

Against the idea of 'rational suicide' is the claim that suicide transgresses a fundamental principle of human existence. I seem to be a necessary part of my world. To intend to end my own life is not simply to change something within my world. It is to 'end it all'. This helps explain why Thomas Aquinas thought that suicide was wrong for a more fundamental reason than killing another person would be. It represents a failure to value existence as such. The philosopher Ludwig Wittgenstein struggled throughout his life with thoughts of suicide, and lost three brothers to separate suicides. He expressed a similar thought to Aquinas when he said, 'If suicide is allowed, then everything is allowed. If anything is not allowed, then suicide is not allowed. This throws a light on the nature of ethics, for suicide is, so to speak, the elementary sin' (Wittgenstein 1961: 91).

Philosophical accounts of suicide

If it seems too much to say suicide is the 'elementary sin', we could say that suicide is a failure to grasp the inherent worth of human life *in my own case*. According to Immanuel Kant, the first rule of morality can be formulated in this way: 'Act in such a way that you treat humanity, whether in your own person or in the person of any other, never merely as a means, but always at the same time as an end' (Kant 1993: 30). Kant was perhaps the greatest defender of autonomy as an ethical principle, but in his view, the act of suicide could not be an authentic expression of human autonomy. It contradicts the basis for autonomy (see Chapter 27 for further discussion of autonomy).

A problem with philosophical accounts of suicide, even those by great thinkers such as Kant, is that they tend to regard suicide as the free action of an individual and then analyse this action. In contrast, since the time of the sociologist Emile Durkheim, we have come to appreciate much more how the action of suicide is affected by social factors outside the person and by psychological factors within the person, that together can seriously undermine a person's ability to reason freely.

Suicide prevention and social solidarity

Suicide is commonly an impulsive act. It is characteristically an expression of desperation. It is not simply an individual decision and is not something that is inevitable. Others can help and suicides can be prevented. The imperative to prevent suicide is not based principally on a moral analysis of suicide but is based on the conviction that 'every suicide is a tragedy' (WHO 2014: 2). Rather than thinking of suicide as a person doing harm, suicide prevention strategies regard suicide as a person suffering harm and ask how we might help avert this.

In thinking of suicide, we should begin, then, not with individual actions taken in isolation, but with social solidarity. It is true that everyone must die his or her own death, but human death is never simply a private matter. It involves us all. This has rarely been expressed better than by the poet John Donne:

No man is an island, entire of itself; every man is a piece of the continent, a part of the main. If a clod be washed away by the sea, Europe is the less, as well as if a promontory were, as well as if a manor of thy friend's or of thine own were: any man's death diminishes me, because I am involved in mankind, and therefore never send to know for whom the bells tolls; it tolls for thee. (Donne 1959: 108–9)

This sense of solidarity impels us to help those who are suicidal by helping them to live. Suicide is not just the person's business. Suicide, and suicide prevention, is everyone's business. The disability rights campaigner Alison Davis, reflecting on a long period of her life when she wanted to die stated that, 'My greatest piece of good fortune was that I had friends who did not share my view that my life had no value … Often all desperate people, disabled or not, need is to be given hope. What they definitely don't need is to be told they are right to feel so unhappy and that they would be better off dead' (Davis 2013; and see Jones 2018: 311). In saying this, Davis was not envisaging a quick fix. She acknowledged that it took 'a very long time to help me just "give life another try"'. Nevertheless, she was bearing witness to the possibility of finding hope again. Where there is life, there is hope.

It is uncontroversial that, at least in general, suicide is a tragedy that society should seek to prevent. Indeed, Jonathan Herring, Professor of Medical Law at Oxford University, goes further and states that people have a right to be protected from dying by suicide (Herring 2022).

Encouraging and assisting suicide

It is to protect people from suicide that the Suicide Act 1961 makes it unlawful in England and Wales to 'encourage or assist suicide'. This law has been challenged in court several times by people who want to legalize some form of physician-assisted suicide. However, the European Court of Human Rights has upheld the current law. The prohibition on encouraging or assisting suicide is a reasonable means by which the state seeks to protect people who are vulnerable to suicide, and any of us may become vulnerable to suicide.

In order to overcome public and political reluctance to legalize physician-assisted suicide, advocates have moved away from the language of 'assisted suicide'. For example, the first official report on the Oregon Death with Dignity Act in 1999 used the term 'physician-assisted suicide', as did the first eight reports. However, the ninth report, released in 2007, dropped this term and it is not used in any of the subsequent reports. The political motivation for this change in language was acknowledged by the philosopher Gerald Dworkin, even though he was in favour of legalizing assisted suicide: 'the use of the term "Physician-assisted suicide" is now politically incorrect, for tactical reasons. I understand that the popular prejudice against suicide makes it more difficult to rally support for the bills I favor' (Dworkin 2015).

The official language used in Oregon has changed, but the practice remains the same. A patient who is terminally ill can obtain lethal drugs from a doctor for the purpose of ending his or her own life. In Oregon, the patient must self-administer the drugs. Lethal injection by a doctor (sometimes termed 'euthanasia') is illegal in Oregon. It is clear that the reason for providing the drugs is so that people can *end their own lives*. This fulfils the definition of suicide, and when the doctor provides the lethal drugs for that purpose, the doctor is assisting suicide.

Consider a recent case from Queensland, Australia (AAP 2024). A woman who had cancer made use of the Voluntary Assisted Dying law to obtain a lethal drug to end her life. She did not use the drug, however; she died from her cancer. After her death, her husband, overcome with grief, used the lethal drug to kill himself. His death was suicide, as everyone admitted, so surely it would also have been suicide if his wife had taken the same drug for the same purpose.

The term 'assisted suicide' remains the ordinary term in the Netherlands and Switzerland and accurately reflects what this practice is about. Physician-assisted suicide is thus a form of suicide, albeit a medically facilitated and socially sanctioned form of suicide (Pierre 2015).

Does assisted suicide decrease the numbers of non-assisted suicides?

Nevertheless, some people have argued that, paradoxically, legalizing physician-assisted suicide could actually help prevent suicide. This is for two reasons. First, some people with a terminal illness who do not have access to assisted suicide, die by ordinary ('unassisted') suicide, so if assisted suicide were available instead, this might reduce unassisted suicide. And second, some people who obtain a lethal drug for assisted suicide do not use it and the reassurance that this option is available can help people live until their natural death.

On the basis of these two points, people have argued that legalization of assisted suicide would reduce the number of unassisted suicides and might also lead to fewer self-initiated deaths overall (assisted plus unassisted suicides).

This is a serious argument that merits investigation, but all the evidence points in the opposite direction. After a change in the law there are more suicides. In all cases there are large increases in self-initiated deaths and, when controlled for other factors, nowhere has seen a decrease in unassisted suicide after a change in the law. In Victoria, Australia, politicians argued that the Voluntary Assisted Dying Bill could help prevent 50 suicides a year among older people but instead there has been an *increase* of 50 such suicides a year (Jones 2023). A recent study from the United States also showed that changing the law on assisted suicide was followed by a statistically significant rise in unassisted suicide of 6 per cent overall and of 14 per cent among women, even after controlling for other factors (Paton and Girma 2022).

Conclusion

The evidence is clear: permitting assistance in suicide encourages suicide; prohibiting assistance in suicide reduces suicide. The current law in England and Wales against encouraging or assisting suicide helps prevent suicide. The current law is an effective safeguard for the vulnerable that should not be abandoned lightly.

References

Australia Associated Press (AAP) (2024) Woman found father dead after he took assisted dying drugs meant for someone else, Queensland inquest hears, *The Guardian*, 20 February. Available at: https://www.theguardian.com/australia-news/2024/feb/21/woman-found-father-dead-after-he-took-assisted-dying-drugs-meant-for-someone-else-queensland-inquest-hears (accessed 9 March 2024).

Davis, A. (2013) Why euthanasia/assisted suicide would have robbed me of the best years of my life, *Catholic Medical Quarterly*, 63 (2): 5–7. Available at: http://www.cmq.org.uk/CMQ/2013/May/Editorial-Euthanasia-Alison-Davis.html (accessed 9 March 2024).

Donne, J. (1959) *Devotions upon Emergent Occasions*. Ann Arbor, MI: University of Michigan Press (originally published 1624).

Dworkin, G. (2015) California dying, *3 Quarks Daily*, 1 June. Available at: https://3quarksdaily.com/3quarksdaily/2015/06/california-dying.html (accessed 9 March 2024).

Herring, J. (2022) *The Right to be Protected from Committing Suicide*. Oxford: Hart Publishing.

Jones, D.A. (2018) Assisted dying and suicide prevention, *Journal of Disability and Religion*, 22 (3): 298–316.

Jones, D.A. (2023) Did the Voluntary Assisted Dying Act 2017 prevent 'at least one suicide every week'?, *Journal of Ethics in Mental Health*, 1: 1–35. Available at: https://jemh.ca/issues/open/documents/Did%20the%20Voluntary%20Assisted%20Dying%20Act%202017.pdf (accessed 11 July 2024).

Kant, I. (1993) *Groundwork of the Metaphysics of Morals*. Indianapolis, IN: Hackett (originally published 1785).

Paton, D. and Girma, S. (2022) Assisted suicide laws increase suicide rates, especially among women, *Vox EU*, 29 April. Available at: https://cepr.org/voxeu/columns/assisted-suicide-laws-increase-suicide-rates-especially-among-women (accessed 9 March 2024).

Pierre, J.M. (2015) Culturally sanctioned suicide: euthanasia, seppuku, and terrorist martyrdom, *World Journal of Psychiatry*, 5 (1): 4–14.

Wittgenstein, L. (1961) *Notebooks 1914–1916*. Oxford: Basil Blackwell.

World Health Organization (WHO) (2014) *Preventing Suicide: A Global Imperative*. Geneva: WHO. Available at: https://www.who.int/publications/i/item/9789241564779 (accessed 9 March 2024).

30 Instability of eligibility criteria for assisted death and its implications[1,2]

Scott Y.H. Kim

Introduction

When I speak with people who have not been steeped in the assisted dying[3] debate (including journalists and most of the public), they tend to think the debate turns on giving a convincing example: if one can describe a case of assisted dying that seems morally acceptable, then assisted dying should be legally permitted. Anyone who is familiar with the celebratory nature of assisted dying reporting (e.g. 'She died a beautiful death on her own terms') will know what I mean. The question 'Who else should qualify, i.e. what is the boundary of permissible assisted dying?' is usually not considered central to the debate over whether to legalize assisted dying or not.

Given the morally charged nature of assisted dying, this is understandable. But I outline here why such an approach to assisted dying policy is incomplete and misleading, and show that the question of 'Who else should qualify?' is not a practical detail but a fundamental question. My argument, in brief, is as follows.

Across jurisdictions, there is a wide variety of eligibility boundaries (terminal illness, terminal illness causing unbearable suffering, any medical illness causing unbearable suffering, etc); there is no obvious, stable boundary. Moreover, this instability works in one direction, as a tendency to expand, i.e. to allow more categories of people to qualify for assisted dying. This is because of a desire for equality. If assisted dying is permissible for terminal cancer pain, why not for non-terminal neuralgic pain? If for pain, why not for physical or mental suffering? It seems unfair and disrespectful to give some people's suffering more consideration than others'. If we do draw a boundary, there will always be those who have cause to complain, and the line will hold only as long as the more privileged who favour that boundary can get what they want. So the ever-expanding boundary ultimately leads to assisted dying without boundary – death on mere demand. This is a dystopia with the form of equality (celebrated by the privileged), but with the substance of inhuman disregard for the weak and the vulnerable. I argue instead that the only meaningfully human equality requires that no-one has the right to end the life of another. It turns out that human equality implies equal respect for all human lives.

Many variations of eligibility boundaries

If there were an obvious, stable boundary for assisted dying eligibility, there probably would not be the wide variation that exists across jurisdictions. Consider the range of distinguishing criteria: 'terminal illness' (with differing definitions in the US states, New Zealand, Australian states); medically based 'irremediable, unbearable suffering' where assisted dying is a last resort option (Belgium, the Netherlands and other jurisdictions); medically based 'irremediable, unbearable suffering' where refusal of curative treatment or lack of access to standard therapies is compatible with eligibility (as in Canada); autonomy only (without any preconditions about illness or suffering, as in Germany and Switzerland). There are variations within these types: for instance, the combination of 'terminal illness' and 'unbearable suffering' (NZ and Australian states) (Waller et al. 2023), or use of criteria at the discretion of private organizations providing assisted dying in Switzerland (Nyquist et al. 2024).

Although 'instability' suggests that the boundary could slide in either direction, the tendency (once assisted dying is legalized) is towards expansion. Canada is the best example, going from a prohibition to the boundary of reasonably foreseeable natural death, then to the erasure of that boundary – in a matter of a few short years (Coelho et al. 2023). But one could also point to the Netherlands, where psychiatric euthanasia was introduced some years after the courts effectively decriminalized euthanasia/assisted suicide, followed by further expansions in the meaning of 'medically based' suffering, as well as the perennial pressure to expand the boundary to include 'tired of living' or 'completed life' as a criterion (Florijn 2022; Kim 2022). Although it is true that US states have maintained the terminal illness condition for years, it is not for lack of arguments (Kious and Battin 2019) or intent on the part of activists (Bergner 2007; Blakespear 2024) to the contrary.

The sources of instability

Why is there this expansionist pressure to broaden assisted dying eligibility? The first reason is easy to miss because it is so obvious: regardless of one's view about assisted dying, *if* something is so morally important as to outweigh the long-standing prohibition against intentional taking of human life by private citizens – a prohibition, we should remember, still respected in 95 per cent of countries – then that consideration, *if* it has *that* moral weight, must be of no ordinary importance. Its moral weight will naturally seem to outweigh most reasons proposed to hem it in (Kim 2021).

Consider 'medically based' suffering as an eligibility criterion. Some might object that if it is the badness of suffering that justifies assisted dying (i.e. weighty enough to overthrow the prohibition against the intentional taking of human life), then that badness must surely outweigh whatever countervailing moral weight is borne by the distinction between medical and non-medical suffering.[4]

This kind of reasoning gains further momentum with the addition of one of the most commonly used arguments – equality or parity arguments – used in favour of expanding assisted dying boundaries (Nicolini et al. 2019). It starts with the (true) thought that it is discriminatory to grant a privilege to someone while another similarly placed is denied it. The argument proposed is that since medical and non-medical suffering are similar enough, to treat people differently in regard to assisted dying based on the source of suffering is to discriminate.

The equality approach is limited only by the ingenuity of 'equality technicians', as one lawyer once described his work to me. As the appeal to addressing suffering is the most common rationale for assisted dying, it is not difficult to imagine how this would go. Once a society deems it permissible for a private citizen to terminate the life of someone at their request because they belong to a group defined by suffering X, an equality technician can surely ask: 'what about the others in the group defined by suffering Y who seem to share salient features with those in group X?'. After all, it seems dehumanizing to rank one person's suffering over another's in terms of their moral significance (Kim 2022). It is only a short step from this to collapsing the definition of irremediable, intolerable suffering – or any other criterion – to that defined solely by the patient. The expansionist pressure is naturally towards prioritizing private reasons, apparently shielding it from intrusive eyes.

Dystopian equality

The German Federal Constitutional Court (2020) recently carried the above logic to its conclusion: 'the right to a self-determined death is not limited to situations defined by external causes like serious or incurable illnesses', the court said, 'nor does it only apply in certain stages of life or illness. Rather, this right is guaranteed in all stages of a person's existence'.'

Such a system at first sight seems truly egalitarian. Any competent adult would be able to access assisted dying, without having to justify their request based on illness, suffering, terminal condition, etc. Equality arguments seem to have run out of boundaries to complain about.

But that conclusion would be too hasty. If 'competence' is a functional concept, requiring sufficient decisional abilities, what about minors who seem capable of making decisions? Both Belgium and the Netherlands already have expanded access to their assisted dying law to minors. But even an expansion to include competent minors would not exhaust concerns about discrimination. Without resorting to some fanciful hypothetical construct, we can consider a widely discussed challenge to the very idea of functional definition of capacity, pushed by an influential UN committee. The United Nations Committee on Rights of Persons with Disabilities has argued that a functional abilities approach to determining capacity is discriminatory, and that everyone regardless of one's disability or functional abilities has legal capacity (United Nations 2014). The Committee has therefore called for the abolition of surrogate decision-making laws.[5]

We have now arrived at our final destination. Existing constructs (human rights constructs, no less) can readily be enlisted to argue that since even functional abilities are not needed for possession of legal capacity, anyone can qualify for assisted dying, merely on the asking. Regardless of one's age, gender, health status or disability, functional decisional abilities, and so on, every person would have access to assisted dying in this egalitarian, if dystopian, scenario.

Hegemony of privilege

Is my argument alarmist? I offer the above as a *reductio*,[6] but in the assisted dying debate, one person's *reductio* is another person's anti-discrimination argument. And given the widespread strategic use of equality arguments, one can be forgiven for some degree of scepticism regarding those who dismiss arguments like mine as unrealistic or morally unthinkable.

If we put aside dystopian equality as pictured above, what are the alternatives? One option is to give up the quest for equality when it comes to assisted dying laws. But is a principled argument for one of the boundaries likely to emerge? It would amount to accepting the following, although what one accepts will depend on one's point of view.

For assisted dying proponents (and those wishing to make use of assisted dying), they would have to accept that on this momentous issue of having a choice about life or death, some human beings deserve that choice but other human beings do not. For assisted dying sceptics (and those who do not want the option of assisted dying thrust upon them), it would amount to accepting that the law should deem assisted dying permissible for some people because their lives are below a certain threshold of value, but other people should be protected because the value of their lives is higher, above that threshold.

It is understandable that people on both sides would find the implications hard to accept. They are hard pills to swallow, regardless of where the boundary is set, as it means *both* that society will deny some people's 'right of self-determination' *and* society will deem some people's lives not worth living. Imagine explaining to someone that their suffering isn't quite up to par for them to earn the right to assisted dying; or explaining to someone, who would rather live despite their suffering, why standard treatments that would make them better are harder to obtain than access to state-approved death, all the while enduring the disdainful gaze of others that say, 'their lives are so bad, why are they hanging on?'. (Note here how much more complex and difficult the task of justifying a boundary is compared with conjuring a single hypothetical example of acceptable assisted dying.)

It seems unlikely that a decisive, *principled* compromise would emerge.

In reality, arriving at a boundary will be susceptible to what usually maintains unjustified inequalities in societies, namely, the inequality of power. Those with more socio-economic, cultural and political influence will likely have more influence getting their preferred boundaries. If there is one great socio-political truth about assisted dying, this is probably it. This hegemony of privilege seems to have so far had the starkest implementation in Canada whose current Medical Assistance in Dying (MAiD) law combined with the country's peculiar health funding situation de facto targets the poor and the weak (Kim 2023a).

True equality

There is, of course, another way of achieving true universal equality among all persons regarding assisted dying. And that is to prohibit all intentional termination of human life, even upon request, by a private citizen. This equality-based conclusion highlights a couple of neglected truths about assisted dying policy-making.

First, it is not some sectarian belief in absolute inviolability of human life that need ground prohibition of assisted dying. It is about showing equal respect for all human life. A prohibition is the only truly principled basis for treating every human being's life equally. Second, it is perfectly coherent to endorse a prohibition even if one believes that in some situations assisted dying can be morally acceptable or, indeed, even if one would want assisted dying for oneself. Endorsing a prohibition only demands that everyone – those who find assisted dying morally acceptable and those who do not – accept that there is a shared, higher principle of common morality we must not neglect.

Conclusion

Ultimately, there are three options when it comes to assisted dying policies: assisted dying with contested boundaries reflecting inequalities of power, privilege and economic resources; assisted dying with no boundaries, an egalitarian dystopia; and finally, its prohibition based on a human rights achievement thousands of years in the making – a deep commitment to the equality of all human beings.

Notes

1. The opinions expressed are the author's and not the policies or views of the NIH, DHHS or the US government.
2. Parts of this essay are adapted from Kim (2023), 'What does true equality in assisted dying require?', the text of which is in the public domain.
3. I will use the terms 'assisted death' or 'assisted dying' to denote the intentional termination of human life that requires the involvement of another (that is, medical assistance in dying, euthanasia, assisted suicide, physician-assisted suicide, physician aid in dying, etc.).
4. As Felicia Ackerman (2020) provocatively puts it, 'many people have suicidal desires grounded in conditions that are very unlikely to change, such as poverty, ugliness, menial and gruelling jobs, lack of love'. This is not just provocative hyperbole. See the brief discussion (in Kim et al. 2016) of a Dutch woman whose grief was dubiously medicalized so that she could qualify for euthanasia.
5. Paragraph 7, General Comment 1 states: '[Substitute decision-making regimes] … must be abolished in order to ensure that full legal capacity is restored to persons with disabilities on an equal basis with others.'
6. That is, the argument has the form of a *reductio ad absurdum*. Dr Kim establishes the reasonableness of his argument by showing that the alternative leads to absurdity [added by editors].

References

Ackerman, F.N. (2020) Commentary on 'Expressivism at the beginning and end of life', *Journal of Medical Ethics*, 46 (8): 548–49.
Blakespear, C. (2024) *End of Life Option Act*, Bill SB 1196, California Senate, 14 February. Available at: https://leginfo.legislature.ca.gov/faces/billTextClient.xhtml?bill_id=202320240SB1196#99INT (accessed 12 March 2024).

Bergner, D. (2007) Death in the family, *New York Times Magazine*, 2 December. Available at: https://www.nytimes.com/2007/12/02/magazine/02suicide-t.html (accessed 20 February 2024).

Coelho, R., Maher, J., Gaind, K.S. and Lemmens, T. (2023) The realities of medical assistance in dying in Canada, *Palliative and Supportive Care*, 21 (5): 871–78.

Florijn, B.W. (2022) From reciprocity to autonomy in physician-assisted death: an ethical analysis of the Dutch Supreme Court ruling in the Albert Heringa case, *American Journal of Bioethics*, 22 (2): 51–58.

German Federal Constitutional Court (2020) Criminalisation of assisted suicide services unconstitutional. Press Release No. 12/2020, 26 February. Available at: https://www.bundesverfassungsgericht.de/SharedDocs/Pressemitteilungen/EN/2020/bvg20-012.html (accessed 20 February 2024).

Kim, S.Y.H. (2021) Ways of debating assisted suicide and euthanasia: implications for psychiatry, *Perspectives in Biology and Medicine*, 64 (1): 29–43.

Kim, S.Y.H. (2022) The unstable boundary of suffering-based euthanasia regimes, *American Journal of Bioethics*, 22 (2): 59–62.

Kim, S.Y.H. (2023a) Canadian Medical Assistance in Dying and the hegemony of privilege, *American Journal of Bioethics*, 23 (11): 1–6.

Kim, S.Y.H. (2023b) What does true equality in assisted dying require?, *American Journal of Bioethics*, 23 (9): 1–4.

Kim, S.Y.H., De Vries, R. and Peteet, J. (2016) Euthanasia and assisted suicide of patients with psychiatric disorders in the Netherlands 2011 to 2014, *JAMA Psychiatry*, 73 (4): 362–68.

Kious, B.M. and Battin, M. (2019) Physician aid-in-dying and suicide prevention in psychiatry: a moral crisis?, *American Journal of Bioethics*, 19 (10): 29–39.

Nicolini, M.E., Gastmans, C. and Kim, S.Y.H. (2019) Parity arguments for 'physician aid-in-dying' (PAD) for psychiatric disorders: their structure and limits, *American Journal of Bioethics*, 19 (10): 3–7.

Nyquist, C., Cohen-Almagor, R. and Kim, S.Y.H. (2024) Expert views on medical involvement in the Swiss assisted dying practice: 'We want to have our cake and eat it too'?, *AJOB Empirical Bioethics*, 15 (1): 41–59.

United Nations (2014) *General Comment No. 1: Article 12 Equal Recognition Before the Law*, UN Committee on the Rights of Persons with Disabilities. Available at: https://www.ohchr.org/en/documents/general-comments-and-recommendations/general-comment-no-1-article-12-equal-recognition-1 (accessed 20 February 2024).

Waller, K., Del Villar, K., Willmott, L. and White, B.P. (2023) Voluntary assisted dying in Australia: a comparative and critical analysis of state laws, *University of New South Wales Law Journal*, 46 (4): 1421–70.

PART 7

Faith and no faith

31 | The place of religion in the public debate about assisted suicide

Nigel Biggar

Introduction: why medicine must reach beyond empirical science

Empirical medical science raises questions that cannot be given an empirical answer. It can tell us about the development of the human foetus, for example, but it cannot tell us what a 'person' is or at what point the foetus becomes such a thing: those are philosophical or theological questions. Nor can medical science tell us under what conditions it is permissible to kill a person: that is an ethical question. Questions of philosophical or theological views of human being, or questions of ethics, cannot be answered simply by appeal to empirical data and thereby to medical science.

That does not mean that their answers are irrational: appeal to hard empirical data is not the only form of reason. So are appeals to moral intuitions about what is good and right, to logic and rational consistency, and even to beauty. However, given the long-standing controversy that attends such issues as the definition of the human person and the conditions for permissible killing, it is clear that applying 'reason' to such matters does not produce consensus, and nor is it likely to any time soon. So, the ideal of medicine as a realm of reason *and therefore* as untroubled by deep metaphysical and moral disagreements is a fantasy. Even if medicine were religion-free, its peace would still be disturbed by disputes between philosophical schools: Aristotelian, utilitarian and Kantian, just to mention the obvious ones.

Why religion is not simply irrational

Religion, therefore, is not uniquely awkward. It is not the only disturber of the peace in the ethics of medical practice. Philosophy can disturb perfectly well on its own. Nevertheless, it is widely supposed that religion should be kept out of 'secular' space – whether medical or educational or political – because it is by nature irrational and dogmatic. After all, religion is a matter of faith, not reason, is it not?

Yes and no. For sure, some religious believers can believe some violently irrational things – for example, that God commands them to detonate suicide bombs on the London Underground. Violent irrationality, however, is not the creature of religion as such: the practice of suicide-bombing was pioneered by the secular, political separatist movement, the Tamil Tigers.

It is true that religious believers believe in things that they cannot put under a microscope or demonstrate mathematically – God's existence, for example, or the natural purpose of the cosmos, or the afterlife. However, many unbelievers have faith in human dignity and in the unstoppable progress of human history, neither of which can be proven empirically or logically, and both of which attract rational doubts.

So, the fact that religion involves faith (in the sense of belief that outruns proof) does not mean that it is bereft of reason. Unbelievers, of course, doubt that religion commands *sufficient* reason. But believers beg to differ.

Plural secularity instead of anti-religious secularism

Secular space – whether in medicine or elsewhere – cannot expect to be free of conflict between rival kinds of reasoning. In medicine, conflict is an irremovable fact of life at the metaphysical and ethical levels. Secular space, therefore, is not and should not pretend to be neutral, transcending conflict. According to its original meaning, developed by Augustine, Bishop of Hippo in North Africa in the early fifth century AD, the word 'secular' refers to the time *before* the complete establishment of divine order in the world. The *saeculum* is the age of spiritual and moral mixture and ambiguity. In this secular age, peace in political society is the result, not of natural uniformity, but of negotiation and provisional compromise between rival viewpoints.

This Augustinian conception of secularity is more consonant with a genuinely liberal, plural political ideal than the dogmatically anti-religious, secularist version. Every citizen, whether religious or not, has an equal right to say what they think in public. And since religion is not simply, invariably, or uniquely irrational, it follows that its representatives should be allowed to sit at the table of public negotiation – not least in Parliament.[1]

To take a seat at the negotiating table, however, implies a readiness to negotiate and so to persuade; and that has implications for what one *does* at the table, for how one *behaves*. To persuade, one must become persuasive.

Persuasive religion

For religious believers, what does this mean? Negatively, it requires the abandonment of all sheer appeal to authority – whether to that of the Bible or of the Pope or of the Quran. Such appeals are imprudent and disrespectful. They are imprudent because they are unlikely to move those who do not recognize them. But they are also disrespectful because they fail to notice that, in a secular and therefore plural context, the people addressed might not share the believer's assumptions. To appeal to religious authority, therefore, is to refuse to engage with the listener's difference, pushing past as if it were so stupid or wicked as to be beyond rational consideration. To unbelievers this is bound to seem insensitive and *gauche*, if not high-handed and insulting.

Positively, if I, a religious believer, am going to succeed in persuading you, an agnostic or atheist or different kind of religious believer, of my moral view, then I will have to invoke values and principles we share in common and show you that your view has weaknesses or problems that cannot be adequately repaired in your terms, but can be repaired in mine.

Since the topic under discussion is a moral issue, and not a specifically religious one, I might not refer at all to the existence of God or the afterlife. I will address the issue in terms of moral principles and the view of human being they assume. If the topic is the morality and legalization of physician-assisted suicide[2] and euthanasia, for example, I will talk about such things as the value of individual human life, the limitation of individual autonomy by social duty, the importance of social norms that dispose us to care for those in adversity, the gap between the fine letter of the law and its implementation by under-resourced healthcare staff, and the real possibility of the abuse of the vulnerable by impatient or greedy relatives.

However, while none of these terms is itself religious, the views they express are nevertheless shaped by religious tenets. Not everyone believes in the value of individual human life, for example, but biblical monotheists such as Jews, Christians and Muslims who view human beings as the beloved creatures of a divine Creator are bound to. And Christians, with their pronounced sense of human sinfulness, will be more sensitive than many to the possibility of the corruption of humane norms, the failure of institutions and the malice of individuals.

The fact that religious believers do not always talk in overtly religious terms does not mean, as some suggest, that they are being disingenuous. It means only that they are attending strictly to the moral nature of the topic under discussion, and giving expression to their religious world-view insofar as it bears upon that.[3]

Christian views of physician-assisted suicide

All Christian traditions, being monotheistic, have a high view of the dignity of human individuals and the value of their lives. Nevertheless, while there is a marginal pacifist tradition that forbids all taking of human life, the mainstream traditions permit it under certain circumstances – for example, where necessary to defend the lives of innocents against grave assault. That said, from very early on the Christian Church set its face absolutely against suicide, partly to discourage members whose over-enthusiasm was driving them actively to court martyrdom. In addition, the example of Jesus who suffered crucifixion has inclined Christians to view suffering in general as something to be borne with faith and courage.

On the other hand, compassion for those subjected to oppression or adversity ranks high among the Christian virtues and inclines Christians to relieve human suffering, not least among the dying. What's more, high esteem for the dignity of human individuals entails respect for a certain kind of autonomy. Christian tradition has long recognized a limited sphere of autonomy, where the individual should be free to make up his or her own mind about what moral obligations and vocations require in a particular case, here and now. That is what is commonly known as 'conscience'. Respect for an individual's conscience, fortified by compassion, has led a minority of Christians in recent times to support the legalization of assisted suicide.[4]

However, from a properly Christian point of view, the freedom of conscience is a morally responsible freedom. It operates within the bounds set by objective moral obligation. Usually, however, the kind of autonomy asserted in the debate about physician-assisted dying is not of this qualified, responsible kind. Rather, it is absolute and libertarian, as in 'My life is my property, and I have the moral right to dispose of it when and how I choose'. To this the Christian response should be: 'Whether or not you *have* such a moral right is not something you can establish merely by asserting it. It depends on whether or not you're subject to overriding obligations to other people, which constrain your choice of physician-assisted dying'. Are there in fact such obligations? There would be, *if* granting a certain class of patient the right to physician-assisted dying would tend to undermine any societal commitment to support human life in adversity, and *if* it would expose a much larger number of patients to abusive manipulation. *If* that were the case, then larger considerations of social good would preclude the granting of a small class of individuals the right to physician-assisted dying.

'*If* that were the case': but is it in fact so? The answer to this is necessarily speculative, but not therefore fanciful. It can appeal to reasonable considerations of logic, of experience, and of finite and fallible human nature. Among these, a Christian formed by religious belief and practice to care for the equal dignity of all humans and to be especially sensitive to the plight of those at the bottom of the social heap, would point to the fact that the minority of those lobbying for the right to physician-assisted dying tends to be economically secure, highly educated, articulate, independent and accustomed to control, whereas the majority of patients are far less self-confident, far more dependent on others and therefore far more vulnerable to abuse. In the UK, at any one time about 400,000 elderly people are being abused, mostly by close relatives (Age UK 2022).

In such circumstances, it is not unduly pessimistic to suppose that, if patients were granted a right to physician-assisted dying, many of them would be persuaded to choose it as a means of ending misery that is socially manufactured. The humanity of a society is to be measured by its care for the most vulnerable: to grant patients the right to physician-assisted dying, where social circumstances such as those described above obtain, would be to abandon many of the poor to the mercy of unscrupulous relatives.[5]

Notes

1. In the British context, advocates of the legalization of assisted suicide sometimes complain about the presence of Church of England bishops in the House of Lords and the baleful influence they exercise there in mustering opposition. However, that influence can hardly be thought dominant. At best, there are 26 Anglican bishops in an upper house containing 784

members. Further, it is good that a secular, as distinct from secular*ist*, House of Lords contains experienced representatives of a wide range of civil social bodies, including religious communities.

2. Proponents prefer to talk of 'dying with dignity' rather than 'assisted suicide'. This is problematic in two respects. First, it confuses palliative medicine and care with intentional killing. And second, it obscures the fact that what 'assisted dying' actually refers to is assistance in deliberate self-killing or 'suicide'.

3. For a fuller discussion of the place of religion in public discussions about issues in medical ethics, see Biggar (2015a, 2015b).

4. These include Anglicans such as the theologian, Paul Badham; the former Archbishop of Canterbury, George Carey; and the late Archbishop of Cape Town, Desmond Tutu.

5. For a book-length discussion of suicide and euthanasia from a Christian point of view, see Biggar (2004).

References

Age UK (2022) New data on domestic abuse in older people, *Age UK*, 9 December. Available at: https://www.ageuk.org.uk/discover/2022/december/new-data-on-domestic-abuse-in-older-people/ (accessed 10 February 2024).

Biggar, N. (2004) *Aiming to Kill: The Ethics of Suicide and Euthanasia.* London: Darton, Longman & Todd.

Biggar, N. (2015a) Why religion deserves a place in secular medicine, *Journal of Medical Ethics*, 41 (3): 229–33.

Biggar, N. (2015b) Religion's place at the table of 'secular' medical ethics: a response to the commentaries, *Journal of Medical Ethics*, 41 (11): 873–74.

32 Assisted suicide: an Islamic perspective

Abdul-Azim Ahmed[1]

The Islamic position on assisted suicide could be simply summarized as overwhelmingly considered absolutely prohibited and against the moral and ethical precepts of the religion of Islam. Such a summary is unhelpfully succinct, without knowing how Muslims arrive at this conclusion, the principles on which it is based, and the concerns assisted suicide raises. This discussion focuses predominantly on the Sunni tradition; the Shi'i tradition arrives at the same conclusion, although through different mechanisms.

Islam is a broad tradition with no universal clergy and no singular authority that dispenses the official position of the religion. It does, however, hold orthodox positions as a cumulative communal endeavour of scholars. Scholars, men or women, who have engaged in prolonged study of the Islam, are invested with religious authority to determine the questions of morality and ethics.

The Quran is the revealed text believed by Muslims to be the literal word of God.[1] An important distinction, often misunderstood by uninformed outsiders, is that while the Quran is considered the literal word of God, it is generally not read literally. Metaphors, images, similes and poetic language abound, and the well-trained Muslim scholar would engage with the Quran on multiple levels from linguistic to historical context (*asbab an-nuzul*) in order to derive meanings (whether for spiritual edification, or legal rulings).

Verses of the Quran often cited include the following:

Do not kill each other, for God is merciful to you (4:29);

… If anyone kills a person – unless in retribution for murder or spreading corruption in the land – it is as if he kills all mankind … (5:32);

It is God who gives life and death; God sees everything you do (3:156).

Quranic verses alone do not establish a clear position of orthodoxy, since a Muslim could interpret them in divergent ways. They would be placed alongside the Prophetic example (often called *the sunna*, and accessed through the *hadith*, or preserved historic narrations about the sayings and actions of the Prophet Muhammad). There are numerous examples of a vocal disapproval for suicide given by the Prophet Muhammad, though there are distinctions over the nature of suicide and the intentions. For example:

There was among those before you a man who had a wound. He was in [such] anguish that he took a knife and made with it a cut in his hand, and the blood did not cease to flow till he died. Allah the Almighty said: My servant has himself forestalled Me; I have forbidden him Paradise. (Hadith 28, 40 Hadith Qudsi[2])

This intentional, and importantly, rationalized, decision to end one's life is condemned by the Prophet Muhammad and God, but suicide during a mental health crisis is generally judged differently (another Prophetic teaching describes three categories of people as having the 'pen lifted', meaning they are not considered accountable for their actions, the one who has lost his or her sanity is among them).

The Quranic verses on God's dominion over life and death, the injunctions against killing others and oneself, combined with the Prophetic teachings warning against suicide (often explicitly in circumstances to avoid pain or suffering from injury) have led to *ijma*, or consensus, among Muslim scholars. *Ijma* holds the highest weight for determining orthodoxy in Islam, an indication that scholars geographically and temporally have all interpreted and understood a particular Quranic verse or Prophetic teaching in the same way.

There is, then, a very strong condemnation of assisted suicide in the Islamic tradition, for the individual seeking it, and for doctors, and others who administer it. It is considered a rejection of the divine gift of life, a rejection of God's Will, and a rejection of God's sovereignty over life and death. Further reading, specified below, provides greater depth from medical and Islamic angles.

Personal moral questions are part of the Islamic principles central to a just society and good life. What does it mean for individuals, a society and a state to assist suicide? If assisted suicide is prohibited for a Muslim (whether the patient or the one assisting), what role should Muslims play if other members of an ethically diverse society wish to pursue it? Should they object, or by not objecting facilitate it? Answering this requires inter-communal, inter-religious and inter-social moral reasoning, of the type this book endeavours to produce.

Notes

1. All translations are taken from Abdel Haleem's *The Qur'an* (2005).
2. Available at: https://sunnah.com/qudsi40:28 (accessed 16 February 2024).

Reference

Abdel Haleem, M.A.S. (2005) *The Qur'an*. Oxford: Oxford University Press.

Further reading on Islam and assisted suicide

Ahaddour, C., Van den Branden, S. and Broeckaert, B. (2018) 'God is the giver and taker of life': Muslim beliefs and attitudes regarding assisted suicide and euthanasia, *AJOB Empirical Bioethics*, 9 (1): 1–11.
Brown, J.A.C. (2014) *Misquoting Muhammad: The Challenge and Choices of Interpreting the Prophet's Legacy*. London: Oneworld.
Harvey, R. (2017) *Qur'an and the Just Society*. Edinburgh: Edinburgh University Press.

Madadin, M., Al Sahwan, H.S., Altarouti, K.K. et al. (2020) The Islamic perspective on physician-assisted suicide and euthanasia, *Medicine, Science and the Law*, 60 (4): 278–86.
Maravia, U. (2021) MAiD or AiD? Seeking 'medical assistance in dying' or 'Allah's (assistance) in dying'?, *Journal of the British Islamic Medical Association*, 9 (3): 7–19.
Van den Branden, S. and Broeckaert, B. (2011) Living in the hands of God: English Sunni e-fatwas on (non-)voluntary euthanasia and assisted suicide, *Medicine, Health Care, and Philosophy*, 14 (1): 29–41.

33 Assisted dying: a Jewish perspective

Alexandra Wright

Judaism affirms the sanctity and value of human life. Deuteronomy (30.19) teaches, 'Choose life, that you and your descendants may live'.[1] The commandments are to be observed so that human beings 'shall live by them' (Leviticus 18.5) and not, in the words of the *Talmud*, 'die by them' (*bAvodah Zarah* 27b), which was understood to mean that no obligation should take precedence over the saving of life, except the laws forbidding idolatry, incest and murder (*bYoma* 82a). The duty to save life is enshrined in rabbinic sources: 'Only one human being was created in the beginning: to teach us that anyone who destroys a single soul is considered by Scripture as if they had destroyed a whole world, and anyone who saves a single soul as if they had saved a whole world' (*mSanhedrin* 4:5).

The duty to heal is found in the phrase from Exodus 21.19, *v'rappo y'rappé* – 'and he shall surely heal him', which is understood by rabbinic literature (*bBerakhot* 60a) to mean that the physician is given permission to practise medicine professionally.[2]

The Jewish legal tradition (*halakhah*) regards the dying person (*goses*) as a living person in all aspects. (The word '*goses*' refers to someone who is expected to die within three days.[3]) Nothing should be done to anticipate or hasten their death. To close the eyes of the *goses*, even as the soul is expiring, is as though one has shed blood (*Shulchan Arukh, Yoreh De'ah* 339: 1–4). The dying person is compared to a 'flickering flame; as soon as one touches it, the light is extinguished' (*bShabbat* 151b).[4]

However, to what extent does *halakhah* require the physician to keep a dying patient alive, especially if they are suffering great pain?

Some halakhic sources state that, while it is our duty to pray for a sick person to recover, there may come a time when we should pray for God's mercy that they may die. The law is based on a well-known incident in the *Talmud* that describes the final illness of Rabbi Judah the Prince. The Rabbis were gathered around his bed praying that he might be kept alive a little longer. But when his maidservant saw how painful it was for her master to get up and attend to his needs, she went up to the roof and dropped a pitcher to the ground. The shattering of the pitcher distracted the rabbis from their prayer and Rabbi Judah died (*bKetubbot* 104a).

No judgement is cast on the maidservant's interruption of Rabbi Judah's 'life support system'. In other texts, it is permitted to stop an intrusive noise that is preventing the soul from departing. Indeed, later mediaeval works, based on the scriptural verse 'a time to be born and a time to die' (Ecclesiastes 3.2), acknowledge that 'just as [a person] has a right to live, so there comes a time when [they have] a right to die' (Freehof 1994: 199).

The story of the martyrdom of Rabbi Chanina ben Teradyon is often invoked in relation to the question of whether it is permitted to shorten the life of someone who suffers unbearable pain (*bAvodah Zarah 18a*). A victim of Roman persecution, he is wrapped in a Torah scroll, surrounded with bunches of branches which are set on fire. Tufts of wool soaked in water are placed over his heart to prolong his suffering. His students encourage him to open his mouth to allow the flames to enter so that death comes more quickly. He replies: 'It is better that the One who gave me my life should take it, than I should harm myself.' When the executioner offers to increase the flame and remove the wool tufts from his heart, allowing him to die more quickly, he accepts, and both Rabbi Chanina and the executioner are summoned to the life of the world-to-come (the executioner having also leapt into the fire and died). The story appears to contradict the stringency of Jewish law regarding hastening death, yet Jewish sources permit 'the withdrawal of any factor – whether extraneous to the patient himself or not – which may artificially delay his demise in the final phase' (Jakobovits 1961).

Those who resist change in the law regarding physician-assisted dying have invoked the abhorrent eugenics programme in Nazi Germany, in which medical professionals implemented a 'racial hygiene' policy against children and adults with mental, physical and social disabilities.

They acknowledge the experience of Holocaust survivors. Rabbi Sybil Sheridan argues that, 'For many, their deaths are traumatic. Having spent so much time holding on to life, they do not know how to give it up' (2014: 28). She advocates a greater focus on 'ensuring adequate pain relief, counselling support and appropriate drugs to help overcome depression' and the expansion of the work of the hospice movement. The role of religion, she argues, plays an important part in the comfort over death.

Others consider that the principle of liberalizing existing legislation is 'hard to resist', especially when modern medicine ingeniously prolongs life, but fails to provide any quality to that life (Rayner 1998: 142–43).[5]

There is no single Jewish response to the question of physician-assisted dying. Jewish literature – legal and non-legal – sees life as sacred, in God's hands, but acknowledges that there may be times when suffering is so extreme and incurable that it is permissible to remove the obstacles that prevent an individual from dying.

For those with a terminal illness who wish to end their lives voluntarily, the Jewish response would always be to support without judgement, pastorally, with compassion and love, the decision that is made by any human being.[6]

Notes

1. The translation of biblical phrases in this chapter are those of the author. The translations from the *Mishnah* and *Talmud* are by Rabbi Adin Even-Israel Steinsaltz. The *Mishnah* is the first major work of rabbinic literature compiled around 200 CE. It records the decisions of Jewish sages on a variety of legal matters and includes some stories about the rabbis. The Babylonian *Talmud* was compiled in Babylonia between the third and eighth centuries CE and is structured as a commentary on the *Mishnah*. It embraces a range of Jewish law and lore. The Palestinian or Jerusalem *Talmud* (fourth to fifth century CE) was compiled in Galilee and is also structured around the *Mishnah*.

2. Also relevant, from Rayner (2005: 53–54): 'But the permission is also an obligation, for those who have an opportunity to heal are obligated to do so.'
3. For further discussion of this notion in a related context, see Gillick (2001).
4. See also: Maimonides, *Mishneh Torah, Judges*, Laws of Mourning 4:5.
5. The Central Conference of American Rabbis' 1994 responsum argued strongly against 'voluntary assisted suicide'. But a more recent responsum (2023) acknowledges that there may be times when 'a reasonable person may reach the point where they see that their *life*, as opposed to their existence, has ended; and that sometimes the greatest compassion one can receive is to be assisted in dying in order to end intolerable suffering'. Available at: https://www.ccarnet.org/ccar-responsa/5783-1/ (accessed 28 February 2024).
6. My thanks to Rabbi Dr Michael Hilton for his help with this chapter and for raising the question of how spiritual and pastoral care can be extended to both the individual who wishes voluntarily to end their life and to their family who may object.

References

Central Conference of American Rabbis (2023) *Medical Assistance in Dying*. Available at: https://www.ccarnet.org/ccar-responsa/5783-1/.

Freehof, S.B. (1994) Allowing a terminal patient to die, in W. Jacob and M. Zemer (eds) *Death and Euthanasia in Jewish Law: Essays and Responsa*. Pittsburgh, PA: Rodef Shalom Press.

Gillick, M.R. (2001) Artificial nutrition and hydration in the patient with advanced dementia: is withholding treatment compatible with traditional Judaism?, *Journal of Medical Ethics*, 27 (1): 12–15.

Jakobovits, I. (1961) The dying and their treatment in Jewish law: preparation for death and euthanasia, *Hebrew Medical Journal*, 2: 251–65 (quoted in F. Rosner and J.D. Bleich (eds) (1985) *Jewish Bioethics*. New York: Hebrew Publishing Company).

Rayner, J.D. (1998) Euthanasia, in J.D. Rayner, *Jewish Religious Law: A Progressive Perspective*. New York: Berghahn Books.

Rayner, J.D. (2005) *Principles of Jewish Ethics*. London: Liberal Judaism (first published in 1998 by the new Jewish initiative for social justice).

Sheridan, S. (2014) Dignity in dying or living less well?, in J. Romain (ed.) *Assisted Dying: Rabbinic Responses*. London: MRJ.

34 | The Humanist case against assisted suicide and euthanasia

Kevin Yuill

Introduction

The Humanist case against assisted suicide and euthanasia (ASE) is not that different from most religious cases against its legalization. That may be surprising, as the case for assisted suicide/euthanasia often presents itself as a progressive and forward-thinking campaign that faces only a few dogmatic Christians imposing their outdated belief system on the rest of the population. But atheists – and liberals – who think long and hard enough about the issue will come to the same conclusion. We need to think again.

Why are we opposed? There are four basic reasons. First, it is the wrong answer to the question of suffering at the end of life. That is, it is not necessary and may even be harmful to those suffering at the end of life. Second, the case for assisted suicide/euthanasia is built upon fear, falsehoods and misinformation. Third, it is certainly harmful to individuals, who have their lives cut short. And fourth, it would be destructive of important moral precepts shared by religious people and atheists alike.

The campaign for legalized assisted suicide/euthanasia is based on unwarranted fears about the end of life. As the American satirist and acerbic writer H.L. Mencken noted one hundred years ago: 'there is always a well-known solution to every human problem – neat, plausible, and wrong' (Mencken 1921: 158). Assisted suicide/euthanasia is that solution.

Most deaths – even according to lead campaign organization for a change in the suicide laws, Dignity in Dying – are peaceful. But that doesn't stop them from frightening people about bad deaths. In 2019, the CEO of Hospice UK, a charity that works with those experiencing death, dying and bereavement, publicly chastised Dignity in Dying for the 'sensationalist and inaccurate' portrayal of death in a video to accompany its 'The Inescapable Truth' campaign. The video showed a man convulsing violently at the end of life. But the man was an actor and as many, many doctors said, that was not how people died.[1]

Falsehoods, misinformation and deception

Does the term 'assisted dying' help public understanding? No, it doesn't. In a UK poll conducted in 2021, when asked 'What do you understand by the term "assisted dying"?', more than half of those polled thought that it included '[g]iving people who are dying the right to stop life-prolonging treatment' and 'providing hospice-type care for those who are dying'.[2] 'Assisted dying' does not distinguish between where the doctor takes the final action (euthanasia) and where the patient does (assisted suicide). Moreover, assisted dying is so loose a term that it might refer to the execution process in areas where capital punishment is legal.

The term 'the dying' is also deceptive. Dignity in Dying campaigns only for those who have a terminal illness with a prognosis of 6 months or less left to live. These people they call 'the dying' whereas everyone else who stands to live for 7 months or more is not eligible for having their suicides validated or assisted, regardless of their level of suffering. Dying is, of course, part of living. As pioneering author of *On Death and Dying*, Elisabeth Kubler Ross, said in justifying her opposition to it, assisting a suicide is 'projecting your own unfinished business' onto that person, cheating them of part of life.[3]

Nor is the campaign about physical pain, as is often implied. Examining the reasons why people opt for assisted suicides in Oregon, according to their official surveys, physical pain has never been in the top five reasons. Being a burden is more important. Nor is legalization of assisted suicide/euthanasia a way to prevent suicides, as *Dignity in Dying* implies and as Australian proponents argued in order to pass the law in Victoria allowing assisted suicide/euthanasia in 2017 (Jones 2023).

No-one disputes that there are difficult deaths. But assisted suicide/euthanasia is not the answer. In the Netherlands, where assisted suicide/euthanasia has been legal for more than 20 years, between 28.5 per cent and 42.8 per cent of deaths still experience pain and restlessness (Heijltjes et al. 2023). Everywhere, there are very few cases where taking action to end a life is necessary and right. But, where the practice is still on the wrong side of the law, they are unlikely to be prosecuted, let alone convicted.

Nor is there really any respect for 'autonomy'. If there were, proponents would support a 'suicide pill' for all competent adults. They would support the autonomy of duellists who, after all, harm only themselves and not others. They would support the right of German cannibals to enjoy their obsessions without any legal interference (Harding 2003).

History shows that consent was merely an afterthought for a campaign that seeks to streamline society, to make it more efficient and less costly. The term 'voluntary' in voluntary euthanasia campaigns was only added in the 1930s. The concept of dignity in dying was pioneered by Dr Walter Sackett in the 1960s. Sackett proposed legislation that would allow 'death with dignity' for the severely retarded in his state of Florida so that the resources spent on them could be diverted to more worthy causes. (US GPO 1972: 15).

History also indicates that the proposals of those who claim the mantle of progressiveness should be investigated thoroughly. One hundred years ago, we humanists were in the forefront of another progressive suggestion – eugenics. In fact, it makes sense to see euthanasia as part of eugenics, which is the 'science' of human betterment. The idea of limiting the number of the 'genetically inferior' in a population through the use of positive or negative eugenic means became widely accepted in a number of countries. And humanists were in the thick of it. Writing in the *New Humanist*, Appleby (2010) admitted: 'It is a sad fact that prior to the 1930s it is a struggle to find prominent British rationalists who were not in favour of some form of eugenics.'

Euthanasia was simply negative eugenics, a way to weed out the weaker members of society not by selectively breeding but by killing them. One can see the outlines of sentiments in favour of euthanasia in a chilling confession by novelist D.H. Lawrence in a letter to his friend Blanche Jennings in 1908. He explained how he would dispose of society's outcasts:

> If I had it my way, I would build a lethal chamber big as the Crystal Palace, with a military band playing softly, and a Cinematograph working brightly; then I'd go out in the back streets and main streets and bring them in, all the sick, the halt and the maimed; I would lead them gently, and they would smile me a weary thanks; and the band would softly bubble out the 'Hallelujah Chorus'. (quoted in Grue 2010: 34)

Harmful

Assisted suicide and euthanasia are harmful to individuals in that they cut lives short. Dr Harvey Schipper, professor of medicine and adjunct professor of law at the University of Toronto, recently estimated that between 2,000 and 4,000 wrongful deaths are likely to have already occurred in Canada. If 2,000 to 4,000 wrongful deaths occurred because of wrongful convictions in capital punishment cases, an outcry would follow (Schipper 2024).

In response to understandable depression when given a terminal diagnosis, dispensers of assisted suicide/euthanasia push the proverbial suicidal man from the ledge. In every country where it has been legal for more than a few years, the so-called 'safeguards' have been overcome. In the Netherlands, at least eight people suffering only from autism have been euthanized. Among the eight patients, one was an autistic man in his twenties. His records said he had been 'unhappy since childhood', was regularly bullied and 'longed for social contacts but was unable to connect with others'. His request to be killed by lethal injection was honoured by his doctor (Tuffrey-Wijne et al. 2023).

We are – rightly, in my opinion – horrified by the prospect that capital punishment might take an innocent life. Yet, few are concerned about lives lost due to inaccurate prognoses or failure to detect suicidality. Why? Oregon – the model for Dignity in Dying – has witnessed deaths that take up to 137 hours after ingesting the poison (Oregon Health Authority 2024: 15). Again, if an execution took 137 hours, people would rightly protest at the cruelty of the process.

The evidence from Canada shows how quickly a culture in which death becomes a desirable outcome envelops a nation once it legalizes any form of assisted suicide/euthanasia. One 55-year-old woman who sought assisted suicide/euthanasia 'identifies poverty as the driver of her MAiD request – food insufficiency and inability to access appropriate treatments' (Zhu 2022). Another patient, 'a 57-year-old man and published author, identified lack of housing and lack of access to medical care among the reasons for his request to die' (Zhu 2022). In Belgium and the Netherlands, people have sought and been allowed to access assisted suicide/euthanasia because of tinnitus, a botched sex-change operation, and the onset of blindness.

Moral harm

The moral harm caused by legalizing assisted suicide/euthanasia may not be as palpable but it is just as real. It undermines the treatment of lives as of equal value under our laws. Right now, it is just as wicked to take the life of an 86-year-old who does not value her existence as it is to kill a 24-year-old with his whole life ahead of him. Why would this be different for suicide?

There is no contradiction between religious and secular morality on this point. As the French sociologist Emile Durkeim observed 125 years ago, 'suicide must be classed among immoral acts; for in its main principle it denies this *religion of humanity*' (emphasis added). Approving suicide would undermine:

> ... a sentiment almost the only bond between its members ... From the moment that the human person is and must be considered something sacred, over which neither the individual nor the group has free disposal, any attack upon it must be forbidden. No matter that the guilty person and the victim are one and the same ... If violent destruction of a human life revolts us as a sacrilege ... we cannot tolerate it under any circumstances. (Durkheim 1970: 302)

We cannot value life by how many years it has left or by the wealth or even happiness of its possessor. We must maintain the principle of the equal value of every human life if we are to maintain our civilization. That does not mean that all individual lives are equal; a doctor faced with a choice of whether to save an 86-year-old or a 24-year-old would be forgiven for saving the latter. But the *principle* must be maintained in order to afford equal protection to all human persons. Assisted suicide/euthanasia – by identifying entire categories of persons as appropriate for suicide simply by their physical characteristics – attacks the fundamental basis of the religion of humanity.

The individual does not decide the value of her life – it is those around her that do. That is why we prevent suicides when we can. That is why it is always a virtuous act to save a life, even if the person who is saved dies the next day. We risk deep harm to our fundamental moral connections if we legalize or in any way legitimize the taking of a human life simply because it is wretched.

Conclusions

Assisted suicide/euthanasia remains now as it was in the past – a method of ridding society of individuals whose continued existence is burdensome to themselves and burdensome to society. It has always been about compassion and utility. There is no doubt that compassion motivates some of those who wish to legalize assisted suicide/euthanasia. However, even that compassion is shaped by a perception that some lives are of less value than others.

There is no contradiction between religious and secular morality on the issue of killing human beings. In fact, a secular morality – the religion of humanity, as Durkheim puts it – must be even more respectful of human life as we have no faith in any afterlife. Human beings, whether infants with their promise and potential or the elderly with their wealth of experience and knowledge, must be accorded respect.

It is time to think again about assisted suicide and euthanasia.

Notes

1. See Assisted dying campaign video accused of 'scaremongering', *BBC News*, September 2019 https://www.bbc.co.uk/news/health-49635646 (accessed 28 February 2024).
2. See https://www.dyingwell.co.uk/survation-appg-for-dying-well-survey-july-2021/ (accessed 28 February 2024). This poll and the complexities of polling are discussed in Chapter 2.
3. Cited in Yuill (2013: 45).

References

Appleby, J. (2010) Rationalism's dirty secret, *New Humanist*, 23 December. Available at: https://newhumanist.org.uk/articles/2471/rationalisms-dirty-secret (accessed 28 February 2024).

Durkheim, E. (1970) *Suicide: A Study in Sociology*. London: Routledge & Kegan Paul.

Grue, L. (2010) Eugenics and euthanasia – then and now, *Scandinavian Journal of Disability Research*, 12 (1): 33–45.

Harding, L. (2003) Victim of cannibal agreed to be eaten, *The Guardian*, 4 December. Available at: https://www.theguardian.com/world/2003/dec/04/germany.lukeharding (accessed 28 February 2024).

Heijltjes, M.T., van Zuylen, L, van Thiel, G.J.M.W. et al. (2023) Symptom evolution in the dying, *BMJ Supportive & Palliative Care*, 13 (1): 121–24.

Jones, D. (2023) Did the Voluntary Assisted Dying Act 2017 prevent 'at least one suicide every week'?, *Journal of Ethics in Mental Health*, 11: 1–20. Available at: https://jemh.ca/issues/open/documents/Did per cent20the per cent20Voluntary per cent20Assisted per cent20Dying per cent20Act per cent202017.pdf (accessed 28 February 2024).

Mencken, H.L. (1921) *Prejudices Second Series*. London: Jonathan Cape.

Oregon Health Authority (2024) *Oregon Death with Dignity Act: 2023 Data Summary*. Available at: https://www.oregon.gov/oha/PH/PROVIDERPARTNERRESOURCES/EVALUATIONRESEARCH/DEATHWITHDIGNITYACT/Documents/year26.pdf (accessed 23 March 2024).

Schipper, H. (2024) Delaying medically assisted death for mental illness will give us time to find an acceptable place for MAID, *Toronto Star*, 13 March. Available at: https://www.thestar.com/opinion/contributors/delaying-medically-assisted-death-for-mental-illness-will-give-us-time-to-find-an-acceptable/article_3d1e6c72-dfc8-11ee-998c-c7c6c82c4f1c.html (accessed 23 March 2024).

Tuffrey-Wijne, I., Curfs, L., Finlay, I. and Hollins, S. (2023) Euthanasia and physician-assisted suicide in people with intellectual disabilities and/or autism spectrum disorders: investigation of 39 Dutch case reports (2012–2021), *BJPsych Open*, 9: e87. Available at: https://doi.org/10.1192/bjo.2023.69 (accessed 5 February 2014).

United States GPO (1972) *Death With Dignity: An Inquiry Into Related Public Issues*, Hearings before the Special Committee on Aging, United States Senate, Ninety-Second Congress,

Second Session, Part 1 – Washington, DC, 7 August. Available at: https://www.aging.senate.gov/imo/media/doc/publications/871972.pdf (accessed 28 February 2024).

Yuill, K. (2013) *Assisted Suicide: The Liberal, Humanist Case Against Legalization*. London: Palgrave MacMillan.

Zhu, Y.Y. (2022) Leaked slides reveal dark side of Canada's euthanasia policy, *Unherd*, 20 December. Available at: https://unherd.com/newsroom/leaked-slides-reveal-dark-side-of-canadas-euthanasia-policy/ (accessed 28 February 2024).

Select bibliography

Biggar, N. (2004) *Aiming to Kill: The Ethics of Suicide and Euthanasia.* London: Darton, Longman & Todd.

Dworkin, G., Frey, R.G. and Bok, S. (1998) *Euthanasia and Physician-Assisted Suicide: For and Against.* Cambridge: Cambridge University Press.

Finlay, I. and Preston, R. (2020) *Death by Appointment: A Rational Guide to the Assisted Dying Debate.* Newcastle upon Tyne: Cambridge Scholars Publishing.

Huxtable, R. (2013) *Euthanasia: All that Matters.* London: Hodder.

Jones, D.A., Gastmans, C. and MacKellar, C. (eds) (2017) *Euthanasia and Assisted Suicide: Lessons from Belgium.* Cambridge: Cambridge University Press.

Keown, J. (ed.) (1995) *Euthanasia Examined: Ethical, Clinical and Legal Perspectives.* Cambridge: Cambridge University Press.

Keown, J. (2018) *Euthanasia, Ethics and Public Policy: An Argument Against Legalisation*, 2nd edn. Cambridge: Cambridge University Press.

Rubenfeld, S. and Sulmasy, D.P. (eds) (2020) *Physician-Assisted Suicide and Euthanasia: Before, During, and After the Holocaust.* Lanham, Maryland: Lexington Books.

Woods, S. (2007) *Death's Dominion: Ethics at the End of Life.* Maidenhead: Open University Press.

Yuill, K. (2013) *Assisted Suicide: The Liberal, Humanist Case Against Legalization.* London: Palgrave MacMillan.

Subject Index

Page numbers followed by lower case *b*, *f* or *t* indicate boxes, figures or tables respectively; *fn* indicates footnote.

Name Index

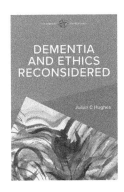

Dementia and Ethics Reconsidered

Julian Hughes

ISBN: 9780335251001 (Paperback)
eISBN: 9780335251018

2023

Ethical issues are involved in every decision that is made in connection with someone living with dementia – from decisions about care and treatment to decisions about research and funding.

This book encourages the reader to reconsider ethics in dementia care with the use of 'patterns of practice', an innovative idea developed by the author. The book highlights the importance of understanding the person's narrative, of good communication, high quality care, and expert interpretation of the meaning of situations for people living with dementia. This book:

- Reviews ethical theories and approaches in connection with dementia care
- Considers issues such as stigma, quality of life, personhood and citizenship in relation to dementia
- Looks at issues relevant to research ethics
- Presents case vignettes to highlight a complete spectrum of ethical issues that arise in dementia care
- Is accessibly written for multiple audiences – from people living with dementia to practitioners

Dementia and Ethics Reconsidered is a comprehensive account of thought and practice in relation to ethical issues that arise in the context of dementia care, which seeks to show how ethical thinking can be put into practice and prove relevant to day-to-day experience.

www.mheducation.co.uk

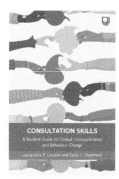

Consultation Skills:
A Student Guide to Clinical Communication and Behaviour

Jacqueline F. Lavallee, Sarah C. Shepherd

ISBN: 9780335251506 (Paperback)
eISBN: 9780335251513

2024

Consultation Skills blends the theories of behaviour change with practical clinical communication and motivational interviewing skills, enabling students to understand the theoretical foundations and know how to apply them in real-world healthcare scenarios.

Bringing together clinical communication skills and behaviour change in one source, this book eliminates the need for students to refer to multiple sources, thus streamlining their learning process and providing a holistic understanding of these topics.

Consultation Skills will also remain a useful reference guide for students after qualification, as they embark in their professional careers. **Key features of this book include:**

- Integrates clinical communication skills and behaviour change theory
- Incorporates the most up-to-date theories and techiniques
- Comprehensive content in one source
- Post qualification utility

Drawing on the most up-to-date theories and techniques, this book equips students with the latest theoretical foundations and practical skills to become the healthcare professionals of the future.

www.mheducation.co.uk

OPEN UNIVERSITY PRESS
McGraw Hill

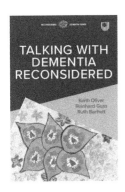

Talking with Dementia Reconsidered

Keith Oliver, Reinhard Guss, Ruth Bartlett

ISBN: 9780335251285 (Paperback)
eISBN: 9780335251292

2024

This book places people living with a diagnosis of dementia at its core, providing each person with the opportunity to express themselves whilst viewing their lives in relation to the Kitwood flower model.

Authored by a person living with dementia, an experienced consultant clinical psychologist and a respected academic, the three combine to amplify and showcase the words of the Fifteen people living with dementia in an original, authentic and unique way. This book:

- Gives readers transparent insight into the lives, hopes and fears of a diverse range of people living with various forms of dementia
- Shows how each petal of the Kitwood flower with love at its centre is a helpful framework for each person to describe their life
- Links the interviews with issues, frameworks, policy and practice
- Examines what stakeholders can take from this book to advance dementia care

Talking with Dementia Reconsidered truthfully adds to the growing knowledge base of what life with dementia is really like in an engaging and informative way. It is essential reading for anyone and everyone directly or indirectly affected by dementia through lived experience, studying dementia or working professionally to support those affected.

www.mheducation.co.uk

OPEN UNIVERSITY PRESS
McGraw Hill